Social-Emotional Learning in the Classroom

Practical Guide for Integrating All SEL Skills into Instruction and Classroom Management

William B. Ribas, Ph.D.

Deborah A. Brady, Ph.D.

Jane Hardin, M.Ed.

RIBAS ASSOCIATES AND PUBLICATIONS, INC.

Published and distributed by Ribas Publications
596 Pleasant Street
Norwood, MA 02062
Website: ribasassociates.com
Phone: 781-551-9120

ISBN-13: 978-0-9715089-9-6

Book design and typesetting by Jane Tenenbaum
Graphic on front cover reprinted with permission from CASEL.org

Printed in Canada

ABOUT THE AUTHORS

In the biographies below, you will see that the authors were chosen carefully to ensure this book has immediate relevance to current and future practitioners. The three authors have experience as teachers and supervisors of teachers at the preK-12 and college levels. Their experience includes general education, special education, English language learning, and counseling. They have worked in urban, suburban, and rural schools.

William B. Ribas, Ph.D.

Bill Ribas has taught all grades K-12 and is a certified guidance counselor. He has been an assistant principal, principal, director of student services, and assistant superintendent. He is also the author of three other books: *Educator Supervision and Evaluation That Works: Addressing the Educational, Legal, Political, and Social Emotional*; *Instructional Practices That Maximize Student Achievement*; and *Inducting and Mentoring Educators New to the District*. Since 2002 he has been the president of Ribas Associates and Publications, Inc., a training, consulting, and publishing company dedicated to embedded professional learning for teachers, school clinical staff, school leaders, paraprofessionals, and parents.

Deborah Brady, Ph.D.

Deb Brady has served as a teacher, director of curriculum and instruction, and assistant superintendent. She has been a college teacher who taught graduate and undergraduate courses in curriculum, reading, literacy, co-teaching, and writing. Deb earned her doctorate in educational studies at Lesley University, where her research focused on the classroom and the impact of a standards-based curriculum on teaching, learning, and assessment. Her special areas of interest include: curriculum assessment, development, and improvement; literacy, reading, and writing; instructional leadership; assessment and the use of data that improves instruction, social-emotional growth, and student achievement; and building the capacity of districts through collaborative work within professional learning communities to address school climate, data teams, and administrator collaboration. She is author of the book *Instructional Practices That Maximize Student Achievement: For Teachers, By Teachers*.

Jane M. Hardin, M.Ed.

Jane Hardin began her career as a teacher in both general education and special education. During her time as a resource room teacher, her program was selected as an exemplary model by the National Council for Exceptional Children. For the last 22 years, Jane has been a member of the Simmons College Faculty, supervising and training undergraduate and graduate student teachers and interns in the field of special education. In addition, she has served as a consultant for a variety of local and national school systems. She is a board member of the Massachusetts Council for Exceptional Children and a member of the Massachusetts Architectural Access Board. Jane is also a published author. She holds a bachelor's degree in general education and a master's degree in Special Education, with advanced training in differentiated instruction and language disabilities. Her areas of training and consultation include classroom and behavior management, the changing face and needs of the student with ASD, teaching students with emotional and behavioral issues, how anxiety and trauma impact the learning process, and the social and emotional needs of students with disabling conditions.

DEDICATIONS

To my four children who have shown me that kindness
to the most vulnerable is the greatest strength.
—Deborah Brady

James, Jennifer, and John Hardin, who have taught me well about
life, love, and the creative spirit.
—Jane Hardin

All the teachers, school clinical professionals, paraprofessionals, and administrators
who give their hearts and souls to the children they teach.
—Bill Ribas

CONTENTS

Social-Emotional Learning
in the Classroom

INTRODUCTION

One Author's Journey to Social-Emotional Learning

My journey striving to influence the social-emotional situations and skills of my students began with my teaching career in 1979 in a high-poverty district. Like so many other educators, I taught during the day, coached during the afternoon and attended classes for my master's degree in counseling in the evening. My counseling studies introduced me to many ideas about the social and emotional well-being of students. I was anxious to try out these concepts in my class.

My school did not have a counselor because it was a poor district, so I began to test some of my novice counseling in my classroom. Student fights that previously were met with punishments for both parties still met with consequences. However, when the punishment was completed, I started having "sit downs" with the combatants to mediate the disagreements. Since all the teachers in the school taught six periods a day, I had to be creative in finding time for these meetings either before school (when the buses arrived and school had not started), at lunchtime, or after school (before the buses pulled out or I had to run to practice for the team I was coaching). These meetings rarely lasted more than 10 or 15 minutes but still proved productive.

In my second year of teaching, I was joined by a colleague who had experience in counseling and social work before she began teaching. She helped me set up a rudimentary counseling session structure. I fumbled through those sessions using some group counseling skills that I learned in a graduate course on group counseling. In hindsight, I realize that I don't know if these meetings had any impact on classroom dynamics; however, they gave me tremendous insight into the way my students thought about themselves and their relationships with other students. These understandings caused me to shift my classroom management from one of reacting to misbehavior to one of shaping positive behavior.

Fast forward eight years and I was now the vice-principal in a K-8 school with the highest parent education level and one of the highest parent income levels in the Commonwealth of Massachusetts. As vice-principal I was the school disciplinarian. I was fortunate to be in a school with a principal who valued students' social-emotional development. The school had a guidance counselor whom I respected and with whom I worked closely addressing students with behavior issues. In the role of vice-principal, I taught the first two periods of the day before assuming my administrative duties. These mixed positions gave me a special opportunity to work on student social-emotional development. I had a classroom laboratory to try out class meetings and other classroom practices as well as unscheduled time to work with the counselor and principal on the social-emotional climate school-wide.

Two years later (1988) I became a principal and had my own school. At a principals' meeting, the superintendent spoke about a new program that had been developed by Wellesley College called Open Circle. It was an innovative classroom meeting model designed to develop students' social and emotional competencies. As an eager new principal, I dove in with both feet, committing my faculty to a school-wide project. Two years later I realized that many of the teachers in my school didn't share my beliefs about the role of classrooms and/or classroom meetings in social-emotional development. I accepted full responsibility for this. I had an experienced and highly qualified staff whose results showed them to be highly effective (student test scores were among the best in the state). I immediately took the time to listen and understand their beliefs.

Looking back, I learned three lessons from this. First, you can't ask people to attend to students'

> *I came to the realization that nearly all the social and emotional behaviors students need to learn are best developed through effective classroom management, group and partner work, and questioning.*

social-emotional development if you don't attend to theirs. Second, many of the teachers who were not implementing the classroom meetings were more effective developing students' social-emotional growth than some who did run the meetings. These highly effective teachers used their multiple daily classroom management, group work interactions, and effective questioning to develop students' self-management, self-awareness, responsible decision making, relationship skills, and social awareness. Third, I came to the realization that nearly all of the social and emotional behaviors students need to learn can be best developed through effective classroom management, group and partner work, and questioning.

The interaction of classroom behavior and the development of social-emotional skills have long been an interest of mine. In 2006, my co-authors and I wrote the first edition of the book *Instructional Practices That Maximize Student Achievement.* In the chapter on classroom management, we identified nine components of effective classroom management. Among those nine components are instructional, social development, and emotional development strategies teachers can use to be more proactive and less reactive in their classroom management. In the 2017 edition (Ribas, Brady, Tamerat, Deane, Greer, Billings), we delved more deeply into the social and emotional components of classroom management. In Chapter 5, we delved deeply into teachers' questioning practices. The social-emotional questioning strategies in this book build on that work. In Chapter 7 (on motivation), we looked at the academic, personal, and interpersonal effects of poverty on students. We examined the use of growth mindset and the nature of intelligence as it impacts all students.

Since the 2006 book had to address 10 areas of effective teaching, we were limited in our ability to focus on how teachers can modify these classroom practices to develop students' social-emotional skills. In this book, we explain how group work, partner work, classroom management, and questioning—the things every teacher does every minute of every day—can be used to effectively develop students' self-management, self-awareness, responsible decision making, relationship skills and social awareness without large commitments of time on the part of the teacher. —*Bill Ribas*

Second Author's Social-Emotional Learning (SEL) Journey

I was shy—painfully shy. I blushed a hot, embarrassed red each time I had to answer a question. I had always been conscientious, had done my work, wrote insightful essays and aced exams, but I never wanted to volunteer an answer. Throughout my years in classrooms, teachers had threatened to take points off if I didn't "speak up" in class. Rarely was there a class where I felt sufficiently safe and accepted to join in the discussions. I sometimes forced myself, with my heart beating and my face beet red, to raise my hand and participate. Although I was a voracious reader, and I loved learning and thinking and reflecting, the thought of public performance made each school day excruciatingly long and uncomfortable. Yet, somehow, I was academically successful.

My introversion, the need to think things out in my own time and my aversion to speaking spontaneously, were seen by most of my teachers as avoiding participation, a character flaw for most teachers. I became aware as I tried to fix my "uncooperative" self over the years that this perspective of my teachers was not necessarily appropriate. My shyness, now recognized as introversion, had life-long and serious consequences in my feeling successful at school. Class participation can be demonstrated in many ways beyond answering teachers' questions, including pair work, in which talking is less intimidating, conferences with the teacher, and using technology to record ideas such as podcasts. My "A" averages belied my feeling of public, social failure in school.

I began my practice teaching in English during the summer after I graduated from college, and despite my shyness, my love of words, encouraging mentors, and my belief in the power of education to elevate the lives of everyone somehow helped me get past my inhibitions and fears. I *loved* the dynamics of a classroom and surprisingly had found my place in the world. I brought to my classroom a recognition that success in education needs to be more than excellent grades. Good classrooms should be both academically challenging and emotionally safe, and I needed to understand that student behavior is not necessarily what I or conventional wisdom thought. I hadn't been resistant to learning; I had been shy.

At this point in my career, I needed to ask myself if a student that I saw as *distracted*, for example, was, in reality, just bored, unfocused, or recalcitrant. Or were those behaviors triggered by other causes that I could not see? And what should I do about those behaviors?

One of my four children (all twins) had a teacher misperceive him. He had spent the summer reading *Island of the Blue Dolphins* and had been totally immersed in reading the book and seeing connections to his everyday 10-year-old life. He had taken notes with the excited anticipation of sharing once he was back to school. He took his book and notes with him everywhere in his back pocket. His notes were insightful, but looked a bit worse for wear.

Unfortunately, his new teacher felt that this lack of neatness represented carelessness, and she never saw his insight or enthusiasm for learning. In our first parent meeting, she told me of every messy or careless mistake he had made. I was at first shocked at how much she had missed, then I became incensed at her emphasis on compliance, neatness, and conformity. I decided at that moment, on my way to vent my frustration to the principal, that my life's work would be to make my classroom and others' classrooms safer for all students, including boys without perfect handwriting or shy and retiring girls as well as the miscreants often called "the frequent flyers." From then on, I attempted to school myself in the possible ways to make a classroom a positive place for learning for every student.

I began to realize that to achieve cultural sensitivity I needed to consider broader issues of our culture including poverty, race, religion, disability, and diversity. Beyond tolerance and patience, I needed to have a deeper appreciation and empathy for others. I also began to look at my own blind spots that caused me to misapprehend the appearance, words, or actions of students.

As an assistant superintendent, I have worked with teams of teachers and with The Collaborative to Advance Social and Emotional Learning (CASEL) to implement social-emotional learning, have created "look fors" in walkthroughs with teachers to self-assess and support the implementation of positive behavior intervention systems, and adapted curricula for all students through Universal Design for Learning. In addition, I've worked with teachers and administrators to bring the Massachusetts Tiered System of Support with three tiers of support, both academic and social, to the schools. I've learned that the work takes time and that the emphasis must stay focused on creat-

> *To achieve cultural sensitivity I needed to consider broader issues of our culture, including poverty, race, religion, disability, and diversity. Beyond tolerance and patience, I needed to have a deeper appreciation and empathy for others.*

ing a positive environment for students to gain these social and academic skills. I realized that this kind of shift in school and classroom culture requires an ongoing effort and sometimes major changes in perspectives and mindsets of teachers, administrators, and students.

In the end, I've seen many positive results: Third and fifth graders were taught through sentence starters to have appropriate academic dialogues providing credit to others' ideas with phrases such as "Building on John's ideas…", and their social awareness expanded; some students spontaneously invited the more reserved students to join in. These elementary students then carried their new skills and their social awareness forward to new classes and to the next year of school. Other examples include an assistant principal who is encouraging moments of mindfulness, and teachers who, for instance, invite students to breathe deeply in the two minutes before announcements every day and others who have become attuned to the emotional atmosphere of their classrooms.

Thus, I come to this book with a major focus on developing a community and an accepting culture for learning together within each classroom. A safe classroom needs to be orderly and calm and focused on high academic expectations. At the same time, it requires that students are seen with empathy and understanding and that both their academic and social-emotional growth is supported by socially and culturally aware educators.

I taught English, then reading, then became a director of a college writing and learning center, then a K-12 director of curriculum and, finally, in my last 17 years, I was an assistant superintendent during which time I spent as much time as I could in classrooms, the real front lines for education. The districts ranged from schools with low socio-economic demographics, to suburban, to large multi-town rural districts where I encountered the devastating forces of poverty on students' lives.

As part of the research for this book, we interviewed teachers, administrators, social workers, and school psychologists for their insight into the needs of teachers and students. The myriad concerns they address daily are at times overwhelming to hear. Their suggestions, including mindfulness and strength-based beliefs, which emphasize what a student can do instead of the so-called deficit model that focuses on remediating weaknesses, have been incorporated into this book. Until recently, these skills were called "soft skills" and educational research had not yet documented that these skills were essential for academic success. This book provides pragmatic support for teachers in every class every day. I see SEL as an organic part of teaching and learning.—*Deb Brady*

Why This Book Was Written

This book provides educators with an easy-to-use guide for developing social-emotional learning in themselves and their students without the need for multiple hours of training and/or time-consuming wholesale changes to the way they teach. The authors of this book each have over 30 years of experience as paraprofessionals, teachers, and administrators. We have collectively worked in more than 100 school districts as trainers and consultants.

All educators are experiencing initiative fatigue. Initiative fatigue is an overabundance of initiatives they are being asked to implement simultaneously. In this book, we designed a program that enables educators to fully develop their students' social-emotional learning within the context of the work they already do every day. The book contains multiple strategies that can be implemented with minimal commitment of educator time. It shows teachers how they can adjust and/or tweak the student interactions they already have multiple times each day and how that results in a significant development of social-emotional learning skills.

What Is Social-Emotional Learning?

The social-emotional learning (SEL) movement is a thoughtfully created structure for organizing what good teachers and good schools have done for decades. It is a structure for organizing the development of affective (intrapersonal and interpersonal) learning.

SEL began as a movement in the 1960s when educators began to recognize that social and emotional skills made a significant difference in improving both behavior and achievement in inner-city schools. Most of the components of what we now call social-emotional learning have been with us for decades. By the '70s, educators were talking about the "affective domain" of teaching and learning, which were at that time the responsibility of guidance counselors. Classroom teachers, on the other hand, were responsible for the

Objectives for the Book

After reading this book, the reader will be able to

a. make social-emotional learning an integral part of every interaction with students by managing academic, personal, and interpersonal activities in a way that develops self-management, self-awareness, responsible decision making, relationship, and social awareness skills.

b. develop teacher and student self-awareness about their beliefs related to student and teacher behavior and use growth mindset strategies to make positive modifications to educator and student belief systems.

c. use teacher questions, student reflections, and metacognition to support the development of students' social-emotional skills in the five areas of social-emotional learning.

d. incorporate effective practices in whole class and group work to support the development of students' social-emotional skills.

e. use the nine components of effective classroom management to support the development of social-emotional learning skills.

f. develop and manage classroom rules, routines, and expectations to maximize the level of respectful, accountable talk, and on-task behavior.

g. create classroom communities that are safe for all students and conducive for learning.

h. obtain, maintain, and engage students' attention throughout the lesson.

i. develop educator-to-student and student-to-student relationships that proactively increase appropriate student personal and interpersonal awareness and behavior.

j. set up a classroom structure which, by providing routines and mode maintains, appropriate student behavior and supports and enhances a student's personal and interpersonal awareness and behavior.

k. create a system of rewards, consequences, and learning experiences based upon SEL theories for reinforcing respectful, on-task behavior, and the development of students' social-emotional skills.

l. use SEL best practices to respond to difficult-to-manage behaviors and develop an individual contingency plan to support the growth of a student whose inappropriate behavior hampers learning.

cognitive domain, and physical education and health teachers were responsible for the psychomotor domains.

The 1970s decade was also a time of great experimentation in the use of counseling in schools by teachers in classrooms. William Glasser and others created schools for students identified as having "behavior issues" by training teachers to use counseling skills to supplement the counseling sessions conducted by mental health professionals. In addition, the work in high-poverty schools resulted in improved behaviors as well as improved academic success. The Collaborative to Advance Social and Emotional Learning eventually coalesced these ideas into the SEL movement based on the positive impact of these "soft" skills. Based on a meta-analysis of over two hundred SEL programs, the academic performance of students improved 11 percent (Durlak et al., 2011). Although these programs varied widely, Durlak et al. discovered the following:

- A safe, caring, classroom climate improves students' SEL skills.
- Student participation in collaborative and group learning situations increases student achievement and student engagement if students have adequate SEL skills to work with others.
- High-risk behaviors decrease when students are working with peers and teachers trained in pro-social skills and their attitude toward school becomes more positive.

Thus, classrooms that provide emotional safety,

> *Classrooms that provide emotional safety, respectful relationships, and worthy tasks support SEL growth and academic achievement.*

respectful relationships between peers and teachers, and worthy tasks with high expectations support both SEL growth and academic achievement (Durlak et al., 2011).

CASEL has done for interpersonal and intrapersonal learning what the professional learning communities structure did for teacher-directed professional development.

The five major areas of social-emotional learning, illustrated in Figure 1, include (Casel, 2016):

Self-Awareness

The ability to accurately recognize one's own emotions, thoughts, and values and how they influence behavior. The ability to accurately assess one's strengths and limitation with a well-grounded sense of confidence, optimism, and a "growth mindset."

Table 1 lists specific self-awareness behaviors in the left column. The right column lists the activities provided in this book for supporting those behaviors.

Self-Management

The ability to successfully regulate one's emotions, thoughts, and behaviors in different situations—effectively managing stress, controlling impulses, and motivating oneself. The ability to set and work toward personal and academic goals. Table 2 lists specific self-management behaviors in the left column, and the

Table 1 Self-Awareness Connected to Classroom Practices

Self-Awareness Behaviors	Classroom Practices Described in This Book That Support Self-Awareness
• Identifying emotions • Accurate self-perception • Recognizing strengths • Self-confidence • Self-efficacy	• Goal setting • Reflecting/Journaling • Classroom meeting • Accountable talk • Socratic seminars • Group work and partner work • Metacognition

Table 2 Self-Management Connected to Classroom Practices

Self-Management Behaviors	Classroom Practices Described in This Book That Support Self-Management
• Impulse control • Stress management • Self-discipline • Self-motivation • Goal setting • Organizational skills	• Goal setting • Self-assessment • Restorative justice discussions • Conflict resolution facilitation • Maintaining attention • Inhibiting inappropriate impulses

activities provided in this book for supporting those behaviors are listed on the right.

Social Awareness

The ability to take the perspective of and empathize with others, including those from diverse backgrounds and cultures. The ability to understand social and ethical norms for behavior and recognize family, school, and community resources and supports. Table 3 lists specific social awareness behaviors in the left column, and the activities provided in this book for supporting those behaviors are listed on the right.

Relationship Management

The ability to establish and maintain healthy and rewarding relationships with diverse individuals and groups. The ability to communicate clearly, listen well, cooperate with others, resist inappropriate social pressure, negotiate conflict constructively, and seek and offer help. Table 4 lists specific relationship-management behaviors in the left column, and the activities provided in this book for supporting those behaviors are listed on the right.

Responsible Decision-Making

The ability to make constructive choices about personal behavior and social interactions based on ethical standards, safety concerns, and social norms. The realistic evaluation of consequences of various actions and a consideration of the well-being of oneself and others. Table 5 lists specific responsible decision-making behaviors in the left column, and the activities provided in this book for supporting those behaviors are listed on the right.

Table 3 Social Awareness Connected to Classroom Practices

Social Awareness Behaviors	Classroom Practices Described in This Book That Support Social Awareness
• Perspective-taking • Empathy • Appreciating diversity • Respect for others	• Service learning • Conflict resolution facilitation • Role playing • Accountable talk • Socratic seminars • Group work / Pair work

Table 4 Relationship Management Connected to Classroom Practices

Relationship Management Behaviors	Classroom Practices Described in This Book That Support Relationship Management
• Communication • Social engagement • Relationship-building • Teamwork	• Classroom meeting • Questioning • Service learning • Conflict resolution facilitation • Role playing • Accountable talk • Socratic seminars • Group work / Pair work

Table 5 Responsible Decision Making Connected to Classroom Practice

Responsible Decision-Making Behaviors	Classroom Practices Described in This Book That Support Responsible Decision Making
• Identifying problems • Analyzing situations • Solving problems • Evaluating • Reflecting • Ethical responsibility	• Classroom meeting • Debating an issue • Problem solving with case studies • Socratic seminars, inner and outer circle • Steps to a procedure as individual and as part of group • Conflict resolution facilitation • Accountable talk

Figure 1
Social and Emotional Learning Graphic
Used with permission from CASEL 2017

The Need for SEL in Schools

The results for SEL are clear: Social and emotional processes have a significant positive effect on learning and on students' behavior and relationships to their peers, their teachers, and their school. Each SEL skill listed above supports the development of self-regulation behaviors, perseverance, and motivation, all of which are linked to academic achievement (Aronson, 2002; cited in Durlak et al., 2011; Duckworth and Seligman, 2005; Elliot and Dweck, 2005; cited in Durlak et al., 2011, Zins and Elias, 2006; cited in Durlak et al., 2011).

Just as clear is the converse: **If SEL is lacking and if relationships in the classroom are conflicted, the classroom environment can result in disengaged students and decreased academic achievement.** Students in conflict-filled classrooms are more likely to have low achievement and to be disengaged from school (Burchinal, Peisner-Feinberg, Pianta, and Howes, 2002; Hamre and Pianta, 2001; NICHD Early Child Care Research Network, 2003; Raver et al., 2008). Further, only 60 percent of students in middle school and high school feel that their schools are caring or encouraging, and less than 50 percent of these students feel that they have SEL skills for making decisions, resolving conflicts, or feeling empathy for others (Benson, 2006; cited in Durlak et al., 2011).

The First Step for Teachers: Determine Your SEL Competency

A teacher's social-emotional competencies (SEC) are at least as important as pedagogy and content knowledge for success in teaching and learning. Teachers' SEL competencies influence the qualities of the relationships established in the classroom, serve as models to students, and are major contributors to the classroom climate. According to Mashburn et al., "When students have high-quality relationships with teachers, they have better social adjustment and higher academic competence" (Mashburn et al., 2008; Raver, Garner, and Smith-Donald, 2007; Pianta, 2003).

Researchers suggest that "awareness, attention, flexibility, and intentionality" are essential dispositions for teachers (R.W. Roeser and colleagues, 2012). In addition, **teachers need to develop calm, organized, and safe classes with carefully created classroom management routines and norms that provide positive climates for students' learning.** The relationship between a teacher and a student was found to be a greater factor in student success than the teacher-student ratio and teacher education (Mashburn et al., 2008).

Everyday occasions for teachers to make use of their social-emotional competencies include the following:

- **Emotional Skills**: showing empathy, cultural awareness, appreciation
- **Social/Interpersonal**: modeling coping skills and appropriate responses to anger, anxiety, or sensitivity
- **Cognitive Regulation**: changing a lesson when it's not working, avoiding anger or sarcasm when it is aimed at the teacher, adjusting the work based on the needs of the class (Jones et al., p. 67)

A teacher's SEL competencies may help her deal with typical everyday stresses and the emotional weight of working with students who have experienced trauma. Stress has a negative impact on the behavior of both students and teachers. With stress, classrooms and schools often become harsher, colder, and more conflicted.

Teachers with positive SEC are more likely to demonstrate positive attitudes and experience higher job satisfaction (Brackett et al., 2010). For their own emotional health and to prevent professional burnout, teachers profit from the SEL tools that support students and address how to cope with the stressors, how to foster positive relationships with students, mindfulness focusing, centering techniques such as deep breathing, yoga, or meditation (Jones, et al., p. 68). Brain research recognizes that stress disrupts thinking, including "attention, memory, and problem solving" (Jones, et al., p. 67).

Cultural Awareness

As SEL programs have evolved, research has recognized that feeling safe and accepted in the classroom makes a profound and positive difference. Researchers have found that "having friends from several different social groups that integrate gender and race increases students' sense of connection" (Zakrzewski, 2016). Specific activities that respond to cultural differences can address the impact of harmful words (questioning) and are provided in this book, as well as activities that encourage students to find their shared humanity (classroom meetings) or that bring out students' kindness and empathy (accountable talk, service learning). In addition, every one of these exercises can be used as part of any academic unit from literature to world languages to history to the social sciences as much as they could be used on their own in a classroom meeting organized to discuss interpersonal problem solving.

Researchers have found that "having friends from several different social groups that integrate gender and race increases students' sense of connection."

These social and emotional competencies are not necessarily natural to all teachers, but they can be learned and embedded into the daily life of the school for everyone—students, teachers, staff, and administrators. This book is focused on providing teachers with practical, everyday practices that support the development of SEL skills for students and provide a safe, orderly classroom.

Fact 1: Classroom behavior problems cause loss of time for teaching and learning.

As Walker, Ramsey, and Gresham (2004) note in their article, a survey of teachers who are members of the American Federation of Teachers indicates the following:

> Seventeen percent (of teachers) said they lost four or more hours of teaching time per week, thanks to disruptive student behavior; another 19 percent said they lost two or three hours. In urban areas, fully 21 percent said they lost four or more hours per week. And in urban secondary schools, the

percentage (who report losing four or more hours of instruction) is 24 percent.

For the typical teacher who has between 20 and 30 hours a week of contact with students, this is a significant loss of instructional time over the course of the year. Even if we take the lowest figure (two hours) and multiply that by 38 weeks in a school year, we see a loss of 76 hours of instructional time. That is equal to more than three weeks of school!

Teachers have long been aware that effective and engaging instruction is an excellent means of avoiding classroom management issues; however, we also know that even the most engaging teacher will have classroom management issues unless he or she has an effective plan for managing students' personal and interpersonal interactions.

Fact 2: Managing student behavior is one of the more difficult skills to teach teachers because it is so situational in nature.

Landrum, Lingo, and Scott (2011), as well as Alderman and Greene (2011), assert the importance of being proactive in classroom management rather than reactive. Predicting and solving problems before they occur is far more productive than addressing behaviors in the moment. Additionally, there are many variables and social structures (factors) that must be considered when developing a classroom management plan. In this book, we look at the variables and social structures that teachers must consider when managing student behavior. We then look at specific steps to take when establishing an effective plan. Later in the book, we look at what we do with individual students who still disrupt even when we have a well-constructed and consistently implemented classroom management plan.

Fact 3: Brain development related to nutrition and other factors in homes in poverty may contribute to lower engagement.

A longitudinal study analyzing MRI scans of 389 typically developing children and adolescents at six US research sites found that children from poor families showed systematic structural differences in brain development, specifically in the hippocampus and in the frontal and temporal lobes. In contrast, there were no statistically significant differences in the brain regions between children of near-poor families and those from higher socioeconomic-status groups.

Fact 4: Poor SEL skills often result in academic failure.

In "Promoting Student Resilience in School Contexts" (2007), Gale Morrison and Megan Redding Allen tell us, "If students have poor social skills, a lack of friends, and have poor relationships with teachers, they are at serious risk of failure" (p. 163).

> *If students have poor social skills, a lack of friends, and have poor relationships with teachers, they are at serious risk of failure.*

Fact 5: SEL has a positive impact on behavior and achievement in K-12 children.

"A major review of 213 experimental-control group studies of K-12 students who participated in SEL programs demonstrated positive results" (Weissberg and Cascarino, p. 11).

- Improved social and emotional skills, self-concept, bonding to school, and classroom behavior;
- Few conduct problems such as disruptive classroom behavior, aggression, bullying, and delinquent acts; and
- Reduced emotional distress such as depression, stress, or social withdrawal.

Integrating These Skills Into the Classroom

This book focuses on the classroom and how SEL can contribute to everyday learning. It also provides practical examples based on research into the ways in which SEL supports classroom culture and students' growth socially, emotionally, and academically.

The Nine Social, Emotional, and Academic Components of Managing Classroom Behavior

Over the past 20 years, the co-authors of other books and other trainers with whom we work have used the classroom management, motivation, and growth mindset sections of those books to train thousands of teachers in effective behavior management within the context of academic teaching. The unique program described in this book has been used with preschool,

elementary, middle school, and high school teachers as well as with undergraduate and graduate college students. The key reason for the success of this program is that it explains all nine factors that must be addressed to create a positive educational environment using effective behavior management and classroom-proven methods that lead to high levels of student academic and social-emotional development. It is a systematic approach to creating classrooms that are orderly, build a sense of community, and support the development of children's control of their personal and interpersonal behavior and their involvement in learning.

One of the skills we look at closely is a teacher's questioning practices (see Table 6). Questioning is the most frequently used instructional strategy. However, its impact is often underutilized. In our book, *Instructional Practices That Maximize Student Achievement*, we looked at all questioning practices. In this book, we zero in on questioning practices as they can be used to develop social-emotional learning.

Throughout each chapter, samples of questions are provided to support students' social-emotional learning. Each chapter's content and the SEL skills it addresses are listed below.

Chapter 1 describes educator and student beliefs about the nature of intelligence as it relates to academic, social, and emotional success and their connection to classroom climate, and teacher and student behavior.

Chapter 2 describes educator-to-student and student-to-student relationships as key components in building a community of learners in the classroom.

Chapter 3 discusses the importance of arranging classroom space and of the teacher's use of proximity to students to optimize students' social interactions, personal feelings, and incidences of positive behavior.

Chapter 4 provides descriptions of how to directly teach and model rules, routines, and expectations that provide students and teachers with opportunities to develop social and emotional skills and understanding as a whole class and in partner and small group work.

Chapter 5 details strategies for obtaining, maintaining, and regaining attention and that build students' self-image, student engagement, and academic success.

Table 6 Academic Purposes of Questions and SEL Connections

Purpose of Questioning	Social-Emotional Connections
Assess learning to inform instruction	1. Self-awareness 2. Student self-assessment skills and metacognition 3. Quality teacher feedback 4. Quality positive responses and appropriate praise 5. Respectful, encouraging relationships
Deepen student understanding	1. Develop higher-order thinking 2. Embed learning 3. Develop social and personal awareness 4. Develop decision-making and relationships skills
Engage students and maintain their attention	1. Develop self-management 2. Engage students in the content 3. Social awareness 4. Respect for others 5. Relation management 6. Social engagement 7. Teamwork 8. Develop decision-making skills
Activate previous learning	1. Connect students to their learning 2. Connect to students' experiences 3. Uncover academic and social misconceptions 4. Generate student involvement and interest

Based on the work in Ribas, Brady, Tamerat, Deane, Greer, and Billings

Chapter 6 provides examples of student self-assessment of personal and interpersonal behavior that lead students to metacognition and reflection.

Chapter 7 details a system of rewards and consequences that maintain positive student actions and interactions while building self-esteem.

Chapter 8 provides techniques for teaching that engage students at all academic, social, and emotional levels of development.

Chapter 9 gives the reader methods for maintaining a classroom environment that develops and nurtures social-emotional learning.

To achieve effective classroom management and social-emotional learning, all nine techniques described in the chapters above must be evident in a classroom.

Chapter 10 discusses the use of classroom meetings in the development of social-emotional learning.

1

Beliefs

We begin with ourselves—the first set of beliefs to consider when constructing a classroom environment that addresses social-emotional learning is our own belief system. If we don't have a clear idea of our strengths and weaknesses, we will have difficulty helping students develop their self-awareness, self-management, responsible decision-making skills, relationship skills, and social awareness. Key among these understandings is how our belief system impacts how we work with students.

These beliefs have an impact on the relationships, responses, and expectations that we hold for students throughout every day.

Our Beliefs About Our Definition of 'Appropriate' Student Behavior

What we believe about the following three areas affects every interaction that we have with students:

1. "appropriate" student behavior
2. intelligence, race, socio-economic background, country of origin, religion, and other personal factors
3. the most effective way to shape students' behavior

These beliefs have an impact on the relationships, responses, and expectations that we hold for students throughout every day.

Our Beliefs About Relationships Among Staff

The second set of educator beliefs we need to understand is the other members of our teaching team. Students see many teachers during a day. Even in elementary grades, students often interact with teachers in specialty areas such as art, music, and physical education, as well as at lunch or recess with other classroom teachers and paraprofessionals from their grade group.

Our Beliefs About School Culture

The third set of beliefs are the beliefs about school culture. Schools often operate with vastly different overt and covert cultural norms related to students.

Our Students' Belief Systems

The fourth set of beliefs we need to understand and consider are the belief systems of our students. Students arrive at school with beliefs already established including their beliefs about their intelligence and self-worth, the intelligence and self-worth of their peers (including their ideas on race, socio-economics, religion, countries of origin, and disabilities). These beliefs have been well established by their prior interactions with parents/guardians, siblings, friends, acquaintances, the media, and other forces.

Parent and Guardian Beliefs

The fifth set of beliefs is the beliefs of the parents and guardians in the school community. Parents' and guardians' education levels, socio-economic strata, religious beliefs, personal beliefs, personal experiences and cultural norms all have an effect on the culture of the learning environment.

With these variables at play, it is little wonder that shaping a classroom culture that supports students' social-emotional development is such a critically important area for teachers to develop each year.

Educators' Beliefs

Social-emotional learning in the classroom must begin with us, the educators, before it will work with the students. Each of us operates with a belief system on two levels. The first level harbors our cognitive **conscious beliefs**. It's what we learned in our pre-service and in-service training and through our experiences working with students.

The second level relates to our **unconscious beliefs**. This is how we react to students' behavior when we don't have the time to clearly reflect on a problem situation, weigh alternatives, and choose the best alternative based on our cognitive belief system. Our unconscious beliefs are the result of how we were parented, the school behavior management we experienced as students, and possibly our religion, culture, or previous trauma. In the stress of the classroom, our unconscious beliefs may control our behavior management decisions as much or more than our cognitive beliefs.

For example, one of the authors of this book grew up in a neighborhood and attended a school where most families lived in poverty or slightly above.

Many of the parents never finished high school and no one had a college degree. It wasn't until high school that I had friends whose parents had college degrees and white-collar jobs. Thus, my conscious and unconscious belief was that people who lived in big houses, had college degrees, and worked in white-collar jobs were smarter than those of us from lesser circumstances. Over the years—as I acquired college degrees and spent more time among educated, white-collar professionals—my conscious belief system changed. I learned that intelligence and achievement was more the result of hard work than of a family's socio-economic level. My conscious beliefs changed with time and experience.

My unconscious belief system, however, was much harder to change than my conscious belief system. In 1995, I became an assistant superintendent in a school district that had the highest parent education level and one of the highest average family income levels in the Commonwealth of Massachusetts. Despite my Ph.D. from Boston College and being one of the leaders of an elite public school system, I still struggled with the unconscious beliefs that had been ingrained in me during childhood and adolescence. I always battled feelings that I was inferior to the doctors, lawyers, CEOs, college presidents, and others with whom I now interacted daily, believing they had more cognitive, personal, and interpersonal intelligence than I had. As I look back at my fourteen years as a classroom teacher, vice principal, and principal, I wonder how those unconscious beliefs may have negatively affected the students with whom I worked.—*Bill Ribas*

My unconscious belief system was much harder to change than my conscious belief system.

There is a physiological reason for regressing to our unconscious beliefs even when they are inconsistent with our conscious beliefs. This typically happens when we are feeling stressed. This phenomenon is probably more prevalent when responding to student misbehavior than at any other time in our work as educators. Our brain is made up of three primary parts: the *brain stem,* the *paleocortex,* and the *neocortex.* Frederic Jones, in his book *Tools for Teaching* (2013, p. 3859 of 8100, Kindle version), and Davis, Eshelman, and McKay, in their book *The Relaxation and Stress Reduction Workbook* (2008), discuss the impact on our brain when we are confronted with a classroom discipline issue.

Student misbehavior is stressful for teachers because it detracts from the learning the teacher is trying to achieve. Each student's misbehavior distracts the teacher and detracts from the teacher's learning goals. Not achieving one's goals produces stress. Confronted with misbehavior, ideally we would want to be able to calmly and rationally assess the situation, draw on our acquired knowledge, generate alternatives, assess each alternative, and select the alternative that is best suited to the situation at hand (the steps to making a responsible decision).

To do this, we need to operate in the higher level of our brain, the neocortex. Unfortunately, when confronted with a stressful situation, the brain's physiological response is to prepare for either **flight, fight, or freeze**. This response has been conditioned in us through millions of years of evolution. The blood leaves the neocortex and the paleocortex and flows to the brain stem and into large muscles. This move prepares us well to flee or fight. Or it can even cause us to freeze and not respond because the decision-making parts of our brain are impaired by lack of blood. It serves us poorly when we're trying to solve complex problems such as discipline situations. We respond by avoiding (self-awareness), becoming aggressive (relationship skills and social awareness), or resorting to conditioned responses (self-management) rather than using our cognitive belief system and problem-solving skills to deal with the situation (responsible decision making). It is important to note that this physiological response is also true for our students when they are afraid, angry, or confronted with other stressful situations. Developing their self-awareness of their reaction to stress helps them use "**cognitive override**[1]" so that they can make good personal and interpersonal decisions rather than reacting without thinking and running away, fighting, or freezing.

In addition, when responding to behavior issues, we need to be cognizant of whether we tend to be **authoritative** or **authoritarian**. Ferlazzo (2015) describes the difference between these two behaviors as follows: Being authoritarian means wielding power unilaterally to control someone, demanding obedience without giving any explanation for why one's orders are important. Being authoritative, on the other hand, means demonstrating control but doing so relationally through listening and explaining. Opting for the authoritative style will make students more likely to respect your authority and probably more willing to cooperate. We all know we should be authoritative in our classroom management. Unfortunately, some of us can slip into an authoritarian tone when we are under stress.

> *Opting for the authoritative style will make students more likely to respect your authority and probably more willing to cooperate.*

of earlier beliefs and not be aware of it. In recent years, we have become more aware of things such as "subtle racism" and myths about poverty.

These beliefs are not just the result of our experiences in our personal lives. They are the result of hundreds of years of mistaken beliefs. Below I will briefly describe some of that history.

Growth Mindset and Fixed or Deficit Mindset: The Nature-Versus-Nurture Debate About Intelligence

For more than 130 years, educators, social scientists, and psychologists have debated the question of whether intelligence is innate (an entity) or acquired (**growth mindset**). It is part of the age-old nature-versus-nurture argument that continues to this day. In this next section we look at these two perspectives on the nature of intelligence and how they affect beliefs about cognitive, interpersonal, and intrapersonal intelligence.

The first is the idea that *all or most of our intelligence is genetic and a single entity.* Theorists in this school of thought say there is relatively little that schools can do to influence the intelligence of a student.

The second idea is that *intelligence is learnable and multifaceted and can be developed incrementally.* More recently, this theory has revolved around grit and growth mindset. The proponents of this school of thought believe that most of a person's school and career success (up to 75 percent, per some theorists) is the result of environment (e.g., school, home), effort, acquired strategies for thinking and learning, and the person's attitude toward success and failure.

The Nature-Versus-Nurture Debate

Working effectively with students requires that we closely examine our conscious and unconscious beliefs about intelligence and how it is acquired. As shared earlier, one author's own conscious beliefs about intelligence and particularly about intelligence and poverty took a great deal of education and experience to change over a period of many years. The unconscious beliefs were slower to change. And, since they are unconscious beliefs, we still may maintain some vestiges

Intelligence as a Single Entity and Primarily Due to Heredity

As early as 1869, British scientist Francis Galton wrote the book *Hereditary Genius: Its Laws and Consequences.* In it, he spoke about genetics as the primary determinant of intelligence. American psychologists extrapolated from this the concept of **Intelligence Quotient (IQ)**. This was a measurable intelligence that was native and stayed constant throughout a person's life (Devlin, Fienberg, Resnick, and Roeder, 2002, p. 2).

In their book, *Intelligence, Genes, and Success*

---

1   Cognitive override is a phrase we coined. It refers to using self-awareness to avoid making bad decisions based on our unconscious reactions to situations. We stop the impulse and make good cognitive decisions about how to react to the situation.

(Devlin, Fienberg, Resnick, and Roeder, 2002, p. 5), the authors describe Galton's work:

Galton was a central figure in the founding of the **eugenics** (a term he coined in 1883) movement and the study of the relationship of heredity to race and talent. From his analysis of biographical dictionaries and encyclopedias, he became convinced that talent in science, the professions, and the arts ran in families so that it would be 'quite practicable to produce a highly-gifted race of men by judicious marriages during several consecutive generations'. (Kelves, 1985)

Interesting to note is that Galton was a cousin to Charles Darwin and was influenced by his cousin's work as it appeared in Darwin's famous book, *On the Origin of Species by Means of Natural Selection*. If evolution was the result of the survival of the offspring of the fittest, then isn't it logical that intelligence is something handed down to the offspring of the "smartest"?

Karl Pearson, one of the founders of modern statistical methods, devised statistical methods for establishing the correlation between hereditary intelligence and success in society. Pearson would later join the University of London and become the Galton Eugenics Professor. He went on to publish some 300 works dealing with the relationships between population traits and social behaviors, occupations, and diseases. In describing intelligence, he was quoted as stating, "No training or education can create [it]. You must breed it" (Kelves, 1985).

The person best known for developing a measurement for intelligence was Alfred Binet, a psychologist at the Sorbonne in France between 1894 and 1911. The first intelligence test described by Binet and a colleague in 1896 involved counting objects in pictures, noting similarities among familiar objects, filling in missing words in sentences, and describing how terms had different meanings (Devlin, Fienberg, Resnick, and Roeder, 2002, p. 9). In 1904, Binet was asked to develop a way to determine which French schoolchildren needed extra help. He introduced his method for measuring a child's performance against the trends of other children in 1908. His system measured a child's mental age in relation to the child's physical age. This was the first step in developing the concept of *intelligence quotient* or *IQ* (Perkins, 1995, pp. 23–26).

Binet, however, was not a proponent of the idea that intelligence was a fixed, single entity that was

This was the first step in developing the concept of intelligence quotient or IQ.

established at birth. Perkins (1995, p. 29) describes Binet's reticence to reach this conclusion:

He (Binet) did not jump from the fact that some people behave more intelligently than others to the presumption that there was one essence, a single mental resource, that some people had more of and some less. ... He feared it would offer educators the excuse to ignore the plight of poorly performing students on the grounds that they lacked the intelligence to do better. It also might give educators grounds for dismissing under motivation and behavior problems as symptoms of low intelligence.

Carol Dweck (2006), one of the leading proponents of growth mindset theory, quotes Binet (1909) from his work *Modern Ideas about Children*:

A few modern philosophers ... assert that an individual's intelligence is a fixed quantity, a quantity which cannot be increased. We must protest and react against this brutal pessimism. ... With practice, training, and, above all, method, we manage to increase our attention, our memory, [and] our judgment, and literally to become more intelligent than we were before. (p. 6)

Binet said this in 1909! It appears from his words above that growth mindset has been around much longer than any of us thought.

Henry Goddard authored the first American version of an IQ test in 1908 and administered it to 2,000 school children in Vineland, NJ. It was the Americans, between 1908 and 1925, who took Binet's individually administered intelligence tests and turned them into paper-and-pencil, group-administered tests. To do this, they created a single entity IQ score to replace the mental age and chronological age scores developed by Binet that were difficult to interpret.

Stanford psychologist Lewis Terman imported Binet's test to the United States and developed the Stanford-Binet IQ test (Gould, 1995, quoted by Fraser, 1995, p. 11). Terman recognized that if IQ tests had to be administered one-on-one by a trained psychologist, they would be too expensive to use widely. He and graduate student William Otis developed the first Army Alpha test that was administered to 1.7 million army recruits between 1917 and 1919. That test would eventually be renamed the Armed Services Vocational Battery and was used during World War II. It continues to be used today by all branches of the military service (Devlin, Fienberg, Resnick, and Roeder, 1997, pp. 9–10).

Terman believed that intelligence was hereditary, as documented in his 1922 article "Were We Born That Way?" that appeared in the journal *World's Work*. In that article, he states

> The common opinion that the child from a cultured home does better in tests by reason of his superior home advantages is an entirely gratuitous assumption. … The children of successful parents test higher than children from wretched and ignorant homes for the simple reason that their heredity is better.

The data derived from the Alpha tests began to drive the belief in American society that certain cultures were genetically more intelligent than others. Princeton psychology professor Carl C. Brigham wrote the book *A Study of American Intelligence* based on the findings from the Alpha tests. Brigham (1923) concluded that the immigration of southern and eastern Europeans to the United States would lower "native" American intelligence. One year later, Congress passed the Immigration Restriction Act of 1924, which enabled a disproportionate level of immigration by northern and western Europeans, who were thought to be more intelligent. In the United States, Supreme Court case *Buck v. Bell* in 1927, the court supported sterilization laws passed in 16 states between 1907 and 1917. In that opinion, noted Justice Oliver Wendell Holmes wrote, "Three generations of imbeciles are enough" (Hernstein and Murray, 1994, p. 5).

In 1912, German psychologist W. Stern improved on Binet's format for determining IQ. Stern (Perkins, 1995, pp. 26–28) developed a system in which a person's mental age was divided by his or her actual age. This number was then multiplied by 100. For example, a 10-year-old who had a mental age of 10 would have an IQ of 100—that is, 10 divided by 10 equals one. One multiplied by 100 equals 100. A 10-year-old with a mental age of 11 would have an IQ of 110. Eleven divided by 10 equals 1.1, and 1.1 multiplied by 100 equals 110. A 10-year-old with a mental age of nine would have an IQ of 90. This gave rise to the bell curve with which we are all familiar (see Figure 1.1).

Stern's method worked well for children but became a problem when applied to adults. The mental-versus-chronological age comparison no longer worked when applied to people in their 40s and 50s. Another method was needed that might be applied to adults and children. Today, psychologists still use a bell-shaped curve such as the one in Figure 1.1. In today's model, IQ is no longer determined by dividing mental age by actual age. Instead, it is normed against the results of many people who are tested to determine average scores and the various standard deviations from the average. The number 100 continues to be used for the average score solely to be consistent with Stern's model. The standard deviation of 15 is also used to continue with the familiar numbers from Stern's work. Stern found a standard deviation of approximately 15 or 16.

In the general population, more than 68.2 percent of the people have an IQ between 85 and 115, while 13.6 percent of the population have an IQ between 115 and 130. Another 2.1 percent of the population have an IQ between 130 and 145. Only 0.2 percent of the population have an IQ above 145. The same is true for the left side of the distribution, with 13.6 percent of the population having an IQ between 85 and 70, 2.1 percent with an IQ between 70 and 55, and only 0.2 percent with an IQ lower than 55.

In the 1930s and 1940s, the United States' public was well on its way to believing that intelligence could be defined by a single score, was genetically inherited, and varied by race.

Figure 1.1 Bell Curve

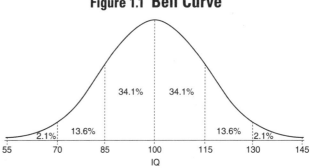

In the 1930s and 1940s, the United States' public was well on its way to believing that intelligence could be defined by a single score, was genetically inherited, and varied by race. Everyone in education has at some time come across the Wechsler Intelligence Scale for Children, commonly known as the WISC. Psychologist David Wechsler developed his first version of the test in the 1930s. This test, in its revised form, is still used in schools to determine student IQ.

In 1957, psychologist Ann Anastasi noted at meetings of the American Psychological Association that the nature (entity)-versus-nurture (growth mindset) debate about intelligence had subsided because geneticists, psychologists, and social scientists had become convinced that nature and nurture were interactive and interrelated as they pertained to intelligence. In 1958, she indicated in an article in *Psychological Review* that the focus on the study of intelligence must be on the interaction of both nature and nurture (Anastasi, in Devlin et al., 1994).

As the 1960s approached, most educators believed that some part of intelligence (or lack thereof) was developmental and not hereditary. Lyndon Johnson's Great Society program brought Head Start to schools to reverse the negative impact of the home environment in socioeconomically deprived homes. The belief was that early intervention would enable students to "catch up" intellectually with their peers from socioeconomically advantaged homes.

Nevertheless, educators were not ready to let go of the concept that intelligence was fixed at some point early in a child's life. They determined that tracking by ability in schools was required to ensure that the less intelligent were not frustrated and overwhelmed and the more intelligent were not held back by the slow pace of the others. Millions of baby boomer children were placed in fixed-ability reading and math groups as early as first grade. Junior high and high schools were tracked by ability. Junior high students were even funneled to either academic college preparatory high schools or vocational high schools, depending on whether they were deemed intelligent enough to go to college.

One school district in southern Connecticut during the late '60s and early '70s went so far as to place eighth graders into fourteen[2] separate "divisions" based on ability. The elementary schools in the city were neighborhood schools from kindergarten to grade seven. All eighth-grade students in the district attended a single school before moving on to high school. Based on the students' grades, scores from the Iowa Tests of Basic Skills, teacher recommendations, and aptitude tests in mathematics and foreign language, each student was placed in one of

The late '70s through the '80s and '90s brought an increased belief in the malleability of intelligence based on home and school environment.

the 14 levels. Each level had a distinct and public number designation from one to 14, which was used to identify the class for various school activities. For example, on school picture day, the secretary would periodically make an announcement when it was time for another class to come for their pictures. "Division 14, please report to the cafeteria for your pictures" would be announced in all classrooms. We can't begin to imagine the negative impact the social and intellectual self-image of the students in the lower divisions.

These educators were not cruel or uncaring. Contemporary wisdom firmly believed that the needs of all the students were best met when grouped by ability. This belief was so strong in society that neither the public nor professional educators saw any problem with grouping students by ability and clearly identifying them, as in this example from the Connecticut school. However, one can only imagine the impact this identification had on the students carrying these labels.

The late '70s through the '80s and '90s brought an increased belief in the malleability of intelligence based on home and school environment. This belief led to a reduction of tracking in our schools, typically occurring first in the lower grades. Fixed reading and math groups were reduced or eliminated first in the primary grades. This change slowly moved up the grades until heterogeneous and flexible grouping became the primary structure in most schools through fifth grade. Many districts changed to the middle school concept (with sixth, seventh, and eighth grades grouped together) and reduced the degree of tracking.

The Nature-Versus-Nurture Debate Continues

Even with these changes occurring in schools, proponents of the concept of intelligence as a single, fixed entity and primarily determined by heredity continued to promote these concepts. In the books *The Bell Curve* (1994) and *Real Education* (2009), the authors reestablished the concept of inherited, fixed, single-entity intelligence as a viable theory of intelligence.

The authors Richard Hernstein and Charles Murray used a comprehensive review of the research on intelligence over the previous 125 years to

---

2   There were 18 separate ability-based divisions in the city. However, because the eighth-grade building was overcrowded, four of the divisions were housed in the high school at a different location. These four classes operated as their own school, with the classes labeled as Divisions 1, 2, 3, and 4. This left 14 divisions in the primary building.

conclude that intelligence was primarily hereditary and that it varied by race and culture. The book reignited a fiery ideological debate in academia and the public between those who adhere to this theory and those who believe that intelligence has multiple components and may be enhanced by home and school environments.

In an article on November 11, 2007, *The New York Times* warns that "nonscientists are already beginning to stitch together highly speculative conclusions about the historically charged subject of race and intelligence from the new biological data." It notes several occurrences of these nonscientists making the case for superior genetic intelligence based on a person's continent of origin or race. The article goes on to describe several recent studies by geneticists that have isolated specific genes to specific races or continents of origin as they relate to a predisposition to certain diseases or illnesses. However, these geneticists are quick to point out that there is no genetic evidence now that supports any genetic link to higher intelligence in people of one race or continent of origin over another.

The research on the variability of IQ continues to uncover new evidence of the importance that both school and home environment play in increasing (or decreasing) IQ.

Intelligence as Having Multiple Components That May Be Enhanced by Home and School Factors

The genesis of the idea that intelligence is a composite of multiple components came from Alfred Binet. David Perkins (1995) credits Binet with presenting us with the first suggestion that there may be multiple intelligences:

> Binet looked at a great variety of kinds of human behavior to gauge intelligence. … He tested children every which way, and the more ways the better. So long as the task did not depend much on unusual rote knowledge or reading and writing it was fine with Binet. … He took this approach because he believed that intelligence, far from being one thing, was a potpourri, a mix of this ability and that ability all jumbled together (p. 25).

For the next 50 years, Binet's thoughts about intelligence containing multiple components were

largely ignored as psychologists, educators, and social scientists strove to find ways to establish a person's innate intelligence as a way of socially engineering aspects of society, including the military, education, and the workforce. As stated earlier, the largest body of work in this area at the turn of the 20th century was for efficiently determining job classifications for the military. Schools used the results to determine effective means of tracking students for efficient instruction.

In the 1970s, University of Pennsylvania psychologist Jonathan Baron examined the relationship between strategies and intelligence. Baron's studies looked at the memories of mildly retarded children versus those of children with average intelligence. In his 1978 article "Intelligence and General Strategies," Baron showed that the significant gap in the achievement on memory tasks that existed between children with average intelligence and children slightly below average might be closed by teaching them strategies that enhanced their memory.

Lloyd Humphreys, a psychologist at the University of Illinois in Urbana, looked at the changes in the IQ test scores between soldiers tested in 1917 and those tested in 1942. Humphreys found a 15-point increase (one standard deviation) in the scores of those tested in 1942. Humphrey credits that increase to the expansion of public education during those years (Perkins, 1995, pp. 77–79).

In the 1980s, University of Virginia psychologist Sandra Scarr examined the relationship between genetics and environment in a series of studies using identical twins, chosen because of their identical genetic makeup. Scarr identified groups of twins who were separated at birth and raised in different homes. Scarr's work, combined with that of others, established that IQ was 50 percent to 60 percent attributable to heredity, with the remaining 40 percent to 50 percent attributable to nurturing factors.

The research on the variability of IQ continues to uncover new evidence of the importance that both school and home environment play in increasing (or decreasing) IQ. Eric Turkeheimer, a psychologist at the University of Virginia in Charlottesville (Jacobson, 2003), found the correlation between IQ and heredity is even lower for children from homes with low socioeconomic status than it is for children in socioeconomically advantaged homes. Turkeheimer's research, based on twins studies, indicates that the correlation for children from homes with low socioeconomic status is 0.1 on a scale with a maximum level of 1.0.[3] This would indicate that the environment, of which schools are an important part, is a significant component of the factors that shape the IQs of children from disadvantaged environments.

Perkins (1995) explains to us that a person's IQ is only 50 percent due to genetics. He further explains that the correlation between IQ and a person's success in school and in the workforce is approximately 0.5 (p. 61). That means that a person's genetic intelligence accounts for only 25 percent of his or her success in school and work. The remainder of a person's success is attributable to learned knowledge, strategies, and effort. This appears to show that 75 percent of a person's school and work success may be shaped by parents, teachers, and other nurturing influences.

In this model of intelligence, teachers, parents, and individuals have little or no control over neural intelligence.

Learnable Intelligence

David Perkins' **theory of learnable intelligence** looks at intelligence as comprising three components. The first is **neural intelligence.** This is the part of our intelligence that is primarily determined by heredity and only changes because of the physical maturation of the brain—i.e., the nature portion of our intelligence. In his book, *Outsmarting IQ* (1995), Perkins defines neural intelligence as

> the contribution of the efficiency and precision of the neurological system to intelligent behavior. This contribution may involve a single unified factor or some mix of several factors. In any case, it is influenced strongly by genetics and physical maturation (p. 102).

The second component of intelligence described by Perkins is **experiential intelligence.** He supports this component of the theory by citing the work of Dutch psychologist A.D. de Groot (Perkins, 1995, pp. 80–81) and others. De Groot studied the similarities

and differences between the cognitive abilities of amateur chess players and those of professional chess masters. He found that amateurs and professionals explored future moves with the same level of depth; however, the professionals easily beat the amateurs. To understand the reason for this, de Groot showed players a chessboard with a typical game situation and quickly removed the board from their sight and study. The amateurs could only remember the exact location of a fraction of the total number of the pieces on the chess board. The professionals, on the other hand, could remember *all the locations of all the chess pieces.* When he repeated the experiment with a random placement of the pieces that would not occur in a game situation, however, the amateurs and professionals had the same level of success in remembering the positions of the pieces. De Groot concluded that the professionals, who played much more frequently than the amateurs, had a much more highly developed memory based on the experience of studying chess pieces during game situations. It was their increased level of experience with the various configurations of pieces as they appeared in games that resulted in a greater ability to remember the location of the pieces during the experiment.

Perkins describes experiential intelligence as

> the contribution of context-specific knowledge to intelligent behavior. **This contribution is learned, the result of extensive experience thinking and acting in particular situations over long periods of time.** While there may be an initial ability to learn efficiently in a domain (for example, musical giftedness), the accumulated knowledge and know-how of thinking in that domain constitutes experiential intelligence (p. 14).

The third component of intelligence is **reflective intelligence**. Perkins (1995) describes this as

> the contribution to intelligent behavior of strategies for various intellectually challenging tasks, attitudes conducive to persistence, systematicity, and imagination in the use of one's mind, habits of self-monitoring, and management. Reflective intelligence is in effect a control system for the resources afforded by neurological and experiential intelligence, bent on deploying them wisely (pp. 102–103).

In this model of intelligence, teachers, parents, and individuals have little or no control over neural

---

3   Correlations between two factors range on a scale of 1.0 to –1.0. A 1.0 correlation between two factors means there is a perfect match. A –1.0 correlation indicates that each factor has an opposite correlation. For example, the correlation between a person's height and his shoe size is a positive correlation. On the other hand, the correlation between days when the temperature is zero in each region and the number of flowers that bloom on those days in that region is probably about 1.0.

intelligence; however, teachers, parents, and individuals have a great deal of control over the development of the experiential and reflective intelligences. Later in this chapter, we will look more at the role of teachers and parents in developing the motivation in students to maximize the growth of their experiential and reflective intelligences. In addition, Carol Dweck's work on self-theory, discussed in the following section, connects to these intelligences.

A Case of Relationship, Growth Mindset, and Grit Changing a Life

The following true story provides an example of how social-emotional factors such relationships, growth mindset, and grit can influence our lives.

Bob and Joe were brothers who were separated in age by four years. They lived in a public housing project with their parents during the 1960s and early 1970s. They attended an elementary school K-7 in which most of the students either lived in the public housing project or lived in a large mobile home park. Their mother supported the family with her job as a waitress in a nearby diner where she walked to work each day. She never had a driver's license and they did not own a family car. Their father was an unemployed alcoholic who would eventually die of cirrhosis of the liver when the boys were approximately 15 and 11 years of age.

Bob was the brother who appeared to have more potential for success (or more "intelligence," as some would say). After elementary school, he attended the local public high school from which most graduates went on to four-year colleges. He played on the basketball team and was in college preparatory courses.

Joe was a likable young man who made friends easily and was a cooperative student. He went to the regional vocational high school rather than the high school attended by his brother. At that time in public education, the move to high school was a filtering process. Those who were "smart" enough for college went on to the local public high school. Those who were not went to the technical high school to acquire a trade.

Joe enjoyed his time at the technical high school and became a draftsman. He went to work for a

Joe exhibited throughout his life what has come to be known as grit.

local company. His boss noticed right away that Joe was a hard worker, was personable, and had the potential to advance in the company. He encouraged Joe to go to college. Joe thought about this idea for a long time, because he was unsure if he was "college material." After all, didn't his elementary and middle school teachers indicate he was not college material by recommending vocational high school, rather than the local college preparatory high school?

Joe finally decided he would give college a try. Since he was now married and needed the income from his job, he decided he would start going to college at night. Joe eventually received a bachelor's degree in business administration. His degree, hard work, and encouragement from his boss earned him a promotion in the company. His confidence in his ability to succeed in the professional and academic worlds (as engendered by his boss and some of his college instructors) rose significantly.

Afterwards, Joe enrolled in an MBA program at night while he continued at his job. He completed the MBA and achieved further success in the company. During his MBA work, he developed an interest in business law, since this area of study was most relevant to his current employment. He decided to enroll in a part-time law school program. He completed law school and passed the bar exam. Joe went on to become a successful attorney practicing business law.

What about Bob? During high school, Bob worked as a cook in the diner where his mother waited tables. After high school, he continued in that position. During and after high school, Bob also began drinking alcohol to excess. Bob continued to work as a cook in the diner until his untimely death at the age of 47 due to alcohol-related physical problems.—*Bill Ribas*

As can be seen from this story of two brothers, Joe exhibited what recently has been labeled *grit* throughout his life. The qualities of grit encompass courage, fortitude, tenacity, and endurance.

In addition, I would add to these qualities one other characteristic: willingness to delay gratification. The gratification that most enjoy after a hard day of work is followed by family time and recreation in the evening and on weekends.

We see in Joe many of these characteristics of grit. It takes significant grit to do the work required to achieve a bachelor's degree, master's degree, and law degree all while working full time. Many hours of sitting in classes and doing homework at night and on weekends takes real resolve when his friends were involved in recreational activities. It took grit to push himself into an academic world that was very foreign to the neighborhood and family life he knew as a child.

We can't measure it, but we can't help believing that the interest and support received from his boss was a factor in his success. Joe's grit may have been enough to achieve as he did. We will talk more about impactful relationships in Chapter 2.

Joe's Social-Emotional Skills

In some ways, Joe may be the poster child for social-emotional learning. His achievements required the self-awareness of the strengths he possessed and the weaknesses he must overcome. It takes a high level of self-management to juggle a job, academic work, and career development simultaneously. Operating in the white-collar world of business law required the acquisition of relationship skills and social awareness that were not modelled in his home. His success required making the responsible decision innumerable times over many years to use his time in a way that would forward his academic and career success rather than in recreational activities.

Let's place the three intelligences discussed by Perkins in the real-life context of Bob and Joe. Bob and Joe came from the same parents, so likely they had similar neural intelligence. One might even argue that, based on Bob's early school success, his neural intelligence may have even been higher than Joe's. At some point during their adolescence and into adulthood, Bob and Joe took very different paths related to their experiential and reflective intelligences. If we track Bob's life after high school, we might argue that Bob experienced no increase in experiential or reflective intelligence.

Joe, on the other hand, acquired increased experiential intelligence as academic and career building blocks. Joe's acquired knowledge and skills at work and in high school led to a sufficient knowledge base to attend college and succeed in college. His acquired learning in college and in his career led to his ability to succeed when attending graduate school. The learning acquired in the MBA program and at work led to his success when attending and completing law school. The building blocks constructed to this point

in academia and in his job ultimately led to a successful career as an attorney.

Reflective intelligence also plays an important role in this story. Joe's decision to attend college at night while working required a high level of self-sacrifice, determination, and the delay in gratification of free-time activities until some future time in his life (a.k.a. motivation). It is the responsible decision almost anyone from any background might make, but it is a decision many people choose not to make. In this example, Joe increased his experiential intelligence and his reflective intelligence.

To understand this idea more clearly, let's look again at brothers Bob and Joe. Let's assume that the decision for Bob to attend the college preparatory high school was based on his having an estimated IQ of 110, along with school grades, Iowa tests, and teacher observations. Let's further assume that Joe's estimated IQ was 90 and that this score prompted the recommendation that he not attend the college preparatory high school. This would indicate a difference of more than one standard deviation between the brothers. If Perkins and others are correct, then 75 percent of what determined Bob's and Joe's ultimate academic and career achievements (or lack thereof) was attributable to family, school, and other nurturing factors, such as the encouragement of Joe's boss for him to attend college. To take this a step further, we may eliminate home as a factor in this example, because both boys grew up in the same home with the same parents. One might then conclude that Bob's and Joe's career achievements are due to nurturing factors outside of the home.

During the 25-year period between Joe's entering ninth grade and his becoming a successful attorney practicing business law, Joe acquired on his own, or with guidance from others, the mental capacity to achieve at a high level. He developed the following traits associated with grit:

1. confidence in his ability to succeed at academic tasks
2. the studying, writing, verbal, and problem-solving strategies needed to succeed in undergraduate, graduate, and law school
3. the perseverance to maintain a full-time job and part-time college study for a span of more than 10 years
4. confidence in his ability to work successfully in a professional environment
5. the verbal, writing, and problem-solving strategies

needed to succeed in both the business and legal professions

6. the motivation to succeed in the competitive environment of business law

Growth Mindset

Many of these characteristics can be developed in schools by using strategies for developing a growth mindset. People who hear the story about Bob and Joe are often left asking themselves why Joe worked to increase his experiential intelligence, while Bob chose to take no action in that direction. Stanford University social psychologist Carol Dweck offers interesting reasons for Joe's and Bob's behavior. In her book, *Self-Theories* (2000), Dweck indicates that some students respond to challenges with an "entity" belief in their intelligence (p. 3–5). This is a belief that intelligence is a fixed entity and, therefore, if a task is difficult for me to do, it must be because I am not smart enough to do it. In her latest book, Dweck (2008, e-book) labels this the *fixed mindset*.

Other students—those who believe that intelligence is what Dweck calls **incremental intelligence**, or intelligence that may be increased with effort and new strategies—see challenges as interesting problems to be tackled step by step. Mistakes are learning opportunities rather than failures. Dweck labels this mindset **the growth mindset**. In her research, she found that, **contrary to popular belief, some students with low confidence in their intelligence still threw themselves wholeheartedly into difficult tasks and stuck with them to fruition.** These students had an incremental belief about intelligence. Other students with high confidence did not want their intelligence tested, and their high confidence was quickly shaken when confronted with a difficult task. These students had an entity belief in intelligence.

In another surprising finding, Dweck (2000, p. 53) found that students who had high achievement during their elementary and middle school years were the most, rather than the least, vulnerable to entity thinking when faced with a difficult task. They worried about failure, questioned their abil-

David Perkins tells us that our intelligence is 40–50 percent learned, and our success in school and life is at least 75 percent—due to the strategies we learn, the effort we exert, and the people who guide the development of these two factors.

ity, and were likely to wilt when they hit obstacles. The other students, those with a history of lower achievement, developed the capacity to stay with a task even when their initial attempts led to failure.

Making Kids Smarter in Schools

David Perkins tells us that our intelligence is 40 percent to 50 percent learned and our success in school and life is at least 75 percent due to the strategies we learn, the effort we exert, and the people who guide the development of these two factors. Clinical psychologist Daniel Goleman, Ph.D., the author of numerous books and articles on emotional intelligence, estimates that IQ only accounts for between 10 percent and 20 percent of a person's success in school and career (1999). That means 80 percent to 90 percent of success in life is in the control of the individual and the people who affect their lives, such as teachers and parents.

Carol Dweck has shown us that how teachers interact with children has a significant impact on how they react when confronting unfamiliar and challenging situations. What an exciting prospect for those of us who work in the education profession, which is primarily charged with preparing students for successful lives.

The next part of this chapter shares ideas that classroom teachers have used to help students develop a growth mindset. By that, we mean developing students who

- willingly exert more effort
- use strategies to more efficiently learn new knowledge and skills
- use strategies to solve problems
- stick with problems until they are solved
- believe in their abilities to succeed in school and life by applying effort and strategies

Dweck (2000) offers some techniques for assessing whether individual students have an entity or incremental approach to their intelligence. The activity sheet in Figure 1.2 may be used to assess students' beliefs about the nature of intelligence. It is designed

---

Figure 1.2

Name: _____

Teacher's Name: _____

Date: _____

Please answer the following questions. It is important that you answer them as honestly as you can and are not influenced by what you think others will answer. **There are no right or wrong answers.**

1. Write a definition for *intelligence*.

2. Think of a person whom you consider intelligent. It might be someone you know personally or know of from the news or another source. Describe what this person does that causes you to think of him or her as intelligent.

3. Are there times when you feel intelligent? If so, when?

4. Is there a time or are there times when you have felt dumb (unintelligent)? If so, when?

5. Fill in the equation below so the total equals 100%:

Intelligence = _____% effort + _____% innate ability

---

for use in upper elementary, middle, or high school; however, it may be simplified or given orally to younger students (pp. 53–63).

In her research with fifth graders, Dweck (2000) found that students with an entity (fixed) mindset defined intelligence as

"What your IQ is or how smart you are."
"Intelligence is how smart you are."
"Very smart, brilliant, or bright."
But the incremental (growth) mindset students defined intelligence as
"I think it is what you know."
"How much you look at a problem and check it over to find stuff wrong."
"I think it is to try your best."
"Studying hard."
"Intelligence is how hard you work to do something" (pp. 61–62).

Entity theorists, those who believe we have a fixed intelligence, tended to answer Question 5 (Figure 1.2) with a higher percentage indicating ability. Incremental theorists, those who believe intelligence can grow, assigned a higher percentage to effort.

Dweck speaks about the need to do "**attribution retraining**" (2000, p. 56) with all students and particularly with those who respond to challenges with the entity reaction of feeling dumb and giving up. **By retraining students to think of intelligence as something we acquire with hard work and strategies (growth mindset), we develop in them the desire to work on challenging school assignments to completion. We motivate students not to give up when something is difficult, but to learn from their mistakes and try again.**

The following are some strategies that teachers use to develop the belief that intelligence is incrementally achieved through effort and learning new strategies.

Implicit or Unconscious Bias and Confirmation Bias

"We absorb bias in the same way we breathe in smog—involuntarily and usually without any awareness." — Beverly Daniel Tatum, quoted by Fairman (2016, p. 11).

Up to this point we have discussed beliefs as they relate to intelligence in general. Some of the more troubling beliefs can be confounded by conscious or unconscious beliefs about student race, socio-economics, or gender.

> Tests of implicit bias (or unconscious bias) show that people of all backgrounds show unconscious preferences on the basis of gender, race, sexual orientation, or other aspects of identity According to these tests, most people favor the group they are a member of—despite claims that they have no preference. The tests also show, however, that people across groups show preferences for the "culturally valued group." Approximately one-third to one-half of the people in "stigmatized groups" tend to favor the "culturally valued group" (Morin, 2015).

The data on student suspension shows that something is amiss in terms of race. Black students are suspended and expelled at a rate three times greater than white students. On average, 5 percent of white students are suspended, compared to 16 percent of black students. American Indian and Native–Alaskan students are also disproportionately suspended and expelled, representing less than 1 percent of the student population but 2 percent of out-of-school suspensions and 3% of expulsions.

One author describes his experience with this dynamic as follows:

> I spent my first two years of teaching in a high-poverty school. I taught second grade one year and third grade the following year. After me, the first male teacher any of the students saw was in fifth grade. Each year the principal would assign him all the boys "who needed a man"—a.k.a. the boys who couldn't behave. I thoroughly enjoyed and had success with these boys the others found highly frustrating or uncontrollable. This was for two reasons. The first is that as an elementary student I consistently received "D" grades in conduct because I couldn't sit still or keep my mouth shut. I was a "frequent flyer" in the principal's office.

These connectors allow girls to have more sensually detailed memory, better listening skills, and the ability to more easily distinguish between different voice tones.

The second is that my female colleagues had all been "good girls" in school. They couldn't understand why these boys behaved as they did. They assumed the behavior of these boys was a choice they made to disrespect the teacher.

It is difficult to teach self-management, self-awareness, social awareness, and relationship skills if you don't understand the underlying reasons why these skills don't exist. Boys represent 79 percent of preschool children suspended once and 82 percent of preschool children suspended multiple times, although boys represent 54 percent of preschool enrollment. The female teachers were dedicated professionals, but they had a strong unconscious bias regarding the behavior of boys.

We now know more about the differences between boys and girls that contribute to boys being less able to "behave" than girls.

A Look Inside Girls' Minds

Gurian and Stevens (2004, 2010) found several characteristics of girls' minds that affect student learning:

- The corpus callosum of a girl's brain tends to be larger than that of a boy's, thus allowing more "cross-talk" between the two different hemispheres in the girl's brain.

- Girls tend to have stronger neural connectors in their temporal lobes than boys do. Thus, these connectors allow girls to have more sensually detailed memory, better listening skills, and the ability to more easily distinguish between different voice tones. In addition, this difference between boys and girls allows girls to use greater detail in writing assignments.

- Girls tend to have a larger hippocampus (a memory storage area in the brain) than boys, which gives girls a learning advantage, particularly in the language arts.

- Girls' prefrontal cortex is more active than that of boys, and it develops at an earlier age, thus allowing girls to have better impulse control than boys. In addition, girls tend to have more serotonin in their bloodstreams, which also makes them less impulsive.

- Girls tend to use more cortical areas of their brains for verbal and emotive functions, whereas boys tend to use more cortical areas of their brains for spatial and mechanical functions.

Although these are just some of the characteristics that define a girl's mind, understanding these factors helps us better understand why girls generally do better than boys in reading and writing (Conlin, 2003, in Gurian and Stevens, 2004, 2010). In contrast, because the girl's brain devotes more of the cortical area to verbal and emotive functioning, it does not use as many of its cortical areas for abstract and physical-spatial functions as does a boy's brain. This difference may in part explain why fewer girls are interested in physics, industrial engineering, and architecture. Children are drawn to activities that their brains find pleasurable. By pleasurable, we mean, "in neural terms, the richest personal stimulation. Girls and boys, within each neural web, tend to experience the richest personal stimulation differently" (Gurian and Stevens, p. 22).

A Look Inside Boys' Minds

Gurian and Stevens (2004, 2010) have also uncovered several characteristics with regards to boys' brains:

- Boys generally use half as much brain space for verbal-emotive functions as girls do because more of their cortical areas are dedicated to spatial-mechanical functioning. For this reason, many boys gravitate toward moving objects such as balls, model airplanes, or their bodies.

- Boys have less serotonin and oxytocin (the primary human bonding chemical) than girls do, which makes boys more physically impulsive. In addition, it is more difficult for boys to sit and listen empathetically to a friend (Moir and Jessel, 1989; Taylor, 2002, in Gurian and Stevens).

- Boys' brains operate with less blood flow than those of girls and tend to compartmentalize learning. Thus, girls are better at multitasking, have longer attention spans, and can transition between lessons and classes more easily (Havers, 1995, in Gurian and Stevens).

- Boys' brains renew and recharge themselves by entering a rest state, whereas girls' brains can

reorient neural focus without ever entering this rest state. Therefore, teachers more often find boys fidgeting or tapping pencils to stay awake. Boys, more so than girls, tend to nod off before completing their work or in the middle of a lecture. Boys generally stay more engaged in a lesson if the teacher uses fewer words and more diagrams, pictures, and movement.

The qualities that characterize a male's brain explain why boys generally perform better in higher-level mathematics and physics than girls when these subjects are taught abstractly; why more boys than girls prefer to play combat-centric video games; and why boys tend to get in trouble more than girls for impulsivity, fidgeting, and boredom, as well as for their "inability to listen, fulfill assignments, and learn in the verbal-emotive world of the contemporary classroom" (Gurian and Stevens, 2004, p. 23).

Deficit or Fixed Perspective

Unconscious biases can also be found when middle-class teachers teach children from poverty backgrounds. Those of us who work with children from low-socioeconomic status (low-SES) or poverty families must be cautious that we do not fall into the trap of believing some of the myths about low-income families. In his article "The Myth of the 'Culture of Poverty,'" Paul Gorski (2008) coined the phrase *deficit perspective*. Deficit perspective is the tendency when some of us consciously or unconsciously focus on what students from poverty (or other groups) lack rather than their strengths. For most of us, this comes from a heartfelt compassion for these children. We recognize the gap between the opportunities they have and those available to middle- and upper-income children. This can lead to lower academic expectations for these children, and lower expectations can, in turn, lead to a self-fulfilling prophesy that results in lower academic achievement on the district standards. This is not to say that these students don't have more obstacles to overcome than middle- and upper-income students to reach the same level of achievement. However, a more respectful and appropriate response to this underachievement is to encourage students, expect high standards, and to support students' growth with scaffolds and tech-

> *Poor working adults often work two and three low-wage jobs, spending more hours working each week than their wealthier counterparts.*

niques that overcome these obstacles rather than to reduce expectations.

The deficit perspective sometimes results from mistaken beliefs about families living in poverty. Below are some examples of these mistaken beliefs and the reality of these families.

1. Lower Motivation Mistakenly Attributed to Those Living in Poverty

There is a "**culture of poverty**" that defines the values of most children and families who live in poverty. For example, some believe these families have less of a work ethic and lower motivation. The National Center for Children in Poverty (2004) found that 60 percent of these families have at least one parent who works full-time year-round. In fact, the Economic Policy Institute (2002) found that poor working adults often work two and three low-wage jobs, spending more hours working each week than their wealthier counterparts.

2. Non-Involvement in Children's School Events

Some believe low-income parents attend few school events because they don't value education as much as higher-income parents. The National Center of Education Statistics found that these parents attend fewer school events because they have less access. Working multiple jobs, having jobs that lack paid leave to attend school events, lack of child care, and the lack of transportation were found to be significant impediments to these parents' ability to attend school events.

3. Substance Abuse

Some believe poor people tend to abuse drugs and alcohol more than their wealthier counterparts. Diala, Muntaner, and Walrath (2004) and Galea, Ahern, Tracy, and Vlahov (2007) found that when alcohol use was grouped with illicit drug use, wealthy people were more likely than poor people to be substance abusers.

Expectations and modified beliefs alone will not equalize achievement among the students from both genders and all socioeconomic levels and races. However, it is important that we start with a high level of self-awareness of our conscious and unconscious beliefs. Otherwise our misguided beliefs about

academic, intrapersonal and interpersonal "intelligence" will become a self-fulfilling prophesy.

Teaching Team's Beliefs

Behavior management plans and the corresponding social-emotional learning that takes place work best when they are well designed, based on principles that support social-emotional development, and are consistent among the teachers in a team (and in the school, which we will talk about next). By *team*, we are referring to those teachers and other educators who have contact with the same students. In elementary schools with self-contained classrooms, the team includes the music, art, and physical education teachers. It includes teachers who may have lunch or recess duty when students are at these activities. In middle schools, teams of teachers often share the same students, with each person teaching a different subject area. In high school, the team is often the teachers in the same department. Over the course of a high school career, a student will have four to six teachers from each department.

A high level of consistency in classroom behavior expectations (and academic expectations) and the way the members of the team reinforce or extinguish behaviors and the awareness of principles that support social-emotional development, will make behavior management more effective for everyone. Later in this book, we will see a plan for teaching the expectations for cleaning up after a science lab. It would be significantly easier for teachers to convey these expectations if all the science teachers established, taught, and consistently required the same expectations and understood supportive SEL principles.

What Causes 'Bad' Behavior'?

Students have spent many years figuring out the adults in their lives. By kindergarten, they have had six years of practice. By their senior year in high school, they have had 17 or 18 years of practice. They become very good at knowing what they can do with whom.

This knowledge is evidenced by the ability students have developed to assess each teacher's behavior limits and "push the envelope" to those limits. One elementary principal with whom we worked could observe lines of students waiting for the bus from his office window without the students' seeing him.

Even though the school had written behavior expectations for the bus lines, teachers would implement these expectations with varying consistency. Student behavior would vary, based on who was on duty.

A middle school assistant principal who was the building "disciplinarian" was often in the position of monitoring the behavior of repeat offenders from the various classes. He found marked improvement in the behavior of the students in all classes when the teachers began responding to inappropriate behaviors in a consistent and SEL-appropriate fashion. He described with excitement the way in which a plan of common techniques for responding to inappropriate behavior, designed to address the behaviors of one or two students, resulted in the improved behavior of all the students.

In general, the more consistent and SEL-principled the expectations and implementation of the expectations among the teaching team, the more effective each teacher will be in managing the classroom.

In general, the more consistent and SEL-principled the expectations and implementation of the expectations among the teaching team, the more effective each teacher will be in managing the classroom. Behavior management is one of those areas in which the consistent whole is more effective than the sum of the parts. Laurie Boyd (2012, p. 63) tells us that even teachers who are masters of classroom management incorporate the key features of the **building behavior management** plan into their classroom plans.

A very good exercise for a teaching team is to examine together their similar and different beliefs about student behavior. This requires raising our self-awareness so we can make responsible decisions about how we address student behavior. This can be achieved by having each person answer the following questions on his/her own:

1.   When children behave in school, why do they behave?
2.   When children misbehave in school, why do they misbehave?

The answers are then shared with the team. The team then discusses the similarities and differences in their answers and works to achieve consensus with the proviso that initially they discussed SEL research that demonstrates that, as stated earlier, they were

• creating a safe, caring, classroom climate to improve students' SEL skills.

• teaching students to participate in collaborative and group learning.
• using pro-social skills by everyone in the school (including both educators and students) (Durlak et al., 2011).

We have done this exercise with thousands of teachers during classroom management and growth mindset training and found in every group a wide range of answers. However, as the discussion progresses, the group's beliefs have moved closer together.

This exercise has two objectives. The first is to create a larger foundation of common beliefs. The second is to understand where our beliefs may differ from those of our colleagues. We don't need to have a robotic consistency of beliefs to work effectively together to create an effective team plan for classroom management. However, we do need to identify our common beliefs and differences and develop a consistent set of rules, routines, and expectations with SEL as a basis.

School Culture

Each school has its own culture. In that culture, we should work to develop common expectations for student behavior; however, this is not always easy to do. There are many educators in a school with many different sets of conscious and unconscious beliefs. The result is that even the best school-wide behavior plan will have gaps because of varying implementation. The goal of the school is to have common expectations and consistent implementation among the staff. This is one of those goals that schools never fully reach; but constant effort from all staff toward this goal will result in more effective classroom management for all teachers.

An example of the value of school-wide behavior routines and expectations was observed in an urban district in a school located in the poorest neighborhood in the city. The governor of the state had come to present a successful achievement award to the school, which had previously been identified as underperforming and was placed under state monitoring. More than 1,000 students from grades K-8 and their teachers were gathered in the school gymnasium to hear the governor speak. The whispering, shuffling, and talking of more than 1,000 people added up to a significant level of noise. The superintendent stepped forward and raised his hand high over his head without speaking a word, and the entire gymnasium fell silent. The raised hand had become the signal for quiet in every classroom, in the entire school, and in the entire district!

It is important that we consider the culture in our school when crafting our behavior management plans. We want to have a plan that the administration supports and that is reasonably consistent with other teachers' plans.

One author taught a workshop on classroom management to a group of teachers from several neighboring districts. In the workshop was a novice elementary music teacher who taught in two schools. Each time the trainer spoke about team consistency and school culture, he could see the teacher's frustration. At the break, the trainer asked the teacher what was frustrating him. He shared with the trainer that, in his district, the four elementary schools were built in a cluster on the same site. Each school had a different philosophy. Parents in that community could choose the school they wished their children to attend. He happened to be assigned to two schools with very different cultures related to student behavior.

One school was "traditional." Most of the classrooms were arranged with students in rows. Students all passed through the halls in lines. The other school was an open concept school. There were large teaching spaces that several classes shared. Students flowed through the halls from one place to another without walking in lines. The students in that school called the teachers and the principal by their first names. The music teacher had tried to develop a classroom management plan that worked in both schools, but he ended up with one that did not work well in either school. The trainer spent some time with the teacher, modifying his single plan by turning it into two plans, one for each school. The teacher reported significant improvement when his classroom management plans matched the culture of each school.

Fortunately, most of us don't have to work in more than one school culture at a time; however, this story does emphasize the importance of understanding the school culture and crafting a plan that is not inconsistent with that culture.

> *The goal of the school is to have common expectations and consistent implementation among the staff.*

Students' Beliefs

Students come to us from a broad range of parenting structures and previous classroom management structures. Each student has taken those varied experiences and integrated them into his or her personality. The result is an individual interpretation of various interpersonal interactions.

Prior learning at home, in the neighborhood, at church, mosque or temple, and at school, coupled with students' innate **emotional intelligence**, results in each student responding differently to a situation. We often see patterns in student behavior, but two students exhibiting the same behavior may be doing so for different reasons. This means that the teacher response that eliminates the behavior in one student may not have the desired result in another student.

Take, for example, two boys who may be constantly talking to each other in class.[4] One may come from a home in which the children hold status equal or higher than the adults. He may be permitted to interrupt adults and choose to ignore adults when they are speaking. This student's belief is that talking to his neighbor during class is an entirely appropriate activity. The other student may come from a home in which he is required to listen to adults, not allowed to disagree or contradict adults, and he is certainly not allowed to interrupt an adult. In school, talking to his neighbor is a form of "pushing the envelope" and "walking on the wild side." For the second student, a firm look (or what we refer to later in the chapter as the *hairy eyeball*) may be sufficient to stop the behavior. For the other student, the look may only cause confusion. In these examples, we see that in our effort to reshape each students' social awareness, self-management, and relationship skills we need to use a different approach with each student. We can be consistent in the way we provide reinforcements and consequences. However, the private discussion after we initially address the behavior may be very different for each boy.

---

4   Jones's research (2007, p. 187) indicates that 80 percent of the student misbehavior in classrooms is students talking to their neighbors. Think how much easier classroom management would be if we could do away with this one behavior!

Figure 1.3 Cycle of Low Motivation and the Impact of Deficit Mindset on Student Behavior

Lack of effort because of the belief that my failures are due to an innate lack of intelligence and so effort will not contribute to the same level of success others enjoy.

Cycle of Low Internal Motivation

This reinforces my belief that intelligence is innate and that I was not one of the people with the good fortune to have been born intelligent.

Disruptive and/or avoidance behaviors (e.g., not doing homework) that hide my perceived lack of intelligence behind a message to my teachers and my peers that my lack of success is due to my indifference about learning and my belief that school success is not important (or even to be reviled).

Teachers (and at times parents and peers) respond to my constant display of these behaviors with frustration that leads to a diminished relationship and sends me the message that they see me as "bad" or not intelligent.

Ribas et al., *Instructional Practices That Maximize Student Achievement for Teachers by Teachers*, 2017.

Growth Mindset and Student Beliefs About Interpersonal Relationships

A great deal has been written about growth mindset as it relates to academic success. Growth mindset is equally important as it relates to intrapersonal and personal development. As seen in Figure 1.3 (Ribas, Brady, Tamerat, Deane, Greer, Billings, 2017), students who feel "stupid" will go to great lengths not to appear that way to their peers. There are two common "masking" behaviors. The first masking behavior is to misbehave. It is far more acceptable in the mind of a child or adolescent to be seen as bad by their peers than it is to be seen as stupid. The second masking behavior is to appear uninterested and/or lazy. Once again it is far preferable in the minds of children or adolescents to be seen as lazy and uninterested than it is to be seen as stupid.

Changing a student's cycle is a process that can be slow in developing. The older the student, the longer it often takes to make the change.

Changing a student's cycle is a process that can be slow in developing. The older the student, the longer it often takes to make the change. We should remember that when the student comes to us, he or she has lived for years within a negative cycle that has contributed to the current lack of motivation. In Figure 1.3 above, we see that failure or the fear of failure has led to masking behaviors (avoidance and disruptive behavior). These masking behaviors have led to reactions from adults and peers that have reinforced the student's belief that he or she is not intelligent (deficit mindset), which in turn leads to more avoidance behavior, and so on.

The next part of this chapter looks at the ways we can reverse this negative cycle and create a new cycle like the one in Figure 1.4. In this cycle, the teacher implements strategies that start the change. We must remember that the change in the student's behavior will come slowly because there have been many previous years in which the old cycle

Figure 1.4 Creating a Growth Mindset and Reversing the Cycle of Low Motivation

Lack of effort because of the student's belief that failures are due to an innate lack of intelligence and that effort will not contribute to the same level of success others enjoy.

Teacher has more to praise, continues relationship-building, continues teaching effective effort strategies, continues to use teaching that engages the student and is matched to his/her learning style, and continues community-building.

Teacher uses relationship-building strategies that cause the student to feel liked and respected by the teacher. The teacher uses engaging and differentiated teaching that enables the student to have small successes. The teacher uses effective praise, strategies that teach the student that success is due to effective effort, and uses strategies that build class community.

Reversing the Cycle of Low Internal Motivation

Student expends more effort, acquires more strategies, and has more success.

Student begins to believe he/she can succeed with effective effort, and experiences the good feelings related to success. This results in a reduced need to use disruptive and/or avoidance behaviors to hide his/her lack of perceived intelligence behind a message to the teachers and peers that his/her lack of success is due to indifference about learning and the belief that school success is not important.

Ribas et al., *Instructional Practices That Maximize Student Achievement for Teachers by Teachers*, 2017.

has been nurtured, resulting in deep roots. In some cases, we may see only small changes during our year with this student. However, the new cycle we set in motion will move on with the student and benefit him or her in future years.

As educators, there are specific ways we can change this cycle in the classroom. We can also work with parents and guardians to help them understand the cycle and support the change at home. However, this may be more difficult in some families because of the barriers to home communication and the difficult family situations that make the parents or guardians less able to assist with this process. In some cases, they may even continue to perpetuate the cycle of low motivation and its accompanying low-deficit mindset.

Before we can seriously embark on changing the cycle, we need to raise our own self-awareness beliefs related to misbehavior and low academic performance.

Monitoring Our Self-Awareness and Self-Management

One of the traps we can fall into when working with low-motivation students is letting our well-deserved frustration with their lack of effort (and, in some cases, with their disruptive behavior) show in our interactions with them. In their article, "The Importance of Teacher-Student Relationships for Adolescents with High-Incidence Disabilities" (2007), Christopher Murray and Robert Pianta tell us the following:

"Historically, teachers have held more negative attitudes and directed more negative behaviors towards students with disabilities and low-achieving students than towards high-achieving students. This includes *lower levels of emotional support, praise, and other positive behaviors and greater levels of criticism, ignoring, and negative behavior.*"

In our work with hundreds of teachers we have found that this behavior toward these students is often unconscious. This dynamic should not be surprising, given that the motivated student who behaves well is easy to praise and enjoyable to teach. The low-motivated students, particularly those who act out in class, generate frustration and even anger in us. Despite our best efforts not to show these feelings, they can sneak through in our tone of voice, facial expression, and even in our words. Oftentimes, we are not even aware of this. After all, we are only human! Unfortunately, the result is that some of the students who are most motivated by the need to be liked and respected by their teachers are the ones who least feel this connection with the teacher.

Parents' and Guardians' Beliefs

The beliefs of parents and guardians as a group may correlate closely with the school culture as in the urban-suburban school district described below or the district describe above. This happens more frequently when students attend neighborhood schools or parents choose schools based on "philosophy." The exception to this is when a school has been deemed in need of a significant change in its culture by a district initiative, an outside agency, or the parents themselves. In those cases, the school's stated culture and its operating culture may be separated by a large gap. In these circumstances, it is important to be aware of both cultures and adjust our classroom plans as the culture of the building changes. The parents' culture might reflect the stated school culture, the operating school culture, or a completely different culture.

There are many situations in which significant numbers of people within the parent and guardian group have a belief system that is outside of the group's belief system. This is less the case in schools such as the ones described above, in which the parents get to match their belief system with the school's culture. Many school enrollments, however, are determined by geography that encompasses neighborhoods beyond those contiguous to the school. This leaves a greater likelihood that there will be parents with beliefs outside of the prevalent group belief system. This difference may be even more pronounced in cities and coun-

As educators, we can best help our students by working to understand our belief systems as well as those of our students, our teaching team, our school, and the parents and guardians of our students.

ties in which students are bused across neighborhood and community lines. In those cases, the socioeconomic, religious, and cultural differences tend to be greater than in schools that draw from a specific geographic neighborhood. We worked with an assistant superintendent in an urban/suburban district with eight neighborhood schools. One school had a parent education level that was in the top 1 percent in the state. The parent income level was in the top 2 percent in the state. Across the district was another school in which more than 30 percent of the students were receiving free or reduced lunch, and many lived in public housing. In a third school, 20 percent of the student population was first- or second-generation Japanese American. In still another school, the population was 40 percent Jewish and 40 percent white Anglo-Saxon Protestant. Another school had a very large concentration of Chinese and Latino students who were predominantly Catholic and had a growing Muslim community. These were all neighborhood schools with their own school cultures and some similarity in family beliefs about student behavior. All eight schools with their different cultures sent their ninth graders to a single high school. One can just imagine the multitude of parental belief systems and school cultures faced by the teachers of these ninth graders.

Conclusion

At the heart of what determines a person's behaviors related to self-awareness, self-management, responsible decision making, relationship skills, and social awareness is their belief system. This includes both their conscious and unconscious belief systems. Becoming self-aware of these beliefs is a prerequisite to changing a person's social-emotional behaviors. As educators, we can best help our students by working to understand our belief systems as well as those of our students, our teaching team, our school, and the parents and guardians of our students.

Discussion Questions for Reflection

Introduction and Chapter 1

1. The Introduction and Chapter 1 define social-emotional skills, intelligence, and beliefs. **Select a passage that resonates with you and relate it to your practice.**

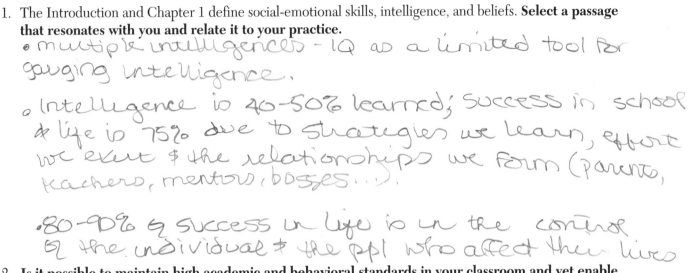

- multiple intelligences - IQ as a limited tool for gauging intelligence.

- Intelligence is 40-50% learned; success in school & life is 75% due to strategies we learn, effort we exert & the relationships we form (parents, teachers, mentors, bosses...).

- 80-90% of success in life is in the control of the individual & the ppl who affect their lives

2. **Is it possible to maintain high academic and behavioral standards in your classroom and yet enable students to feel relaxed and safe in your class?**

Absolutely! Modeling & think alouds in growth mindset strategies, communication

3. **Are there particular student behaviors that trigger your anxiety or an over-reaction—for example, high-pitched voices, students not doing homework, off-task students?**

- Disrespect - backtalk, bullying, aggression

Discussion questions continue on next page

4. Recognizing beliefs about social emotional learning is essential if you are to effectively implement the strategies for SEL. These beliefs may apply to any student, including the gifted, the so-called average, students with special needs, and English Language Learners. The school district from southern Connecticut that divided students into multiple divisions highlights the struggles that children with learning disabilities or other challenges have faced within the structure of public schools. **What might have been the impact on a student's identity and self-esteem with this type of public identification?**

Students in "lower" divisions would receive the message that they were incapable of teaching/learning - Fosters cycle of low internal motivation

5. **Upon reflecting on the story of "Bob and Joe," how can teachers in all settings adjust their practice to develop high expectations for all students? What are some of the circumstances that encouraged Joe's intellectual and educational progress, despite being identified as "not smart enough" for college?**

Joe need ppl who recognized his strengths and gave him the confidence to pursue them through employment/education.

Differentiating instruction/assignments/ assessments to give students choice & develop strengths improves motivation/effort

6. Too many students today, both those who are typical and those with special needs, are driven by the need to be perfect. "Anxiety disorders are the most common mental disorders experienced by Americans." **How can you encourage the strategies of "growth mindset" to help students see "mistakes as learning opportunities rather than failures?"**

Modeling
Emphasizing process over product

7. Boys are more often recommended for special education services than girls. According to the National Education Association, "Boys comprise 67% of all special education students. Almost 80% of these are Black and Hispanic males." (USDOE and Schott Foundation Report) **How can educators use the knowledge of how males learn versus how females learn to change this equation? How does "deficit or fixed perspective" contribute to this statistic?**

Differentiation/choice in how to assess learning

8. Chapter 1 examines some of the underlying issues of "bad behavior" and how creating "common expectations and consistent implementation" increased the probability for improved behavior management. **What are some of the issues within your own classroom and school that would benefit from some of the strategies outlined within the text?**

Classroom Culture → School Culture = Consistency

Teacher-Student, Student-Student Relationships

Impact on Classroom Management and Social-Emotional Learning

Students need a sense of belonging to succeed academically. A good relationship between the student and the teacher is a strong motivator for positive behavior and academic achievement. All of us can remember an educator or adult in our lives whom we genuinely respected and who genuinely liked and respected us so much that it was important to us to please this person and keep his or her respect. This adult motivated us to work harder at our academics, at a sport, in our job, and perhaps on the appropriateness of our behavior. This person motivated us to try hard because we wanted his or her approval and respect.

Chapter 2 focuses on the importance of relationships and emotionally safe spaces to support social-emotional and academic growth. For learning to take place, the learning environment needs a positive school climate that has (1) positive interpersonal relationships, (2) emotionally, academically, and physically safe spaces, and (3) challenging and engaging learning (Yoder, 2014, p. 5).

Impactful Adult Relationships

Impactful relationship is a term we coined for adult relationships that can positively "impact" a student's academic success, social awareness, self-awareness, decision making, relationship skills, and self-manage-

> *A good relationship between the student and the teacher is a strong motivator for positive behavior and academic achievement.*

ment skills. These relationships result in the student having great respect for a person and valuing this person's opinions and advice.

One author's life-changing experience because of an impactful relationship with an educator is provided below.

In the Introduction, I mentioned my less than stellar career as a student in elementary school and high school. Growing up in a neighborhood in which no one went to college and many never finished high school, the idea of going to college never crossed my mind. In the fall of my senior year in high school, I began to think about what I wanted to do upon graduation. I knew two things. First, I didn't want to follow my father and work in a factory for the next 45 years. Second, I knew that I could not make a decent living if I stayed in the city where I was raised unless I worked in the factory. I felt that my only option was to enlist in the military. In October, I had my physical and took all of the armed services placement exams. I was on a delayed enlistment and would enter boot camp after graduation. I did have the option of withdrawing up until the time I swore the oath of allegiance. I was scheduled to go back to the enlistment center in early December to take the oath.

One afternoon early in November, I was sitting in the locker room getting ready for football practice. Football was the only thing I ever loved about school. My football coach from my freshman year, who had also been my guidance counselor, sat down beside me. His name was Tony Maturo and he was the educator I most respected and by whom I felt most respected. The conversation started about football and then moved to some people he knew who were playing football at a Division III school in New Hampshire. He had attended a state school in New Hampshire and talked about how great it was to move out of the city and live on his own.

As an afterthought he said, why don't you go up for a weekend and visit the school and meet the football coach and some of the players he had coached when he had taught in New Hampshire. I agreed because this was a man for whom I would have done anything he asked. I borrowed my parents' car and drove 5 hours to New Hampshire and met with the admissions person and the head coach. The coach assigned a football player to be my guide for the weekend. This was the first and only time I had been on a college campus.

Our schools are filled with Mr. and Ms. Maturos—people who can build relationships that enable them to develop students' social-emotional learning.

I was hooked. I drove home and told my parents that I changed my mind and was going to college if I was accepted. Mr. Maturo helped me submit the application (it was the only school I applied to) and rest is history, almost. Ten years later in 1985, I had my B.S., M.Ed., and had begun my doctoral work while teaching in the Boston area. I went to Connecticut to visit my parents for Thanksgiving. At dinner, my mother said, "It is a good thing that your father and I went to Mr. Maturo's house and asked him to talk to you about going to college. We knew if we said anything to you about it you would have never listened." This was the first time they told me the locker room visit by Mr. Maturo was a set-up they had planned!—*Bill Ribas*

Looking back, I now see that teaching and working with children was my calling. Forty years in education and I cannot imagine spending my life doing anything else[1].

I tell this story because it is consistent with what the research shows about relationships and shaping the social-emotional development of our students. My parents had the social awareness of the importance of having the right messenger (Mr. Maturo) talk with me about another option for my future.

I'm sure they struggled with their decision to intervene in the way they did. Mr. Maturo's relationship skills had made him the most impactful adult in my life. Their choice of actions increased my awareness of other life options and led to my making a responsible life decision.

Our schools are filled with Mr. and Ms. Maturos—people who can build relationships that enable them to develop students' social-emotional learning.

Robert Marzano (2007, p. 150) reviewed 100 studies related to classroom management. His meta-analysis found that "teachers who had high-quality relationships with their students had 31 percent fewer discipline problems, rule violations, and related problems over a year's time than did teachers who did not have high-quality relationships with their students." That means the outcome is 31% fewer negative interactions and 31% or more positive interactions with students—interactions that can include statements and questions that develop social-emotional learning.

For teachers, feeling frustrated by a student who exhibits a lack of effort and demonstrates disrespect and even disdain is difficult to handle. Jessica Minahan, special educator, behavior specialist, and author, recommends in *The Behavior Code* (2012) that teachers reconsider the way that they look at student misbehavior. She says it is not always helpful to assume that a student can act in an expected way or to assume that it is easy for students to change what are considered negative behaviors. Instead of classifying all misbehavior as deliberate defiance, **Minahan suggests that we look at misbehavior as yet-to-be-developed skills.** For example, a student who refuses to write in class may lack self-regulation or be fearful that his or her lack of ability to write on demand might be revealed to the teacher and classmates. Also, Minahan recommends that we look at some misbehavior as a form of communication by a student lacking the ability to express emotions. For example, a student who avoids tasks may be telling you (though in a way that may look like obstinate resistance) that she doesn't know what to do next or has had a bad experience with this kind of activity.

Speaking to teachers, Minahan says: "The only behavior that teachers have control over is their own" (2012, p. 317). Although we have some capacity to control feelings when we see a student "acting out," the reality is we feel what we feel. Even though our emotions toward a certain low-motivated student may

---

1   No one should read this and think the military isn't an excellent option for some. I have had friends and cousins serve in the military and it is a noble calling.

not be positive, we should work to ensure that our behavior and words are appropriately adult: calm and respectful. We need to remember that we serve as models for our students and by responding with respect and patience, we give our students an example of self-awareness and self-management and how to respond in a socially acceptable manner.

*A*cting-out behavior can continue a downward cycle of low motivation, deficit perspective thinking, and academic and social failure.

In addition, teachers who can manage their emotions are more likely to display positive affect and higher job satisfaction (Brackett et al., 2010). Thus, looking at their own emotional response helps teachers recognize the emotional nature of their work, identify and reflect on their emotions and their causes, and cope with difficult emotions through reframing, problem solving, and emotional management (Chang, 2009).

Teaching is emotionally challenging. We can only reduce the stress in teaching if we have the self-awareness to know we feel negatively about one or more students and have self-management tactics to use cognitive override to change our behavior. As noted in Figure 1.1 in Chapter 1, searching for small successes to praise[2] in a sincere fashion is an essential first step to getting students to begin reversing their deficit perspective behavior.

Some low-motivation or disenfranchised students feel isolated from their peers. Their lack of connection with the teacher is compounded by a lack of connection with classmates. This lack of connection with peers and the teacher can lead to acting-out behavior. As we saw in Figure 1.1. in Chapter 1, this acting-out behavior can continue a downward cycle of low motivation, deficit perspective thinking, and academic and social failure.

On the positive side, we all have had students who produced high-quality schoolwork for us who would not produce similar quality work for other teachers. We have also known students who don't produce quality school work for us but do produce it for another teacher. One example is the student athlete who shows no motivation or interest in any class except the one taught by his or her coach. Another example is the student who loves acting, participates in the school plays, and produces his or her best work for the English teacher, who also happens to be the head of the drama club. Sometimes, unfortunately, motivation can be caused by fear. However, more often, it is due to the relationship that has developed between the teacher and student, within and outside of the classroom.

Developing relationships with students can be challenging because of time and schedules. Although students often spend the full day with the same teacher in most elementary classrooms, where they have ample opportunity for the teacher to connect with students and for students to connect with one another, some elementary music, art, and P.E. teachers, as well as middle and high school teachers, see multiple groups throughout the week. In middle schools, the students may or may not stay with the same classmates all day, and these students generally have two, three, four, or more teachers a day. Connecting to students in high school can be even more challenging for teachers since students see few of the same students from class to class and students have five, six, or more teachers in a week.

Research-Based SEL Programs That Work in Elementary School

To support the development of positive peer and teacher relationships, SEL programs generally work on the importance of belonging. Often teachers and staff model positive interpersonal behaviors that may include greeting each child as he or she walks into the classroom or conducting meetings each morning to address the social and emotional concerns of the day. These programs frequently recognize nonacademic skills by celebrating friendship or helpfulness in assemblies or celebrate being connected with "random acts of kindness." In addition, these programs often have a curriculum in which students discuss, problem-solve, and reflect on self- and social-management skills that they encounter during their school day.

---

2 For these students, we will need to decide whether public praise or private praise is the best match for the student. Some of our low-motivation students have spent years criticizing school success, with their words and actions in front of their peers as a defense against their feelings of inadequacy. Praising them in public for academic or behavioral success could negatively affect their behavior as they seek to prove to their peers that success in school is something to be shunned, not sought.

Research-Based Programs That Work in Secondary Schools

To support a positive school culture and to foster relationships between students and teachers, many middle and high schools have adopted advisor-advisee programs in which each teacher is assigned a small group of students with whom he or she meets regularly, sometimes for the three years of middle school or four years of high school. The activities in these group meetings often include academic counseling, self-awareness activities, self-management skills, responsible decision-making skills and relationship skills training. During these small-group sessions, students have an opportunity to build strong connections to a small group of students and at least one member of the faculty. By supporting relationships, these programs confirm for students that they belong in this academic community, a major support for positive school culture based on research.

Developing positive relationships and supporting social-emotional learning skills with our students and among our students can feel overwhelming, given the demands of the curriculum and the focus on academics.

Developing positive relationships and supporting social-emotional learning skills with our students and among our students can feel overwhelming, given the demands of the curriculum and the focus on academics. To avoid our own frustration and feelings of failure at not being able to do this as well as we would like, it is important that we start small and remain realistic about the level of change that will occur. For example, try the following:

1. Choose one low-motivation and/or deficit-perspective student to work with and work to build the relationship with this one student.
2. Acknowledge to yourself any negative feelings you have toward this student, and then commit yourself to consciously ensure that your words, facial expressions, and tone of voice don't betray your frustration when interacting with this student.
3. Next, you can move toward looking for opportunities to praise the student and finding small pieces of time when you can have a private conversation with the student about something that is important to him or her.
4. Remember, it is important that you don't expect to see significant change in this student, as this will result in your feeling disappointed and perhaps feeling like a failure. Remember, this student has had many years of negative feelings related to school success building in him or her prior to coming to you. Any change will be slow in coming and will often be followed by periods of regression. Like so many things related to changing student behavior, this is a two-steps-forward, one-step-backward process.

School psychologist Allen Mendler, author of *Discipline with Dignity* (1999) and *As Tough As Necessary* (1997), writes in his book *Connecting With Students* (2001):

Many educators wonder how they are going to find the time to build and sustain relationships with students when there are so many demands for achievement. In fact, successful educators realize that a strong relationship with students leads to better discipline in the classroom, which means more time for instruction. A 2013 study by Reichart and Hawley of "middle school boys and their teachers in the US, Canada, UK, and South Africa found that … varying degrees of resistance boys brought to the classroom were dissolved by a variety of relational gestures by teachers."

The positive actions described in this book can be incorporated into the school day without taking time for a separate curriculum. Teachers can accomplish positive classroom culture, a sense of belonging, and a safe, challenging environment by using the techniques and tools described here. Deci and Ryan identified three key human needs—competence, autonomy, and relatedness or personal connection. Students feel a sense of relatedness when they perceive that their teachers like, value, and respect them. They feel competent when they work at challenging tasks (Tough, 2013, pp. 74-5). These three feelings are far more effective motivators for students than "a deskful of gold stars and blue ribbons." Deci and Ryan recognize that throughout the day, teachers convey to their students "deep messages about belonging, connection, ability, and opportunity" (quoted by Tough, 2013). Boynton & Boynton recommend nine measures for developing positive relationships with students. Examples for each are added below each measure (Ribas et al., 2017, p. 86).

Nine Measures to Develop Positive Relationships with Students

1. Communicate Positive Expectations

- for elementary school, send home frequent newsletters or emails about the class
- for high school, send home a syllabus and a cover letter welcoming the student and family into the class
- post assignments with examples and rubrics as well as your own positive encouragement and recommendations
- make it clear to students in words and behaviors that we are committed to help them succeed
- write notes to students for good work done in or out of class
- work with struggling students before and after school
- be clear about expectations and support rules consistently and fairly[3]
- make phone calls home to inform parents of good news!
- in goal setting, make sure each student has challenged him or herself

2. Call On and Treat All Students Equitably

- give students an interest survey about their in-school and out-of-school likes and interests
- make eye contact with individual students when you talk to the group
- take their insights and ideas seriously
- greet students when passing them in the hallway
- stand physically close to all students at different points in the class
- when working with seated students, get down to their level so you are not looking down at them
- share common interests with individual students (e.g., soccer, jazz, NASCAR racing, gardening)

3. Increase "Wait Time" Periods When Questioning Students

- after asking a question or after a student has responded, wait, that is, give the student time to invite more ideas or to give the student time to process the question
- take students' insights and ideas seriously and prompt with, "Anything else?", or wait for more of their insights during discussions

4. Give Hints and Clues to Help Students Answer Questions

- if a student is not sure, provide hints or let them call on a friend to help them out
- instead of letting "I don't know" become a final answer, try to jog their memory

5. Tell Students They Have the Ability to Do Well

- describe precisely what students have done well instead of the generic "Good job." For example, say, "Your answer is really clear. Great detail, too."
- post students' work

6. Correct Students in a Constructive Way

- follow the grading formula, three positive comments for every word of constructive criticism
- never use sarcasm to embarrass a student in front of the class

7. Develop Positive Classroom Pride

- send home newsletters or emails that describe the class' progress and notable events
- make it clear to students that you enjoy your job and getting to work with them
- be passionate and enthusiastic about teaching
- let students name their class: The Third Block Stars

8. Demonstrate Caring

- talk informally with students
- greet students outside of school
- greet students at the door when they enter class
- single out students for conversations in the lunchroom

---

3   "Schools can best encourage prosocial behavior by using consistent positive disciplinary practices that include clear expectations, discussions, and modeling" (Kidron and Fleishman, 2006, p. 91).

- comment on important events in the students' lives
- compliment students on important achievements outside of school
- attend students' sporting events and performances
- smile

9. Prevent and Reduce Frustration and Stress

- model tasks showing how you might change your mind or make a mistake
- occasionally share stories about your own experiences as a student
- take a few moments of Monday class time to ask students about their weekends
- be flexible about deadlines when it is appropriate
- whenever possible, handle disciplinary conversations in private
- recognize that making mistakes is an essential part of learning

If you review the nine points made in this list, you'll see that you already do many of these acts in the course of an average week. The behaviors listed above can take place during a normal day of school and require little or no preparation, yet they send important messages to students about belonging, safety, and that they are capable.

Questioning to Support Social-Emotional Learning

Teachers have hundreds of verbal interactions with students every day. Research indicates that questioning is second only to lecturing in popularity as a teaching method and that classroom teachers spend anywhere from 35 percent to 50 percent of their instructional time conducting questioning sessions (Cotton, 2012, p. 3).

Table 2.1 The Five SEL Competencies Connected to Reflective SEL Questions

Self-Awareness	• Label and recognize own and others' emotions • Identify what triggers own emotions • Analyze emotions and how they affect others • Accurately recognize own strengths and limitations • Identify own needs and values • Possess self-efficacy and self-esteem	• How did it make you feel when he called you that name (or hit you)? • Why do you think he called you that name (or hit you)? • How do you think he felt when you called him a name (hit him)? • Did you want to make him feel that way? If so, why?
Self-Management	• Set plans and work toward goals • Overcome obstacles and create strategies for more long-term goals • Seek help when needed • Manage personal and interpersonal stress	• When do you do your homework? • Where do you do your homework? • What gets in the way of your getting your homework completed? • What can you do to overcome that obstacle to getting your homework completed?
Responsible Decision Making	• Identify problems • Analyze situations • Solve problems • Evaluate • Reflect • Consider ethical responsibility	• The next time you have an assignment that is due in a week, what can you do to avoid doing it all the night before it is due? • Why did you skip my class? • How was your life shaped by choosing to skip my class? • What can you and I do to make it less likely you will want to skip my class?

The sources for this table include: CASEL, 2003; Durlak, Weissberg, Dymnicki, Taylor, and Schellinger, 2011; Elias, 2006; Kress & Elias, 2006; Zins, Payton, Weisberg, and O'Brien, 2007.

In addition to classroom questions, teachers can ask questions in multiple school settings outside of the classroom. Each question is an opportunity to develop social-emotional learning.

In Table 2.1 (facing page), you'll find questions teachers can ask specifically to develop metacognitive awareness about social-emotional skills and to support students' reflection. In the next section of this chapter (student-student relationships) and in Chapter 5 (group and partner work), we will continue this work with questions to look more closely at developing relationship skills and social awareness.

The reflective SEL questions in Table 2.1 have been incorporated into specific examples throughout this book. For instance, for self-management and "set plans and work toward goals," teachers can use the goal-setting template in Figure 2.1, which is based upon the work of middle and high school teachers who developed descriptions of successful student habits and created a goal-setting process for students to self-assess their progress. In the process, the student selects SEL goal and tracks and reflects on his progress throughout a term.

In the example below, the student has selected "seeking out help" and "motivate myself" because he has not always been able to finish his math work, but he also did not ask the teacher for assistance. He also knows he's not all that enthusiastic about doing this work, so he's going to set a schedule to do his work to motivate himself.

As you can see, at the end of the month, he evaluated his progress on the goals in the two reflection

Figure 2.1 Goal-Setting: Habits of a Successful Student

Name_____ Class_____ Date_____

My **Goal for Habits for Successful Learners** for the month is to focus on:

(Look at Skills for Successful Students in Table 2.4. Select one of the SES Skills from the first column and one or possibly two Skills for Successful Students from the second column as a focus for your goals for this term.)

1. My **Self-Management** Goal(s)
   Select one or two:
   - **Seek out help when I need it**
   - **Motivate myself**

2. Explain when you will work on this goal: If I don't understand something in math, I never ask for help in the classroom. I will make sure I get started on my work as soon as I come into class or as soon as I get off the bus when I get home.

3. My **self-assessment** of my goal
This month I **went to seek out help when I needed it and I worked on motivating myself**.

Circle the description that best describes your goal this month. Then explain below your self-evaluation.

I nailed it!	Mostly, I did it	I didn't do it much or at all
I asked for help during class just about every day and even went to a Flex-block math session before the test.	I was pretty motivated to get started on my work when I got to class, but when I get home, I'm too fidgety and too hungry to start my homework.	

Reflection question: What can you do to overcome that obstacle to getting your homework completed?
  I really didn't think Miss James liked me, but when I asked her questions, she was OK. I went to her math session before the test. My algebra grade went up to a B.

Reflection question: What gets in the way of your getting your homework completed?
  I'm too hungry and have to eat, plus I just want to run around, so I'm going to move homework time to after dinner or after I get to go outside for a while.

questions, found some success, but felt he still had some changes to make because he didn't go directly home and start his homework. So, he made some changes in his strategy for the next term.

Table 2.2 provides students with the five social-emotional, self-awareness, self-management, social awareness, relationship management, and responsi-ble decision-making skills. In the second column are Habits of Successful Students, behaviors that connect to the five skills that are listed, and in the third column are reflection questions. Students can select any of the five SEL skills, one or two of the Habits of Successful Students and can select an appropriate reflection question for each term.

Table 2.2 SEL Skills, Habits of Successful Students, and Reflective Questions

SEL Skills	Habits of Successful Students	Reflective Questions to Think About SEL
I CAN Self-Awareness	• Identify my emotions, needs and values • Accurately understand my reasons or triggers for doing and saying things • Recognize my strengths and needs • Be self-confident • Feel that what I do makes a difference	• How did it make you feel when he called you that name (or hit you)? • Why did you call him that name (hit him)? • How do you think he felt when you called him a name (hit him)? • Did you want to make him feel that way? If so, why?
I CAN Self-Management	• Set goals, work toward them, and monitor (measure) progress • Seek out help when I need it (self-advocate) • Control my impulses • Display grit, determination, perseverance • Exhibit positive emotions: hope, optimism, motivation • Manage my stress • Control my behavior • Motivate myself • Organize my day	• When do you do your homework? • Where do you do your homework? • What gets in the way of your getting your homework completed? • What can you do to overcome that obstacle to getting your homework completed?
I CAN Social Awareness	• Recognize social cues from others • Listen closely and accurately • Look at things from others' points of view • Feel empathy for others • Appreciate diversity and differences among people • Respect others feelings and reactions	• The next time you have an assignment that is due in a week, what can you do to avoid doing it all the night before it is due? • Why did you skip my class? • How was your life impacted by choosing to skip my class? • What can you and I do to make it less likely you will want to skip my class?
I CAN Relationship Management	• Communicate my ideas and feelings effectively • Engage with people, make friends • Show leadership skills • Build relationships, help others • Work with a team, cooperatively • Work toward group goals • Prevent interpersonal conflict • Resist inappropriate social pressures	• When you are the leader, how do you determine if someone is doing too much of the talking and not giving others an adequate chance to speak • If you see this happening, what can you do to correct the situation?

I CAN Responsible Decision Making	• Identify problems • Analyze situations • Solve problems • Use strategies to resist peer pressure • Evaluate ideas • Reflect on my actions and thinking • Be ethical and fair	• In what ways do these expectations help with the learning in this class (yours and that of the others)? • Are there any ways in which these expectations will detract from the learning? • If a student raises a way in which the expectations may detract from the learning, a follow up question may be: What is an alternative expectation that better meets our goal of respectful behavior and maximum learning?

Adapted from Yoder, N. "Teaching the Whole Child" (2014), American Institutes for Research, pages 4-5; CASEL

Student-to-Student Relationships Within the Classroom and Wider School Setting

It is also important to establish a community of trust and care in our classrooms, as this goes hand in hand with building relationships with our students. Students need to know and understand that both their teacher and their classmates are going to do their best to take care of them throughout the year. Providing opportunities both for us and for our students to get to know one another, celebrating the successes of others, and helping peers get through difficult times, are all critical components to creating a trusting and caring community. Mendler (2012, p. 27) found that building student relationships and making students accountable decreases bullying.

In his book *Relationship-Driven Classroom Management* (2003, p. 81), special educator John Vitto sums up the importance of developing a community and building peer relationships with the following: "When students feel they belong, they are in a better position to learn; when they feel they do not belong, they often turn to misbehavior." Students who lack social skills are distracted from learning by the tremendous amount of energy they expend trying to fit in. Teachers cite social skills deficits as the most frequent cause of classroom behavior problems (Brophy and Good, 2000). Marzano states, "The teacher must provide clear direction to students and generate an atmosphere in which all

When students feel they belong, they are in a better position to learn; when they feel they do not belong, they often turn to misbehavior.

students feel valued and intellectually challenged" (Marzano, 2011, p. 85).

Creating a feeling of belonging for students can take many forms in classrooms. Some teachers use activities known as community builders that are designed to help students get to know one another. An example of a community builder is Four Things We Have in Common. In this activity, students are placed in groups of four or five. Instead of giving the students an academic task, the teacher has them identify at least four things they all have in common. To complete this task, the group members must give the others information about their lives, such as number of siblings, place of birth, pets, favorite movie, etc., until they can find at least four things they all have in common. Through this process, the students get to know one another on a personal level.

Community building can also be achieved through academic tasks. The cooperative learning jobs grid provides an opportunity for students to get to know one another through the division of the jobs based on personal information in the left column in Table 2.3, for example, the person with the oldest sibling or who lives farthest from the school. Structuring the jobs grid with criteria by which the students tell something about themselves is another way of building community. As the year progresses, different jobs grids can be used to learn different facts about one another. A more complete description of role definitions and responsibilities is found in Chapter 5. In addition, the eleven components of effective group work are in Chapter 4, along with other academic activities that encourage positive social interaction, for example, jig saws and Socratic seminars.

Table 2.3 **Cooperative Learning Jobs Grid**

Description Column	Activity 1	Activity 2	Activity 3	Activity 4
Oldest sibling	Leader	Gopher	Reporter	Scribe
Born the farthest from the school	Scribe	Leader	Gopher	Reporter
Oldest living relative	Reporter	Scribe	Leader	Gopher
Whoever is left	Gopher	Reporter	Scribe	Leader

At times, students can take these roles and take responsibility for them during the time of the exercises, but at times these jobs can be connected to the SEL expectations to validate the importance of SEL skills in an academic activity and to verify students' growth in these important social and emotional skills. When accountability is first explained, when students are assessing their participation in a group, or when students are setting goals as "Habits of Successful Students," the connections between the roles and the SEL skills detailed below in Table 2.4 can be used. Setting SEL goals and connecting SEL skills with classroom behavior will be more fully developed in the discussion of group work in Chapter 4 and of self assessment in Chapter 5.

All classroom routines should be structured with expectations that they enhance rather than detract from the sense of community. For example, group work expectations should include expectations about tone of voice and types of comments that are unacceptable because of the detrimental effect they may have on relationships among students. We discuss classroom routines and accountable talk in Chapter 4 and specify opportunities for teachers to provide feedback to students through reflection activities, goal setting, and rubrics.

Developing Self-Awareness, Social Awareness, and Responsible Decision Making

The first way to help students feel ownership of the class is to follow this advice: **Don't do anything for students that they can do for themselves**. Instead, follow the lead of an elementary school colleague of ours who, each year, creates a job wheel that lists approximately twenty-five classroom responsibilities. At the beginning of each week, she uses the job wheel to assign a responsibility to each member of the class. These jobs range from taking attendance

Table 2.4 **Cooperative Learning Jobs Connected to SEL Skills**

Classroom Responsibilities	SEL Skills
Leader	Self-Management—Set goals and work toward goals. Relationship Management—Work with a team cooperatively Relationship Management—Work toward group goals Responsible Decision Making—Identify problems, use strategies, be fair
Scribe	Social Awareness—Listen closely and accurately Relationship Management—Work with a team cooperatively
Reporter	Relationship Management—Communicate ideas effectively Relationship Management—Work with a team cooperatively
Gopher	Relationship Management—Work with a team cooperatively Relationship Management—Work toward group goals Social Awareness—Recognize social cues from others

to collecting homework to hanging up student work. Another example of accountability is a high school science teacher who, by the second month of class, could expect the students to start each lab and obtain all necessary equipment from the appropriate storage area and set it up for the lab. After the lab, they cleaned all the equipment and area and returned the equipment exactly where it belonged. All of these tasks were done with little or no prompting by the teacher by October because he had gradually, and precisely, taught each step and supported students' independence, self-management skills, and sense of self-efficacy. These classroom roles show the important link between creating a smooth-running, academic classroom and the SEL skills that are essential components as well.

*A*nother way in which we help students take ownership of the class and their behavior is by requiring them to actively assess their own adherence to classroom routines.

How does assigning students responsibilities within a classroom relate to creating an effective context for teaching and learning? By creating a classroom structure in which students play a role in the effective operation of the classroom, the teacher sends the explicit message to students that they are active participants and are not in class to sit passively and let the teacher do all the work. They have a role to play in making the classroom one in which effective teaching and learning occur through collaborative teamwork. This clear message may have a powerful impact, not only on the jobs that students are assigned, but also on helping them see their role in their own learning. In a collaborative classroom, students have an opportunity to develop self-awareness, social awareness, and responsible decision making.

The second way to help students feel ownership of the class is to be clear with them about why the routines exist from the perspective of their own benefit (self-awareness), the benefit of other students (social awareness), and the teacher's benefit (responsible decision-making). Classroom participation can take many forms. Some teachers operate on the **democratic classroom** principle of allowing the students to establish the rules, routines, and expectations within reasonable parameters. Other teachers operate as "benevolent dictators." The teacher establishes the rules, routines, and expectations but gives students the opportunity to comment and offer suggestions for improvement. The teacher then modifies the classroom management plan if he/she feels the students' sugges-

tions will indeed improve the overall classroom environment socially, emotionally, and/or academically.

Another way in which we help students take ownership of the class and their behavior is by requiring them to actively assess their own adherence to classroom routines. Table 2.5 on the following page is an example of a rubric that teachers can use to assess a student's behavior as an audience when another student or group of students is presenting ideas. In addition, Table 2.6 provides another rubric for audience responsibilities.

Resolving Student Conflicts in Ways That Develop Social-Emotional Learning

There are many times when educators are in the role of resolving conflicts between students. Student conflicts take many forms—from two preschoolers in conflict over who gets the most blocks in the block corner to two fourth-graders arguing over whether the kicker in a kick ball game is safe or out at first base, to two middle schoolers shoving each other in the lunch line, to two high school students having a fist fight in a hallway. In some schools where I have worked, conflicts can reach the level of gang violence. For the purposes of this book, we will talk about the types of conflicts that are typically resolved by classroom teachers, counselors, and administrators.

***Ending the conflict* and *resolving the conflict* are two very different processes.** Ending the conflict typically makes everyone safe by stopping the behavior that can be physically, emotionally, or interpersonally detrimental. However, ending the conflict does not resolve the conflict. Resolving the conflict requires getting to the root of the conflict with the antagonists and resolving the root cause. Ending conflicts alone between students rarely has any positive impact on the students' social-emotional learning.

It is during the resolution of the conflict that social-emotional learning takes place. The first decision we must make in resolving the conflict is when is the best time to do this. Sometimes the intensity of the conflict is so high that the time immediately after ending the conflict is not the best time to resolve

Table 2.5 Analytical Rubric for Audience Responsibilities

CATEGORY	4	3	2	1	Comments
Attentive Listening	Student gave full attentive listening to each speaker with his/her eyes, ears, and heart.	Student showed attentive listening most of the time.	Student showed attentive listening some of the time.	Student didn't show attentive listening.	
Comments and Opinions	Student withheld his/her comments and opinions during the presentations, but asked appropriate questions after many presentations.	Student withheld his/her comments and opinions during the presentations, but asked appropriate questions after some presentations.	Student withheld his/her comments and opinions during the presentations.	Student didn't withhold his/her comments and opinions during the presentations, and/or didn't ask questions after any presentation.	
Body Language	Listener responds appropriately all of the time to comedic and/or dramatic moments of the presentations. Demonstrated by body language, laughter, and/or silence.	Listener responds appropriately most of the time to comedic and/or dramatic moments of the presentations. Demonstrated by body language, laughter, and/or silence.	Listener responds appropriately some of the time to comedic and/or dramatic moments of the presentations. Demonstrated by body language, laughter, and/or silence.	Listener rarely responds appropriately to comedic and/or dramatic moments of the presentations. Demonstrated by body language, laughter, and/or silence.	
Curiosity and Respect	Student shows curiosity and respect all of the time through body language and questions.	Student shows curiosity and respect most of the time through body language and questions.	Student shows curiosity and respect some of the time through body language and questions.	Student doesn't show curiosity and respect through body language and questions.	

Adapted from Rubistar.4teachers.org, rubric ID 1153873 (May 9, 2005). Copyright ALTEC at the University of Kansas (2000–2008).

the conflict. Some "cooling off" time may be needed before we take steps to resolve the dispute.

Most resolutions consist of some form of Peer Conflict Resolution Protocol. This conference includes the two antagonists and a person who is facilitating the resolution. Below is a protocol for resolving a conflict between two students. It is important to note that no single series of fixed steps is the way to resolve every conflict. However, we offer the following as a template to begin planning your facilitating such a conference.

Peer Conflict Resolution Protocol

Introduction

The facilitator begins by explaining the steps that the conference will follow (e.g., who will speak first, etc.). He or she also provides some ground rules if necessary and explains the objective of the conference. Some ground rules can include:

1. Speak in a calm voice
2. Don't interrupt another speaker
3. No name calling
4. Listen to the speaker

One of the decisions the facilitator makes after framing the rules is whether the facilitator will share what he or she knows first or if one of the antagonists will begin by stating their side of the story. The advantage of having the antagonists start is that they each feel heard before the facilitator says too much. One of the advantages of having the facilitator share what he or she knows first is the information may compel the antagonists to be more truthful. A third option is to tell the parties that you have gathered information about the issue but want to give them the first opportunity to talk. Knowing you have information may dissuade them from fabrications. They don't know what you know and will likely not want to be caught in a lie. Part of the decision of the best way to start depends on what you know about the two students.

Once all the information is "on the table," the facilitator should then frame the issue. Framing the issue is an explanation by the facilitator of what the facilitator sees is the reason for the conflict and the issues that need be addressed to resolve the conflict.

Preparing for the Conference

It is important, prior to the conference, to gather as much information as possible about the situation. Some of the information will come from the antagonists, some will come from witnesses to the conflict or other sources. Once as much information as possible is gathered, the facilitator can then begin to think about the situation and be ready with questions or comments that may help resolve the issue. In some circumstances, this will enable the supervisor to bring additional information that may be helpful in resolving the conflict.

Presentation

Each student is asked to describe the issue as honestly and clearly as possible. During the presentation, the facilitator ensures that the speaker gets to make his or her case without interruption. After the presentation, the supervisor may also ask questions to gather additional information or to obtain clarification on a point.

Once the first student is finished and the issue is on the table, the other student explains or defends his or her point of view. "Managing the response stage well—responding calmly and professionally—is essential to preventing the meeting from degenerating into an argument" (Elmore, 2008). At this point, there are often conflicting views or events introduced into the discussion. The students will be tempted to vigorously defend their view and cast aspersions on the views and integrity of the other student. A firm repeat of the rules and an assurance that everyone will have adequate time to speak is important. It is again important that the facilitator enable the speaker to tell his or her side without being interrupted. After the response, the facilitator also may ask questions to gather additional information or to obtain clarification of a point.

continued on next page

Understanding

The facilitator gets each student to restate the other student's position in a way that shows that he or she heard and understood the issue from the perspective of the other. In some circumstances, the facilitator may believe that restating what the other has said will be counter-productive. In those circumstances, the facilitator can restate what has been said by both parties. Before moving to the next step, the facilitator ensures that all the information has been stated and that each party's position is understood by all.

Generating Solutions

The facilitator opens the discussion to both parties to begin suggesting possible solutions. The facilitator asks questions that help the parties to come to a solution. As ideas are expressed, the facilitator may repeat or paraphrase to ensure that everyone has the same understanding. The facilitator may also suggest solutions.

Best Options

Once some possible solutions are on the table, students usually begin to feel less tense and discuss the solutions, working toward consensus on the one that will work best. At the end of this stage, an agreement is put in writing. If possible, it is good to have all parties sign the agreement before the meeting ends. In circumstances in which this is not possible, it is important to have the agreement written up and given to all the parties as soon as is practicable. The more time that passes, the greater the likelihood that recollections of what was agreed to may change or one party may change his or her mind. *— use a laptop/ chromebook connected to a printer to take notes & make copies*

Ending

At the close of the meeting, it is important for the facilitator to bring closure to the meeting by thanking the students and dispersing them promptly. The end of the meeting is often what Elmore calls "the danger zone." He says, "As students relax and think the ground rules have ended, there is a high likelihood that someone will misinterpret what is being said or begin to revisit the issue. When this occurs, the meeting that should be ending quickly circles back to the presentation and response stages. The hostility returns and the students are likely to distrust the outcome of the meeting. The longer the meeting stays in the danger zone, the more difficult it becomes to implement a solution" (Elmore, 2008).

Follow Up

It is important for the facilitator to ensure that what was agreed to is, in fact, implemented. Every solution requires a certain level of compromise by both parties. Each party has probably agreed to one or more things that they were (or are) reluctant to do. This reluctance may cause them unconsciously (or consciously) to delay following through on what was agreed upon. Lack of timely follow-through will result in the quick resurfacing of the tension between the parties and is likely to undermine the agreement.

Conclusion

Significant relationships with adults (educators and other adults in a student's life) play an important role in social-emotional learning. Some students are fortunate to have parent or guardian relationships that help them develop these important competencies. Many are not. They must rely on educators, clergy people, recreation department counselors and coaches, bosses, and other impactful relationships to develop these important skills.

Developing the social-emotional skills to build positive relationships with peers also varies greatly among students. Table 2.6 provides an overview of possible connections between SEL skills and the questions used during the protocol. These skills are developed through interactions with peers. Howard Gardner argues that some students have more interpersonal intelligence than others. Whatever the students' level of skill in developing interpersonal relationships, educators can further develop these skills by improving students' self-awareness, self-management, relationship skills, social awareness, and responsible interpersonal decision making throughout their daily classes.

Table 2.6 **Self-Awareness and Social Awareness Connected With Peer Conference Protocol**

Self-Awareness Behavior	Questions That Support the Development of SEL in This Area
Label and recognize own and others' emotions	• How did it make you feel when he called you that name? • Why do you think he called you that name? • Why did you call him that name?
Analyze emotions and how they affect others	• How do you think he felt when you called him that name? • Did you want to make him feel that way? Why?
Social-Awareness Behavior	
Listen closely and accurately	• Were you able to listen closely and accurately retell the other person's story? • If the other person disagreed with your version of the story, were you able to understand why there was confusion?
Look at things from others' points of view	• Did the other person understand your point of view? • Did you understand his or her perspective?
Respect others feelings and reactions	• Were you able to stay calm throughout the meeting? • If the other person was upset or angry, were you able to respect those emotions or not react to them?

Discussion Questions for Reflection

Chapter 2

1. The focus of Chapter 2 is about teacher-student and student-student relationships. **Select a passage that resonates with you and relate it to your practice.**

    A strong relationship w/ students leads to better discipline and more time for instruction... Students feel a sense of relatedness when they perceive their teachers like, value & respect them. They feel competent when they work @ challenging tasks... Students who lack social skills are distracted by learning by the amt of energy they expend trying to fit in

2. Students with special needs, especially those students with nonverbal learning disabilities or autism spectrum disorders often lack "social awareness." Students who come from a different culture or who are English learners may need additional support in adjusting to language and social customs. They may need explicit instruction and practice on how to read another student's point of view or understand body language. **What are some practices that you might implement to help these students increase their ability to connect with their classmates?**

    Questioning/Modeling
    - What do you notice?
    - How does ___ look?

3. Students with nonverbal learning disabilities or autism spectrum disorders may have a difficult time when unexpected situations come up that can alter the schedule of the day. In addition, general education students can be disrupted by unexpected events. **What are some classroom strategies that a teacher could implement, for example, routines or posters that would help with classroom management and social-emotional learning?**

    Model flexibility
    Explain need for changes

4. Teachers who successfully use the strategies of social-emotional learning often use humor in their instructional practice. Sometimes, an educator might confuse sarcasm for humor. **What is the difference? Why is it essential for a teacher to avoid sarcasm when dealing with all students?**

   Sarcasm can send the message that someone is incompetent; ppl may not understand the intent of sarcasm & take it literally.

5. In the effort to curb a potential conflict within the classroom, some teachers may choose to squelch a disagreement with a decree of "stop that now or go to the office." This approach may end the conflict but may not resolve the conflict. **Reflect on some occasions when you observed this situation or participated in this approach. Using the practices you have learned in this chapter, how might a difficult situation (conflict) been more effectively resolved?**

   Sending a student to the office for an infraction w/o hearing out their reasons for the behavior... No follow up

Creating Physically and Emotionally Safe Spaces

Classroom Space and Teacher's Proximity to Students

Classroom space and safety, the subject of this chapter, is the second essential component of a positive classroom climate (Yoder, 2014, p. 9). The way in which we arrange our classroom and place ourselves in the classroom can have a significant impact on students' behavior, sense of belonging, and safety. It enables teachers to facilitate student-to-student interactions, preempt misbehavior, and can break down the physical barriers that may inhibit our relationships with students. As noted in the previous chapter, these relationships are an integral part of helping our students develop self-management, self-awareness, responsible decision-making, relationship skills and social awareness.

Let's take, for example, a high school classroom in which the desks are arranged in rows, the students get to choose their seats, and the teacher primarily teaches from the front of the classroom. In this situation, the students who are the most prone to misbehavior tend to sit in the back of the room, placing them at the farthest point from the teacher. The most effective arrangement of classroom space would be to move those students close to the teacher. Teacher proximity to students is an excellent deterrent to inappropriate

The way in which we arrange our classroom and place ourselves in the classroom can have a significant impact on students' behavior, sense of belonging, and safety. It enables teachers to facilitate student-to-student interactions, preempt misbehavior, and can break down the physical barriers that may inhibit our relationships with students.

behavior, and it encourages the development of social-emotional learning.

Proximity also enables the teacher to use some of the subtler attention moves (see Chapter 5) such as a hand on the shoulder or a quick glance of the "hairy eyeball" to regain the attention of these students without openly embarrassing them with a negative statement. It also enables teachers to assess students' seat work and support them without embarrassment to the student.

In many classrooms, the "front of the room" changes during the lesson so there is no consistent "front of the room." Thus, teachers need to circulate to ensure proximity to all students to minimize misbehavior, maintain attention, and seek opportunities to personally connect with students. To circulate well, they need a classroom arrangement that permits easy access to all the students in the room.

This type of negative attention may have achieved the desired result in the short term; the student stopped misbehaving. However, the embarrassment of the student caused by this strategy often resulted in increased levels of misbehavior over the course of the year. The use of positive and negative responses will be discussed more fully in Chapter 5.

It is far more effective to arrange classroom furniture and move about the room while teaching in ways that ensures proximity to all students at various points in the lesson. This movement will proactively decrease acting-out behavior, rather than putting teachers in the position of reactively responding to inappropriate behavior. Marzano states that "**desk arrangements should provide access to any student within four steps from where the teacher spends most of his time**" (2007, p. 121). Students' social-emotional development can be improved by proactively setting up the room for student academic and behavioral success. As we saw in the cycles of deficit mindset and growth mindset in Chapter 1, the fewer instances when we need to address misbehavior, the more we can affirm appropriate behavior, and the more likely we are to reverse the cycle of deficit mindset. Room arrangement and teacher proximity is an important first step in creating a positive learning environment.

A variety of classroom arrangements can maximize the teacher's ability to remain near the students, including paired rows, table groups, and the double horseshoe discussed below.

Paired Rows

In this arrangement, student desks are positioned in pairs. This allows the teacher to position more students near the front of the room and enables all students to be looking forward. This also allows for easy partner support during the learning. For this to work effectively, the teacher needs to be sure to move between the rows during instruction to avoid spending a disproportionate amount of time in the proximity of those student pairs who are in the front of the room. In this arrangement (see Figure 3.1), it is important to have both horizontal and vertical pathways for the teacher to ensure teacher proximity to all students.

Table Groups

In this arrangement, either the teacher uses tables in place of desks or the teacher arranges the desks into tables. Students sit in groups of four or five. This setup enables the teacher to have quick and efficient group

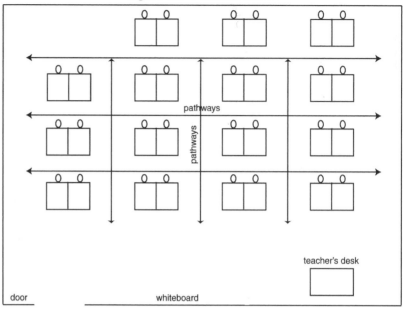

Figure 3.1 Paired Rows

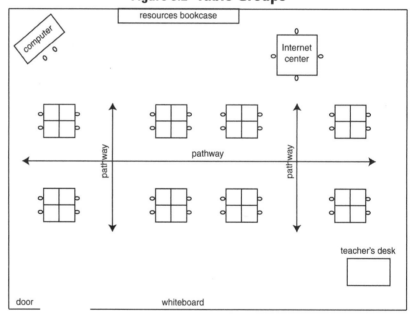

Figure 3.2 Table Groups

processing. It also creates more space for pathways for the teacher to circulate and ensures equal proximity to all students (see Figure 3.2).

Double Horseshoe

In a double horseshoe setup, the desks are arranged in two horseshoes with one inside the other. In this arrangement, the teacher teaches from the inside of the horseshoe. When inside the horseshoe, the teacher's proximity is never more than one desk and student away from any student (see Figure 3.3).

Figure 3.3 **Double Horseshoe**

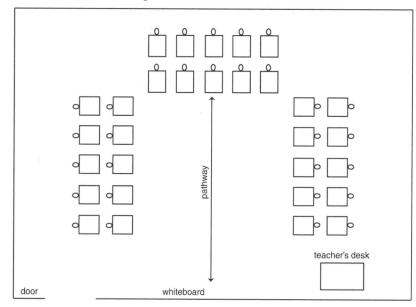

In any student arrangement, it is important that the teacher move throughout the room during the class period. Teachers want to ensure an equitable distribution of teacher proximity to all students.

Table Groups With Learning Centers

In elementary school classrooms with learning centers, and middle and high school classrooms with interest centers, it is important to place the centers for easy access with minimal disruption. Pathways to the centers should be unobstructed so other students are not disrupted by those going to the centers. Figure 3.2, above, shows a middle or high school mathematics classroom with two interest centers. One is a computer workstation for accessing websites for mathematics enrichment, remediation, and application. The other is a table at which small groups of students can work together on mathematics problems that are real life applications of the concepts taught in class.

Figure 3.4 is an elementary classroom configuration with several learning centers. In this classroom, the teacher has instructional times when all the students are in centers. Thus, the teacher needs enough centers to accommodate all the students, and the centers need to be spaced so groups do not disturb one another. Teachers who only have space or furniture for two or three center areas can modify this setup by using some of the grouped desks as centers. For example, a table at the back and one on each side could contain three of the centers. The other four centers could be set up one at each of the four grouped desk tables.

Figure 3.4 **Elementary Table Groups With Learning Centers**

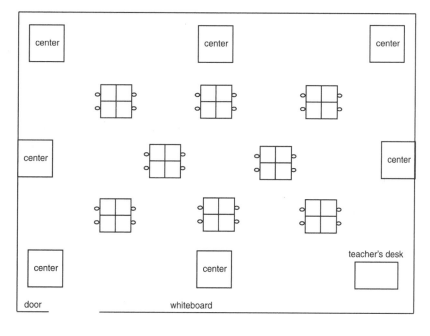

Conclusion About Physical Space

Classroom arrangement and physical proximity are an important component for organizing space that allows for maximum academic and social-emotional learning. Strategic placement of where each student sits, coupled with differentiated physical proximity to students on an "as needed basis," allows teachers to have the level of personal contact with students that preempts misbehavior thereby increasing the frequency of positive reinforcement and decreasing the need for negative reinforcement that allows immediate assessment of learning and subtle, but effective support.

Creating Emotionally Safe Places

Planning classroom spaces carefully as has been discussed in the first half of this chapter demonstrates that spaces where people stand and sit and work are important in developing a safe and smoothly functioning classroom. Equally important is to create a classroom in which students feel emotionally safe so that they can take risks and learn in a supportive place.

Teachers create the culture in a classroom, sometimes knowingly, sometimes accidentally. Whole schools often have a clear culture. I know that when I walk into some classrooms I can feel the positive energy or, sadly, sense the discomfort or tension. Often the culture that we build is like the air that we breathe: we have no awareness of it or how, for example, what we think of as an innocuous statement can cause distress to students. Thus, teachers need to have cultural awareness and to work to understand the different cultures and expectations that students bring to the classroom and, as important, they need to understand the cultures they are creating.

> *Create a classroom in which students feel emotionally safe so that they can take risks and learn in a supportive place.*

Emotional Safety and Cultural Awareness: Acculturating English Language Learners

In the following section, an EL teacher becomes your guide to seeing an American classroom as a new English language learner. The narrator, points out the areas that are strange or disquieting to a new member of the classroom who may also be a newcomer to the country.

Colleen Billings (in Ribas et al., 2017, p. 136) provides an introduction to the cultural awareness teachers need to deal effectively with English language learners:

> In my years of teaching English learners, I realized how essential it is to create a safe environment so that they can acclimate to a new culture as they learn in their new culture. **English learners require an environment that is both supportive and tolerant to fully understand expectations, behavioral norms, rewards, and potential consequences for conflicts or rule breaking.** New to the culture of the school and classrooms of their new community, these English language learners must feel safe and respected before they are expected to start decoding messages and navigating sociocultural contexts.

An effective technique that supports acculturation and language development is to welcome linguistically diverse students by showing interest in home cultures and encouraging the use of students' home languages as support when needed (Elms, Miller, and Sore, p. 17). By having the teacher recognize that each of these English learners arrives with rich life experiences and offers a variety of skills, knowledge, and proficiency in their own culture, the teacher can validate this new member of the school community as a learner with expertise.

In addition, teachers can use more subtle approaches to put English language learners at ease, including gestures to demonstrate friendliness and a positive tone when attempting to communicate the message that school is a safe, comfortable place to learn. Many schools have mentoring programs in which groups of peers are trained as "ambassadors" or "buddies" to welcome new students. Partnering with an empathetic, friendly peer will facilitate the transition of the EL into school routines, rules, and schedules.

Teachers need to be culturally aware of what the transition to a new community can mean for the new student. The first few weeks in an American school can be shockingly different from English learners' previous school experiences. They do not just feel "first day jitters." Most may have had a recent sequence of anxiety-causing experiences, such as saying good-bye to family and friends and leaving the familiarity of their home setting. They then arrive to a new place with cultural and academic factors and rules that may conflict with the norms from their home culture. A group of English learners in grades six through eight generated the following list when asked what was new for them during their first month in the US:

- not understanding any people or street signs
- American paper money and coins
- unusual fashion and food
- malls, stores, and too many choices of products
- snow and winter weather
- drivers on the left and driving on the right

- not knowing anyone in the neighborhood and not knowing what to say
- riding a school bus
- school start/end times, schedules, and changing classes
- desks set up in pairs or groups
- having a locker and a combination
- bell tones to change class
- snack time and buying/eating lunch at school
- noise in the cafeteria
- recess
- the Pledge of Allegiance and "moment of silence"
- student voices on the public announcement system
- fire drills and alarms
- time needed to complete homework
- being "swarmed" by peers the first week and left alone after that
- feeling isolated, lonely, and homesick
- feeling stupid and being unable to read
- hating school

New students may have experienced trauma, such as leaving or losing a family member, witnessing violence, or experiencing poverty and/or neglect. Insightful teachers will be mindful of students' varying abilities to cope with change.

Students with limited or interrupted formal education will have faced additional factors that may cause a higher level of anxiety. These new students may have experienced trauma, such as leaving or losing a family member, witnessing violence, or experiencing poverty and/or neglect. Insightful teachers will be mindful of students' varying abilities to cope with change. Teachers may need to plan for what may lead an English learner to withdraw, act out, or break down in social and academic environments.

Once a student has been given a warm welcome, and possibly partnered with a student peer mentor, teachers need to assure that messages for ELs are comprehensible. For ELs who are developing oral-language proficiency and initial literacy skills in English, visual support such as modeling, pictures, graphs, symbols, and signs facilitate the demonstration of expectations and routines. Explicit instruction may also include scripted teacher cues with student choral responses or mantras and consistent demonstrations of praise to reinforce desired behaviors. ELs with advanced oral proficiency and literacy will continue to need language support in the form of slower speech rates, modeling, and regular references to posted classroom standards and resources.

Regardless of proficiency level, and recognizing the fact that most English language learners have been born in the United States, the behavioral norms of a student's home culture may differ from what is expected in American schools. As teachers develop rules for classroom etiquette, task standards, and homework routines, it is important to investigate social and cultural factors that might influence classroom behavior. Respecting students' experience and home cultures is essential as a teacher works to create a nurturing learning environment for culturally diverse students. Investigating multicultural literature and bringing students' home cultures into curricula and lesson activities will pique student interest, promote students' self-esteem, and lower anxiety. Cloud, Genesee, and Hamadan (2009, p. 28) refer to Luis Moll's research (2005) when they encourage teachers to investigate students' funds of knowledge to support a learning environment that provides continuity with ELLs' past and supports them as they learn new skills and subject matters.

Direct and effective communication with parents and families will further support and reinforce the students' understanding of expectations and norms. To provide information in a language parents understand, schools are required to locate interpreters and translation services when necessary. Parent handbooks and discipline policies and procedures are included in the list of required information schools must communicate with parents (U.S. Department of Education Office for Civil Rights and U.S. Department of Justice, 2015).

ELLs who have school experience in their home countries may be at an advantage when they acculturate to American schools, because they have participated in a system of rules and consequences. However, what may put some of these students at a disadvantage is having to learn an entirely new set of rules. ELs are unique from other new students in that they must learn these new rules while they acquire English language skills. Informal dialogue with the student, interviewing or surveying parents, or researching school culture of the country of origin can provide valuable insights for teachers. The following questions serve as a launching point for understanding the school culture in a student's home country.

Launching Points for Teachers to Understand the Students' Home Country School Culture

- Did students have to raise their hands to speak?
- Did students stand to speak in class or address adults?
- Were students expected to stay seated during class?
- Were there certain phrases or titles students used to address adults?
- Were students separated by gender, age, or skill level?
- Were meals served at school?
- Was there a mid-day break or recess?
- What was the expectation about attendance?
- Were students expected to take turns speaking?
- Were students permitted to talk at the same time?
- Were desks or chairs in rows or groups?
- How did the teacher handle discipline?
- Was good behavior rewarded?
- How often did teachers communicate with parents?
- What was the nature of parent-teacher communication?
- How often did teachers assign homework?
- How many hours of homework were assigned?
- Were parents expected to assist their children with homework?

Teachers need to remember that each student has a unique set of circumstances and has his or her own personal story to tell if or when they choose to do so.

The teacher who considers other belief systems and cultures will certainly be at an advantage for creating a supportive atmosphere for successful learning for their students. Particularly for ELLs, who come from unstable political or struggling economic communities, formal schooling may be a new experience. Students may not be accustomed to being at school for more than three or four hours at a time. Other ELLs may never have attended school with the opposite gender or have only attended religiously affiliated schools in which the behavioral norms were directed by faith and explicitly taught with a focus on doctrine. Students often report that changing classrooms for different content areas is new to them. Changing classes may not be a practice in their home country schools or teachers may have moved from class to class while students remained in the same room for all or most of the day. Other typical American school experiences such as field trips, use of technology, cafeteria culture, electronic communication, project-based learning, borrowing library books, health topics, or physical-education class may require prior consideration and preparation to facilitate success for students who come from non-US schools.

When learning about ELLs' experience in school culture, it is crucial that teachers realize that they can't necessarily generalize about the experiences of students who came from the same country, community, religious faith, or language group.

Teachers need to remember that each student has a unique set of circumstances and has his or her own personal story to tell if or when they choose to do so. Even though some students may have common experiences, assumptions about cultural or ethnic groups may lead to stereotyping, generalizations, and misunderstandings. In examining home cultures, the acculturation process and life experiences of culturally and linguistically diverse learners, teachers can anticipate obstacles, predict confusing elements, and consciously prepare students and students' parents for new rules and standards.

A new student arrives at your classroom door, and as you have just read, this child may never have spoken English before, may have just left a war-torn country, or may have just said good-bye to an extended family. We need great insight to make this new environment and new culture safe for these newcomers to make friends, to work effectively, and to learn.

A Safe Environment and Cultural Awareness: A Special Education Teacher's Perspective

Just as challenging for our skills as the leader of a classroom may be supporting children who have learning or behavioral challenges. At times, we may need to seek out support to make sure these students succeed in our classrooms. In the following description, our guide looks at the classroom from the perspective of a student who may face academic, social, or emotional challenges.

By Victoria Greer (Ribas et al., 2017, p. 134)
As a new special education teacher, I was thrilled to have my own class. As I look back now, I see that students' needs have become more complex and have increased since I began teaching. Students are entering school with diagnosed and undiagnosed disabilities, including sensory processing disorders, learning disabilities, anxiety, and trauma that affect their ability to be regulated and to access the curriculum successfully.

> *Teachers learn not to react to the behavior but to the underlying cause of the behavior.*

During this time of Common Core in the United States, and national curricula in other countries, teachers are worried about how to help students meet the demands of the standards. In addition to curricular concerns, teachers are as concerned about the climate and structure of their classrooms, given the complex makeup of their students. **There are many areas of disability that often leave teachers believing that students are intentionally disruptive and have behavior problems. In fact, however, these behaviors are a result of the impact of the student's disability.**

A 2006 report from the Spiral Foundation estimated that from 5 to 13 percent of children entering school have a sensory processing disorder (SPD) with boys affected more than girls. Three out of four children identified are boys. Sensory processing disorder leads children to experience challenges with how they use sensory information for self-regulation and skill development. These disorders manifest themselves in a variety of ways such as sensory modulation disorder, sensory discrimination disorder, postural-ocular disorder, and dyspraxia. Children with SPD often have challenges with attention and behavior, social skills, play skills, gross and fine motor skills, daily living skills, sleeping, and eating. SPD is most often associated with other disability areas, such as learning disabilities, attention deficit disorder, autism spectrum disorder, language disorders, anxiety disorders, and behavioral disorders. Table 3.1 (next page) compares the types of sensory processing disorders and common characteristics of each (May-Benson et al., 2013). According to the Center for Educational Statistics (2013), students with learning disabilities make up the largest group of individuals with disabilities: 42 percent. Students with learning disabilities often suffer from low self-esteem, low expectations for themselves, underachievement, and underemployment as adults. Students with learning disabilities will often act up and act out to hide their embarrassment.

Teachers sometimes view students with disabilities who act out because of their disorder as oppositional and defiant. Teachers who understand the cycle of **fear**, **avoidance**, **stress**, and **escape** (FASE) understand what "saving FASE" means. Teachers learn not to react to the behavior but to the underlying cause of the behavior. Teachers who understand FASE recognize that all human behavior sends a message. By looking for the message and reframing the behavior as a way of communicating, teachers can see the oppositional behaviors, frequent trips to the nurse, being unprepared for class, and frequent absences as attempts to avoid the shame of underperforming in the classroom (Schultz, 2011, pp. 137–142). For teachers to have success with managing their classrooms, it is imperative for them to understand that the students are not unmotivated or oppositional, but are sending a message about their need for help.

Anxiety and trauma are among the leading causes of children disrupting classrooms in urban public schools across the nation. Unfortunately, children who live in poor, urban communities experience more incidences of violence, whether as a victim or a witness. These children are in a perpetual cycle of disruption and dysregulation, which causes them to be more susceptible to maladaptive coping strategies when faced with the demands of the classroom. In urban school settings, many of the students have experienced some form of trauma; in some instances, it creates more aggressive, explosive, and oppositional situations in classrooms (Rawles, 2010).

Trauma-informed intervention is an evidence-based approach to addressing the needs of students who have been affected by being victims or witnesses of violence. The approach consists of skill development, exploring values, relationship building, and rewards for positive behavior. Creating a trauma-informed approach to prevention and intervention of school violence and behavior outbursts must explore the role of trauma in the development of school aggression and the way it influences every aspect of the student and the systems in which they engage (Rawles, 2010). Teachers and other students in the classroom are often the recipients of unwarranted aggression and disruptive behavior. However, teachers can design classroom systems for prevention and

Table 3.1 Common Disorders That Contribute to Challenging Behaviors

Disorder	Definition	Common Signs
Sensory modulation disorder	Problems regulating responses to taking in sensory information from our bodies and environment and organizing it in an effective, functional manner	• easily distracted by noises • overly sensitive to sounds • dislikes nail/hair cutting • dislikes clothing of certain textures/fits • upset about seams in socks • difficult time falling/staying asleep • reacts defensively to tastes/textures of food • easily distracted by visual stimuli
Sensory discrimination disorder	Problems processing body sensations from touch, muscles, joints, and head movements	• jumps a lot (beds, sofas, chairs) • bumps or pushes others • grasps objects too tightly or uses too much force • frequently drops things or knocks things over • mouths, licks, chews, or sucks non-food I tems • craves movement, likes to spin around • afraid of heights/swings or slides • has poor balance
Postural Ocular Disorder	Problems controlling posture, quality of movement	• seems weaker than other children • fatigues easily • frequently moves in and out of seat • slumps while sitting • difficulty making eye contact/tracking with the eyes, reading • falls and tumbles frequently
Dyspraxia	Problems planning, sequencing, and executing unfamiliar actions, resulting in awkward and poorly coordinated motor skills.	• problems with daily life tasks like dressing or using utensils • eats in a sloppy manner • difficulty following multistep directions • strong desire for sameness or routines • has an awkward pencil grasp • has poor handwriting • dislikes or reluctant to participate in sports

May-Benson, "Parent Fact Sheet: Signs and Symptoms of Sensory Processing Disorder." The Spiral Foundation, 2013, http://www.thespiralfoundation.org/toolkit_parents.html

intervene successfully by fully understanding the approaches used in creating more trauma-informed classrooms.

Anxiety in children is often a direct result of some level of trauma that the student has experienced. While a level of anxiety is a natural part of a child's development, the number of children entering school who have experienced trauma has resulted in an increase in the number of students suffering from anxiety. Through maturation and the development of coping skills, most children learn to manage their anxiety; however, approximately 3 percent to 24 percent of children under the age of 12 experience significant anxiety problems that interfere with their daily functioning. The level of anxiety that students experience affects their ability to learn, which results in lower academic performance than those not suffering from anxiety. Anxiety in children can present itself in many ways. These students are often misunderstood and labeled as lazy, oppositional, rigid, or aggressive. Students who suffer from an anxiety disorder often struggle with peer and adult interactions and relationships, poor parental relationships, and poor self-esteem (Headley and Campbell, 2011). The following are simple strategies that teachers can embed into daily classroom practices to support a well-managed classroom environment:

1. Embed classroom community-building into the classroom structure as a daily practice for students to engage with their peers and the teacher.
2. Implement a strong social-skills curriculum that focuses on developing coping and self-regulations skills.
3. Create safety zones in the classroom for students to access as part of developing coping and self-regulation strategies.
4. Develop visual cues for students to be redirected. This can be extremely helpful when students experience times of heightened anxiety (Headley and Campbell, 2011).

Although the instances of trauma and anxiety have increased for children entering our schools and classrooms, teachers should be aware that recognizing early warning signs for students with a trauma background or anxiety disorder, and implementing preventative measures, ensure a well-managed classroom.

If a student goes into the acting-out cycle, supporting students before they reach the peak phase of the cycle ensures students' success and classroom order. As teachers, we are not able to control what has happened to our students that can affect their success. We can, however, be thoughtful and responsive to their needs in a way that minimizes disruption but still builds strong classroom communities (IRIS Modules, 2015).

Safe Spaces in Which All Students Can Grow, Learn, and Thrive

The conditions for creating safe spaces are addressed in this book. The last two chapters provide a specific and concrete guide to ensure that you have considered the major keys to providing a safe classroom. The chapters incorporate:

- Defining learning and growth and growth or mastery mindset create high expectations, but assures students that they will have the support they need
- Building relationships with students and among students
- Designing classroom spaces to provide smoothly functioning work, discussion, and movement
- Supporting cultural awareness by modeling and practicing norms as a group
- Creating an orderly, respectful classroom through routines and rules
- Carefully scaffolding and modeling group work to support social, emotional, and academic growth
- Creating conditions for positive student engagement with meaningful, worthwhile work
- Speaking to one another so that it is clear that everyone in the classroom is at times a learner and at times a leader or expert
- Setting goals, student self-assessment, reflection, and peer assessment are techniques through which students gain self-awareness
- Creating a classroom plan to incorporate all essential elements into the classroom
- Building community through carefully developed classroom meetings

Each chapter adds a new perspective and new techniques for creating a classroom culture that supports social, emotional, and academic growth.

Discussion Questions for Reflection

Chapter 3

1. Chapter 3 focuses on the creation of physically and emotionally "safe spaces." **Select a passage that resonates with you and relate it to your practice.**

   - Teacher should be w/i 4 steps of every student at all times (see p. 66-67)
   - cultural awareness, multi-cultural understanding Home or native School awareness (p70)
   - Save EASE : fear, avoidance, stress, escape: All behavior is a form of communication. See behavior such as acting out, frequent flyer, or oppositional beh. as a way of avoiding the shame of underperforming
   - Trauma informed interventions

2. The awareness of what a safe space constitutes can vary depending on the student's cognitive level, cultural background and special learning needs. For example, preferential seating is a term that is often used when making a recommendation for a student with unique learning needs. However, what might be advantageous for one learner with attention issues, may be a disadvantage for another student. For example, a student with attention issues, who is fascinated with anything to do with computers would not be best served by close proximity to the computer center within a classroom. **As you reflect upon some of the recommendations within Chapter 3, think about the term** *preferential seating* **and how that may vary depending on the student's profile. Can you provide an example?**

   - close to location of instruction - near the board
   - teacher moving around students/groups
   - flexible seating

3. Students with special needs may require a different type of classroom environment to feel safe and supported. In some cases, teachers can provide two different seats for the same student so when he or she is having a difficult day, he or she can go to his or her "other seat" within the same classroom. Sometimes, this small adjustment of scenery can assist the student in "rebooting" his or her focus and behavior. On other occasions, a student may experience sensory overload and may need to take a physical break from the classroom or move to another section of the class that is delegated for that purpose. **In reflecting on your own classroom design, what setup would you find most conducive to providing this safe environment for a student who may have a sensory issue.**

   Flexible seating: different areas and types of furniture

4. English Language Learners come from a variety of backgrounds and prior experiences that may or may not have provided a positive association with public education. In addition to creating a welcoming classroom environment for these students, teachers must find ways to communicate effectively with the families of these children. The typical approach of "parent-teacher night" may not be effective in creating a strong bond between the home and school. **What are some strategies that you might implement to increase the communication between home and school despite a language barrier (e.g., letters home translated to native language when feasible)?**

   Use Google Translate for notices/info
   Questionnaire o/ educational expectations/experiences
   Questionnaire of preferences - ie. learning style,
   interests...

4

Developing a Classroom Community

Using Group Work, Partner Work, and Effective Classroom Routines to Support Social-Emotional Learning

Effective routines for group work, partner work and other class functions aid in the development of social-emotional learning in two ways. First, well-established routines proactively eliminate the need for correcting students and increase the opportunity to affirm students. Second, group and partner work are opportunities to develop self-awareness, self-management, social decision-making, relationship skills, and social awareness.

Directly Teach and Model Effective Rules, Routines, and Expectations

In thinking about classroom routines (of which group and partner work are two), we focus on three levels of behaviors. The first level includes our classroom rules. There tend to be only a few of these, and they are generally posted. We try to write rules and expectations for behavior in terminology that is positive rather than focusing on the negative. Samples of rules/standards include the following:

1. We will treat everyone in the class with respect (self-management, social awareness, interpersonal decision-making, relationships skills, and social awareness).
2. We will treat all school and personal materials and supplies in an appropriate manner (self-management, responsible decision-making).
3. We will support the learning and growth of all

members of the class (self-management, social awareness, interpersonal decision-making, relationships skills, and social awareness).
4. We will arrive to class on time with our materials, and we will complete our work in a timely manner (self-management, responsible decision-making).

These rules create the framework for developing social-emotional learning within the classroom. Rules and standards are sometimes established on a school-wide basis. If they are not, then it is important that we start our work in developing our classroom management plans by creating the rules or creating rules in the words of the students in your classroom. Expectations should be posted in a prominent place in the classroom, based on Marzano's research (2011):

> To provide academic direction, a teacher must have clear learning goals coupled with instruction and assessment that help students achieve those goals. To provide behavioral direction, the teacher must have well-designed rules and procedures[1] (usually established at the beginning of the school year) that s/he continually updates and reinforces throughout the year. In addition, these rules and procedures need to be the basis for interacting with students regarding behavior: When students follow the rules and procedures, the teacher thanks them; when they don't, the teacher reminds them of behavioral expectations (2007, p. 85).

---

[1] In this book, we use the term *routine* in the same way Marzano uses *procedure*.

To help students understand and appreciate the rules, some teachers ask the students to brainstorm a list of behaviors and expectations that they think would be important to have in their classrooms. Students usually contribute a long list of specific behaviors. As a class, students categorize these behaviors into four or five general rules. For example, the following expectations could all be categorized under the rule: *We will treat everyone with respect*. Yet describing exactly what respect looks like merits the attention of the class.

1. I will listen when the teacher or another student is talking.
2. I will raise my hand when I have something to say in class.
3. I will ask permission if I would like to use another student's materials.
4. I will keep quiet when we are doing independent work.
5. I will make sure everyone is included when we are at lunch and recess.

After the class agrees on approximately five general rules, the students or the teacher creates a poster or class rules document showing the rules, and students are asked to sign their names to the poster as if they are signing a contract, which can add to a sense of belonging in the classroom. There is a common understanding that if a student breaks a rule, s/he will face consequences that are also known and discussed ahead of time.[2]

A high school special education teacher that we work with has a more informal way of setting classroom norms and an interesting method for establishing the norms. Her classroom is consistently a pleasant place to visit and runs smoothly, and every year she thoughtfully develops along with her students, a responsive, respectful class. To get them started, she asks the students to list all the things that "drove them crazy" in any classroom. After students listed things like "Yelling out the answers without waiting," and "Tapping pencils like the desk is a drum," the class discusses the list, combines some suggestions, then posts "Block A Rules of the Class" prominently. The teacher described the language that they have to use as "rules but nicer." So, she tells them not to write, "No yelling out answers," and instead to write, "We talk at appropriate times." The students find it amusing to use "formal language and big words."

---

2 Many middle school and high school teachers incorporate these rules into their classroom management plan, which they send home for parent and student signatures.

To reinforce the importance of the rules, at the end of each class during the beginning weeks of school, they were asked to vote Yes or No on a note card if the rules were followed by everyone. If they answered no for any rule, they have to explain what had happened. The next day, the teacher gives the class feedback (never mentioning any names) about their self-appraisal of their rules. In this way, the students take ownership for defining good behavior, for owning their classroom, and for making sure nobody "drove them crazy." The students knew their norms, supported their validity, and visitors needed to abide by them as well.

Routines and Expectations That Operationalize the Rules

After creating classroom rules, the second level of the classroom management planning is to establish everyday routines—from what to do to find makeup work to where to find and put away materials. To run a classroom smoothly, these routines need to happen automatically once the year has begun. Later in this chapter (Table 4.2), you will see a comprehensive list of classroom routines and expectations one teacher developed for her classroom.

The third level is making the expectations explicit. These are the observable descriptions of the behaviors a student must exhibit to demonstrate successful implementation of the routine. McLeod, Fischer, and Hoover, in their book *The Key Elements of Classroom Management* (2003, p. 79), warn us that "the student must be able to do what you are asking him to do." Our expectations should be behaviors that students can succeed in doing. Later in this chapter, you will see the specific expectations for one teacher's classroom routine for using the bathroom.

Starting Off Well

Teachers may start the year poorly with their classroom management if they fail to devote adequate time during the first weeks of school to teach students the routines and expectations that *operationalize* the rules. Many teachers state and post their rules at the start of the year and never go beyond that point. The problem with only stating the rules is that words may mean different things to different students, based on their beliefs. The definition of *respect* may vary in different homes and in the classrooms of the various teachers the students had during prior years. The definition also changes for people as they enter different stages of their lives. Treating a person with *respect* means one thing to us when we are five years old, another when we are 10, another when we are 15, another when we are 20, and still another when we are 40. Therefore, it is important that we clearly state the routines and our expectations for the behaviors that lead to success in each routine. Respect is a good word for our rules, but it is not sufficiently observable for stating expectations.

In one of my former districts, I always looked forward to the first day that the new teachers began and when the high school English department head who taught Advanced Placement students, among others, taught all of the new teachers and even the new administrators her routines. She had streamlined homework makeup with a period-by-period notebook maintained by students from that specific class that provided every day's homework. I always enjoyed the way that she modeled for high school seniors (no less) how they needed to talk to one another. She had them practice their "one-inch voices" and sitting "nose-to-nose and knee-to-knee, and make eye contact!" Whenever I visited her classroom, students had internalized the expectations, and their academic conversations were serious, focused, and, of course, nose-to-nose and knee-to-knee.

On the other hand, if a class doesn't have well-established routines and expectations, often the class will have a disproportionate level of inappropriate behaviors. The teacher is forced to use frequent negative statements and punishments to maintain order. As we saw in the cycle in Chapter 1, negative words and punishments reinforce a deficit perspective, which leads to lower academic motivation and more misbehavior. This kind of classroom makes establishing positive relationships difficult. Order may be restored with authoritarian actions, but this kind of controlling response will diminish the possibilities of supporting social-emotional learning throughout the year.

Teaching Routines and Expectations to Maximize Social-Emotional Learning

The time spent teaching routines and expectations is time well spent. Over the course of the year, a teacher will save a great deal of instructional time if

> *A teacher will save a great deal of instructional time if s/he devotes adequate time at the start of the year to teaching routines and expectations.*

s/he devotes adequate time at the start of the year to teaching routines and expectations. Well-established routines reduce the number of times teachers need to address negative self-management behavior and increases the opportunity to affirm appropriate self-management behaviors. It also frees the teacher to have conversations with students designed to develop their social-emotional learning skills and to have them feel part of the class.

In his book, *Tools for Teaching*, Fred Jones states, "Research has repeatedly shown that the teachers with the best-run classrooms spend most of the first two weeks of the semester teaching their procedures and routines" (2013, p. 3359 of 8100, Kindle version). In our experience, poor classroom management only gets worse as the year progresses, causing an even greater loss of instructional time. In most cases, the time for student learning is far greater over the course of the year if teachers adequately teach the routines and expectations at the start of year and re-teach them whenever they notice a regression in students' compliance. Returning from a vacation or at the beginning of a term are good points at which to change seats or provide a "refresher" lesson on the rules, routines, and expectations.

Before a teacher can teach routines to students, he or she must have a clear and specific understanding of the expectations for each routine. For example, we were teaching a group of second-year high school teachers about developing routines. Several had expressed concern that the flow of the class was often interrupted by student requests to go to the bathroom. We asked the teachers to write down their expectations for bathroom use and the time they spent telling and/or teaching[3] the routines to students. Several gave a one-sentence explanation of routines, such as, "You must ask permission to use the bathroom in my class." Everything indicated they spent a minute or less telling students the bathroom routine and its expectations at the start of the school year. A series of questions was asked of one of the teachers who had given a single sentence as his bathroom expectation.

---

3 We differentiate between the words *telling* and *teaching* in the following way: *Telling* is an activity done solely by the teacher. Tellers give out the requisite information but do not assess and ensure the students' level of understanding. *Teaching* transfers a body of information in a way that maximizes understanding and retention. It includes an assessment of the students' understanding of the information and their mastery of any behavior required in the learning.

The class continued contributing their expectations. At the end of the conversation, the class saw that they had generated a list of fifteen observable behaviors. Their list follows:

1. No asking to go to the bathroom unless it is an emergency.
2. If you have a doctor-confirmed medical reason indicating you need to use the bathroom frequently, you should speak to me privately.
3. Emergency use is restricted to after the first ten minutes and before the last ten minutes of class.
4. You must raise your hand to ask permission.
5. You must sign out and include the time you leave.
6. You must walk directly to the door without detours and without talking to or touching anyone or anything.
7. You must go directly to the bathroom and directly back without disturbing any other classes along the way.
8. You may not take your backpack with you.
9. You must return in five minutes or less.
10. You must sign in and include the time you return.
11. You must walk directly to your seat without detours and without talking to or touching anyone or anything.
12. You must quietly check with a neighbor to see what you missed.

It soon became obvious to all that they needed to explicitly teach these behaviors and explain the reasons behind these expectations to their classes. Students needed to know what was expected before they could correctly follow the routine. And, students must understand the reason for the expectations and that they and their classmates benefit by following the expectations. Creating understanding of the benefits of following the expectations is as important as being clear about the expected behaviors.

Creating this awareness of the benefits is a valuable way of developing self and social awareness. For example, you don't need to have every student agree with you on the expectations. Some students will argue because they don't want to follow the expectation rather than because they have a better idea. You are still an authoritative teacher (as opposed to authoritarian), so you can make the final decision on what is best for all. You will find that most students will be relieved that the expectations are in place even if they don't challenge the person (particularly if he or she is a bully) who is unreasonably arguing against the expectation. Table 4.1 provides sample questions one may use when establishing classroom expectations.

Figure 4.1 is a list of specific routines and expectations that need to be thoroughly taught at the start of the school year. Put a check next to each routine for

Table 4.1 SEL Skills Connected to Reflective SEL Questions

Social Awareness	Questions That Develop Social Awareness
• Predict others' feelings and reactions • Evaluate others' emotional reactions	• How do you think a person feels when you interrupt them and don't wait your turn to speak? • What impact do you think it has on others when you talk while I'm talking?
Responsible Decision-Making	**Questions That Develop Responsible Decision-Making**
• Identify problems when making decisions, and generate alternatives • Implement problem-solving skills when making decisions, when appropriate	• In what ways do these expectations help with the learning in this class (yours and that of the others)? • Are there any ways in which these expectations will detract from the learning? • If a student raises a way in which the expectations may detract from the learning, a follow up question may be: What is an alternative expectation that better meets our goal of respectful behavior and maximum learning?
Self-Awareness	**Questions That Develop Self-Awareness**
Label and recognize your own and others' emotions	You looked nervous when I announced the upcoming transition. Were you nervous about the transition? If so, why?
Self-Management Behavior in Group Work	**Questions That Develop Self-Management**
• Set plans and work toward goals • Overcome obstacles and create strategies for more long-term goals • Seek help when needed • Manage personal and interpersonal stress	• What can you do or I do to help reduce your anxiety before the transition? • Is there a way I can structure the transition that will make you feel more confident?

which you have already created specific expectations for your students. Put an "X" next to every expectation for which your students know why it is important. As you read through this list, you may write down any notes you wish to remember about any of the listed routines.

Figure 4.1 Comprehensive List of Classroom Routines

Beginning Class Routines and Expectations

- _*_ Entering the class
- _*_ Roll call, attendance (including procedures for tardiness)
- _*_ Seat work requirements when students first enter the class (e.g., Do Now expectations)
- ___ Distribution of materials
- _*_ Sitting in assigned seats
- _*_ Procedure for checking and/or turning in homework
- _*_ Procedure for students absent the previous day to collect missed handouts and assignments and get caught up on missed material
- ___ Writing down that night's homework assignment
- _*_ Materials students are expected to have with them in class each day

General Classroom Routines and Expectations

- ___ Shared materials
- ___ Teacher's desk
- ___ Food and drinks (water)
- ___ Gum
- _*_ Bathroom
- ___ Distributing and collecting materials
- ___ Pencil sharpener
- ___ Student storage, lockers, cubbies
- ___ Dismissing class
- _*_ Lining up for assemblies, trips to library or computer lab
- ___ Attendance and tardiness
- ___ Use of electronic devices in class
- _*_ Class Jobs

Routines and Expectations for Behavior During Independent and Group Work[4]

- _*_ Is talk among students permitted?
- _*_ If so, when and how?

- ___ Identification of resources, such as Internet and dictionaries, and how they may be accessed during the work time
- ___ Passing out and collecting books and supplies
- ___ Assigning tasks to the group members (e.g., leader, scribe, timekeeper, reporter)
- ___ Interim checkpoints
- _*_ Teacher's signals for students' attention (see the section later in this chapter on obtaining and regaining student attention)
- _*_ Students' signals for obtaining the teacher's attention
- _*_ Activities to do when work is done
- ___ How does a student get help from the teacher?
- ___ How and when can a student get help from other students?

Student Participation

- ___ Turning in work
- ___ When and how students return assignments when requested by the teacher
- ___ How does the teacher get back assignments after the student has them signed by parents (or in other situations)?
- ___ Missed work
- ___ Laboratory procedures
- ___ Movement in and out of small groups
- ___ Bringing materials to school
- _*_ Expected behavior in group[5]
- _*_ What to do if you finish early
- ___ Homework expectations and procedures
- ___ Putting away supplies, equipment
- ___ Cleaning up
- ___ Organizing class materials

(continued on next page)

---

4 Later in this chapter, we discuss the components needed for effective classroom work groups.

5 Monitoring the level of conversation during small group work that is on-task and off-task may be difficult when we are helping individual groups with their work. One technique we have used to teach the expectations for appropriate group discussions and, at times, to monitor that expectation is to ask the students to video or record their work.

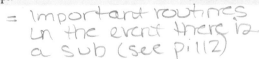
* = Important routines in the event there is a sub (see p.112)

Expectations for Appropriately Completed Work Notes

___ What headings to use on written assignments

___ When students should use pen, pencil, or word processor

___ Is writing on the backs of papers permitted?

___ What are the standards for neatness and legibility?

___ How is incomplete work handled?

___ How is late work handled?

___ When do students use manuscript, cursive, or typing?

___ What margins, fonts, and spacing (single- or double-spaced) are used?

___ Spacing of written work (e.g., writing on every other line)

___ Difference between draft quality and final copy quality

Grading Policies and Procedures

___ Determining grades

___ Recording grades

___ Grading long assignments

___ Closing date for grades

___ Penalties for incomplete work

___ Extra credit work

___ Keeping papers, grades, assignments

___ Grading criteria

___ Contracting for grades

___ Rewrites and retests

___ Makeup work policy (if absent)

Homework Routines[6]

___ When and where does a student write down assignments?

___ Who can assist a student?

___ What are the limits on the assistance others can give a student?

___ What Internet resources may a student use or not use (e.g., translations.com, Moodle, class website)?

___ How does a student get the homework assignment when absent?

___ What are the plagiarism guidelines and penalties?

___ What is the late-homework penalty system?

Other Routines and Expectations

___ Fire drills

___ Lunch procedures

___ Student helpers

___ Safety procedures

___ Out-of-seat policies

___ Consequences for misbehavior

___ Behavior in the computer lab, library, auditorium

___ Locker visits

___ Behavior in the halls

___ Medical emergencies

___ Expectations for when conflict arises

___ Behavior during tests

___ Expectations for how to address teacher and fellow students

---

6   Later in this chapter, you will see examples of plans teachers use for establishing an effective homework routine.

Teaching Classroom Routines

It is never enough just to tell students our expectations for classroom routines. It is important that we *teach* the routines until the students master them, in the same way that we teach academic concepts until they are mastered. As stated earlier, teaching routines should also include helping students understand the value of the routines in insuring safety (physical and emotional), maximum learning, and optimum social interaction. To effectively teach student classroom routines, teachers should follow the following four steps.

Step 1. Make clear what successful and unsuccessful completion looks like.

This should include making clear the impact on learning and safety when the routine is followed in contrast to when it is not followed. Wording the expectations in language that is observable will help you teach the expectation clearly. In the example above of the high school teacher's bathroom routine, we saw that at the expectation level, words such as *appropriate* were replaced with observable behaviors that the teacher could monitor and that students could use to monitor their own success.

Step 2. Test the reality of the expectations for the routine.

The teacher in the earlier example originally wanted no one to go to the bathroom. Upon reflection, he realized this was not a viable routine based on school policies.

Step 3. Ensure that the routine you have planned is consistent with the expectations of the school and team.

In Chapter 1 we talked about the positive impact when teacher teams have expectations that are consistent with one another.

Step 4. Create a plan for teaching the routine.

Some routines are more complex than others. The "plan" for teaching how to set up a paper for an assignment may be no more than showing an example and explaining each part. Whereas teaching effective group work is complex and will take more steps before students can master the routine. It will be helpful to model and/or role-play routines as part of teaching the routine. For example, if one of your expectations as an elementary educator is that students should try to include others that they see are being excluded during recess time, it would be helpful to have a few students role-play this scenario while the other students observe. The social awareness and relationships skills this involves will take direct teaching and practice. After role-playing, the class might discuss other means that will make sure everyone is included. In addition, a routine can be scaffolded, that is, taught in sequential steps. Later in this chapter, a Socratic seminar, whose goal is to have students discuss an issue independently is gradually modeled and practiced beginning with members of a small group who have a specific number of note cards that they will share.

One high school teacher role-plays leaving the classroom to go to the bathroom, assigning himself the role of the student. The first time he shows the students how not to leave the class. He takes on the persona of the student by getting out of his chair and swaggering on a circuitous route around the room, before eventually getting to the door. On his way, around, he pauses at the desks of a couple of his friends to make a comment or flip their books shut. This role-play always results in laughs from the students, as many of them can see themselves in his behaviors. He then role-plays the appropriate way one leaves the room to use the bathroom after receiving permission from the teacher.

Once a routine is taught, we need to expect students to consistently use it, and we should consistently assess students' success in carrying it out. We should look for opportunities to consistently reinforce successful performance of the routine. We should also be ready to reteach the routine if we see student performance regressing. One of the most important parts of establishing and maintaining good routines is consistent enforcement and reinforcement! **The three most important things for teachers to remember when establishing effective classroom management are consistency, consistency, and consistency.** Although there are too many classroom routines to post them all, it may be helpful to post those routines that are particularly important and/or complex at the start of the year. For example, you may want to make a poster listing activities for students to complete when work is finished. You may also want to post a list of expectations for students engaged in group work (explained in depth later in this chapter).

Teacher Provisioning of Materials

It is important that we have all our materials prepared and ready at the start of class. If students are waiting for us to locate materials, the lesson loses its momentum, and this can lead to acting-out behavior. Effective teacher provisioning requires the following measures:

1. We anticipate all the materials that will be needed for the lesson.
    This can include the obvious lesson materials, such as the books, activity sheets, paper, equipment for labs and demonstrations, and appropriate technology. It also includes expecting the unexpected. For example, this can include an extra bulb for the LCD and/or document projectors, extra pencils for students who forget their own pencils, extra books for students who forgot their own, and even a tissue for the student who sneezes and is without a tissue or handkerchief.
2. All the materials needed for the lesson are prepared prior to the lesson and placed in a location where they are readily available.

As described previously in this chapter, we also need to teach students expectations about obtaining these materials. One of the advantages to being well provisioned is that students can then distribute materials or get their own materials. This frees the teacher to teach and/or facilitate appropriate behavior.

Routines and Expectations for Group Work

Many teachers struggle with getting students to work effectively in groups. Teachers who are unsuccessful at getting students to work effectively in groups often avoid doing group work. Unfortunately, we cannot adequately develop social-emotional learning skills nor support the opportunity for students to practice applying and exchanging ideas together unless students have frequent opportunities for group work and can work effectively in groups. Group work is also an important skill for life. Quinn (2012, p. 46) tells us, "Collaboration is included in every list of 21st century skills." See Table 4.2 for questions a teacher can use to support group skills for social-emotional learning.

Eleven Areas of Effective Group Work

There are 11 areas of group work that teachers should address to have effective groups.

1. Alert students to impending transitions. Students do not typically do well with surprises.

They need some time to get physically and mentally ready for transitions.[7] Alerting students to transitions, such as the time when group work will begin, when the group needs to shift activities, or when the group work will end. One way we do this is by indicating this information on our class agenda. Another is to provide students with verbal notice before the impending transition. The length of time we alert students prior to the transition will depend on the how complex the transition will be. In some cases, the notice can be as little as two minutes. In other cases, it may need to be as much as five or ten minutes.

How well students respond to transitions varies depending on certain social-emotional factors. For ex-

ample, some students on the autism spectrum become anxious during a change. For these students, helping with their social awareness and self-management skills is important. At times these conversations can be with the full class. In cases such as a student with a disability in this area, a private conversation is best.

2. Create an effective group size.

Groups should be no larger than four or five students (or they can be as small as two students). In our experience, once groups exceed this limit, some students get lost and/or lose interest because they do not get adequate opportunity to participate. This can lead to loss of learning by these students and, at times, misbehavior. Some people believe that in lower elementary grades, groups should have no more than three students.

You want your groups large enough to provide for more complex social interactions. This provides you with an opportunity to develop students' social-emotional skills. However, you don't want them so large that one or more students can avoid the social interactions because others dominate the conversation time.

3. Assign responsibilities and accountability.

A quick and efficient way to do this is to use the cooperative learning jobs grid. Dean, Hubbell, Howard, and Pitler (2012, p. 37) tell us that "to foster positive interdependence, teachers must ensure that the workload of each individual is reasonably equal to the workload of other team members." Assigning jobs and creating a system of individual accountability (see Area 8 below) are key components of ensuring reasonable equity in the workload. It is also important that the jobs rotate at certain intervals so that everyone experiences every job over the course of the year. Different jobs provide opportunities to use different social-emotional learning skills.

Tables 4.3 and 4.4 are examples of cooperative learning jobs grids. When using the jobs grid, we start by putting the students into their groups. We then explain to the students that each student may only have one job at a time. Beginning with the first descriptor, the students discuss the criteria and figure out who best fits the description in each description column box. Once the leader is established, he or she is out of the running for the scribe position in the second description box. Once the scribe is set, the final two members of the group vie for the recorder

---

7   This is true of all transitions and not just transitions in and out of group and partner work. Alerting students to an impending end of the class or expected classroom disruption makes them better prepared to respond appropriately.

Table 4.2 SEL Skills Connected to Questions That Support Group Work SEL Skills

Self-Awareness Behavior in Classroom Management	Questions That Develop Self-Awareness During Transitions
Label and recognize own and others' emotions	You looked nervous when I announced the upcoming transition. Were you nervous about the transition? If so, why?
Self-Management Behavior in Group Work	Questions That Develop Self-Management During Group Work
• Set plans and work toward goals • Overcome obstacles and create strategies for more long-term goals • Seek help when needed • Manage personal and interpersonal stress	• What can you do or I do to help reduce your anxiety before the transition? • Is there a way I can structure the transitions that will make you feel more confident? • How do you request assistance from other groups when you get stuck?
Relationship Skills in Cooperative Group Work	Questions That Develop Relationship Skills in Cooperative Group Work
• Exhibit cooperative learning and working toward group goals • Evaluate own skills to communicate with others	• When you are the leader, how do you determine if someone is doing too much of the talking and not giving others adequate chances to speak? • If you see this happening, what can you do to correct the situation?

Table 4.3 Cooperative Learning Jobs Grid for Four Students

Description Column	Activity 1	Activity 2	Activity 3	Activity 4
Wearing the most red	Leader	Gopher	Reporter	Scribe
Traveled to the farthest place on summer vacation	Scribe	Leader	Gopher	Reporter
Most unusual pet at home	Reporter	Scribe	Leader	Gopher
Whoever is left	Gopher	Reporter	Scribe	Leader

Table 4.4 Cooperative Learning Jobs Grid for Five Students

Description Column	Activity 1	Activity 2	Activity 3	Activity 4	Activity 5
Tallest	Leader	Timekeeper	Gopher	Reporter	Scribe
Shortest	Scribe	Leader	Timekeeper	Gopher	Reporter
Longest hair	Reporter	Scribe	Leader	Timekeeper	Gopher
Shortest hair	Gopher	Reporter	Scribe	Leader	Timekeeper
Whoever is left	Timekeeper	Gopher	Reporter	Scribe	Leader

position. The last person without a job is the gopher (this name is derived from the fact that he/she is the person to "go for" whatever is needed).

Each job has specific responsibilities (see Tables 4.3 and 4.4). The leader's job is to ensure that the job gets done correctly in the time allowed. The leader must ensure that everyone contributes to accomplishing the task. This means that the leader must encourage the reticent to speak and contain any member who tries to disproportionately dominate the discussion. To do this successfully requires the largest number of social-emotional-learning skills. In classrooms, often the students who most need to build these skills are least often (or never) in the leadership position that requires them to use the skills and gives the teacher an opportunity to develop his or her leadership skills.

The scribe keeps notes as a record of the group's work. The notes must be legible enough so that the reporter can read them to give the group report or so that others can copy the notes if that is required. The reporter gives the oral report of the group's work to the entire class.[8] The "gopher" is the one who gets any materials the group needs. He or she is the one who fetches the dictionary from the bookcase, goes to the library if a research material is needed, or goes to the cabinet for the science lab equipment. He or she can also be designated as the person who gets the teacher if the group needs teacher assistance or goes to another group if the group needs peer assistance. In cases in which you have groups of five, a timekeeper can be added as the fifth job. If you only have four and need a timekeeper, then timekeeping can be assigned to the gopher or to one of the other job areas. Another job that can be given to either the timekeeper or gopher is the assessor. The assessor uses the class rubric or scoring mechanism for the effectiveness of the group in accomplishing their task as a whole and of the effectiveness of each member within the group. Often teachers are concerned that not all students are doing their jobs; the self-assessment along with an alert teacher's frequent check-ins particularly as group work is being established can help students stay focused and accountable for the goals of the work.

All members of the group are responsible for monitoring themselves and others, following the basic group work expectations such as voice volume, good listening, courtesy, etc.

All members of the group are responsible for monitoring themselves and others, following the basic group work expectations such as voice volume, good listening, courtesy, etc. Later in this chapter, you will find methods for teaching students to do this monitoring.

Once the grid is set, the teacher has the group jobs ready for four or five different activities. Since the students rotate through the jobs, there is little concern about fairness. Students typically find the initial placement in jobs by the randomly set descriptions more fair than when the teacher assigns the jobs. However, in circumstances when the teacher thinks it is best, the teacher may certainly assign the first set of jobs and then let the students rotate through the jobs during the next three activities. For example, early in the year the teacher may want a student who already possesses many of the skills of a certain job. This provides an opportunity for the teacher to highlight the skills and their impact as an instructional tool with the other students in the group. The Cooperative Learning Jobs Grids (Tables 4.3 and 4.4) significantly reduce the time it takes to assign jobs each time there is a new activity and eliminates the bickering that may occur over who will do which job.

4. Some groups will need more of your time than others.

Some will need this time because they are struggling with the concept and need more re-teaching and prompting. Some will need this time because they have quickly completed the task and need to be directed toward extension work. Some will need this time because their social-emotional learning skills are less developed and need more teacher instruction and coaching.

If you recognize in advance that you will need to spend a large amount of time with a group, plan activities for other groups in which minimal direction is needed. In some cases, this extra time may be needed because those students are more likely to struggle with an academic task. In some cases, they may need more time so the teacher can facilitate the social-emotional skills of the students in a group.

---

8   Requiring the scribe to record notes that are neat enough for the reporter also makes the notes neat enough for the teacher to collect and review. At times, we will collect the group notes as a way of assessing the quality of the work done by the group.

5. Construct tasks that students will be able to complete independently after you have explained the directions.

Provide students with step-by-step written directions and clear criteria for assessment, such as rubrics or criteria sheets. These directions can also require a final summary and can then be given to the teacher at the end of the group's work or at the end of the class as a ticket to leave. If possible, share examples of student work that successfully meets the criteria. During the group work, you want to be able to differentiate your academic and social-emotional instruction as needed. If students are able work with a high level of independence, if frees the teacher to differentiate the level of interaction based on the needs of individual groups.

6. Set clear expectations with regards to appropriate and productive behavior.

It may be helpful to post your expectations for group work that include levels for each. Teach these expectations (including why they are important) as described in the section on routines that appears earlier in this chapter. See Table 4.5 for an example of a self-assessment for group participation.

Each student can use this rubric as individual accountability for positive group participation and submit it at the end of class.

7. Establish a system for how students may get assistance from the teacher or their peers when needed.

Some teachers use a designated spot on the white board in which students write their names when they need help. When the teacher is available, they know the teacher will either call them to his or her desk or will come to visit with them. Students also understand that they are to continue working (on an alternative activity if necessary) until the teacher can meet with them.

Another strategy is to give the students three colored plastic twelve-ounce cups (preferably red, green, and yellow). The students begin the independent work time with the cups stacked on the corners of their desks, so only the green one is showing. The green signals to the teacher that the student or group is working well and does not need any help. When the student or group needs the teacher, but has an alternative activity on which to work, the student puts the yellow cup on top. When the student or group is completely stuck and has no alternative work, the red

Table 4.5 Student Self-Assessment of Group Participation

Name: Group Participation Skill	4	3	2	1
I shared my ideas and offered suggestions.				
I asked others questions				
I built on others' ideas				
I gave credit to people for their ideas				
I listened closely and attentively				
If I disagreed, I was respectful				
I gave evidence for my ideas				
I made sure everyone had a chance to contribute				
My strongest contribution was Explain:				
An area I'd like to do better in was Explain:				

cup is placed on top of the stack. The teacher attends to the students with red cups showing before going to the students with the yellow cups on top. Some teachers use a variation of this activity. When the yellow cup is on top, a student with a green cup may go and assist the student(s) with the yellow cup. A red cup on top indicates that the student has already received peer help but still needs the teacher's assistance.

8. Create an accountability system.

Below is a description of how some teachers record or videotape groups as a method of assessing the group's effectiveness at achieving their task and working collaboratively (see Table 4.7). Some group work is such that all the students produce a product, and the teacher has the students place their work in a work-in-progress folder that the teacher may view at any time. At other times, students turn in the work they completed during the class period so the teacher can make comments and return their work the following day. A third method is for each role to have a specific task and to self-assess their work at the end of the group's task.

9. Establish procedures for what students should do when they have completed the assigned task.

Should they turn in their finished work? If so, where? What should they do when they are done? When this important step is missing, student misbehavior usually increases.

10. Provide a time for summary reports from the groups.

Make time either at the beginning or at the end of the class session for students to share their work. Doing so sends the message to students that everyone's work is valuable. If one student is designated as the reporter, he/she should understand that the report is to be on the group's work, not his or her individual ideas and contributions. This is also a good time to have the group report on their social-emotional dynamics such as those they self-assessed using the rubric below.

11. Provide time for group and self-assessment.

This should include assessment of the task and assessment of the group's work as a group. There should be both teacher assessment and student self-assessment. Tables 4.6 and 4.8 are samples of student self-assessment scoring guides that can be used for this purpose. As with assessment of academic growth, assessment of behavior should follow the gradual release or responsibility from teacher-implemented assessment to student self-assessment. Below are some tools that can assist students and teachers with assessments.

Student Self-Assessment of Problem-Solving Skills

Evaluating My Problem-Solving Skills

Carefully look over your corrected work and answer the questions below.

1. I used a strategy that made sense. Yes No
2. I found a correct solution. Yes No
3. I explained my strategy clearly and step by step. Yes No
4. My score was _____.
5. Explain what you feel you did well on this task.

6. Explain how you will improve your work in the future.

Developed by Dr. Deborah Brady

Assessment Form for Discussion Groups

Names:
Date:
Group's discussion topic:

Circle the appropriate responses. Provide evidence where possible.

1. Everyone participated and shared in the discussion process.
   Yes   No   Sometimes
   Evidence:

2. The group was supportive of its individual members.
   Yes   No   Sometimes
   Evidence:

3. Group members often asked questions for clarification and elaboration.
   Yes   No   Sometimes
   Evidence:

(continued at bottom of facing page)

Table 4.6 Student Self-Assessment of Group Work on Elementary Level

About My Learning Today	Great!	So-so...	Not Really
I followed directions			
I managed my time			
I cooperated with others			
I participated in the discussion			
I worked on my own (when I needed to)			
I worked in groups			
I completed my work			
I brought all the materials I needed			
I find these things easy to do. Explain why			
I find these things difficult. Explain why			
I really like these things. Explain why			
The person I work best with is Explain why			
The goal that I'm working on is Describe the progress you're making on your goal:			

Adapted with permission from Joyce Silberman, fifth-grade teacher, Newman Elementary School, Needham, Massachusetts.

4. The group discussion stayed on topic.
    Yes   No   Sometimes
    Evidence:

5. The group was energetic and enthusiastic.
    Yes   No   Sometimes
    Evidence:

6. What was the best thing about the way this group worked together?

7. What was one problem this group had? Did we violate any norms?

8. How did you solve it?

9. What else might you have done?

10. What specific plans do have for improving your group's performance the next time you meet?

Adapted from Saskatchewan Education (1996).

Table 4.7 Teacher Assessment Form for Collaborative Work Skills

CATEGORY	4	3	2	1
Participation	Consistently provides useful ideas when participating in the group. A definite leader who contributes a lot of effort.	Generally provides useful ideas when participating in the group. A strong group member who tries hard!	Sometimes provides useful ideas when participating in the group. A satisfactory group member who does what is required.	Rarely provides useful ideas when participating in the group. May refuse to participate.
Support for group members	Is supportive of group members by listening and helping the discussion when needed.	Is generally supportive of group members.	Occasionally is publicly critical of the project or the work of other members of the group. Does not always support group members.	Often is publicly critical of the project or the work of other members of the group. Does not usually support group members.
Communication	Consistently asks questions for clarification and/or elaboration when appropriate. Can clarify confusion other group members have through answering questions and through elaboration.	Generally asks questions or asks for clarification and/or elaboration when appropriate. Can usually clarify confusion other group members have through answering questions and through elaboration.	Sometimes asks questions or asks for clarification and/or elaboration. Sometimes can clarify confusion other group members have through answering questions and through elaboration.	Rarely asks questions or asks for clarification and/or elaboration. Is unable to clarify confusion other group members have through answering questions and through elaboration.
Focus on the task	Consistently stays focused on the task and what needs to be done. Very self-directed.	Focuses on the task and what needs to be done most of the time. Other group members can count on this person.	Focuses on the task and what needs to be done some of the time. Other group members must sometimes nag, prod, and remind to keep this person on-task.	Rarely focuses on the task and what needs to be done. Lets others do the work.
Group dynamics	Consistently has a positive attitude and is energetic and enthusiastic throughout the process.	Generally maintains a positive attitude and is energetic and enthusiastic throughout most of the process.	Sometimes maintains a positive attitude about the task and is energetic and enthusiastic throughout some of the process.	Often maintains a negative attitude about the task and is not energetic and enthusiastic throughout the process.

Adapted from Rubistar.4teachers.org, rubric ID 1004399 (September 18, 2003). Copyright ALTEC at the University of Kansas (2008).

Table 4.8 Student Self-Assessment Form for Collaborative Work Skills

CATEGORY	4	3	2	1
Participation	All group members routinely provide useful ideas when participating in the group.	Most group members provide useful ideas when participating in the group.	Some group members provide useful ideas when participating in the group. One group member may refuse to participate.	Most group members do not provide useful ideas when participating in the group. One or more group members may refuse to participate.
Support for group members	Group members are never publicly critical of the project or the work of others. Group members are supportive of other group members.	Group members are rarely publicly critical of the project or the work of others. Group members are usually supportive of other group members.	Group members are occasionally publicly critical of the project or the work of other members of the group. Group members do not always support other group members.	Group members are often publicly critical of the project or the work of other members of the group. Group members do not usually support other group members.
Communication	Group members routinely ask questions for clarification and/or elaboration when appropriate. Group members can clarify confusion others have through clearly answering questions.	Group members usually ask questions or ask for clarification and/or elaboration when appropriate. Group members can usually clarify confusion others have through answering questions.	Group members sometimes ask questions or ask for clarification and/or elaboration. Group members sometimes can clarify confusion others have through answering questions.	Group members rarely ask questions or ask for clarification and/or elaboration. Group members are unable to clarify confusion others have.
Focus on the task	All group members consistently stay focused on the task and what needs to be done.	Group members focus on the task and what needs to be done most of the time.	Group members focus on the task and what needs to be done some of the time. At times, group members must sometimes nag, prod, and remind one or more group members to keep them on-task.	Group members rarely focus on the task and what needs to be done. One or two group members may end up doing all the work to complete the task(s).
Group dynamics	All group members consistently have a positive attitude about the task(s) and are energetic and enthusiastic throughout the process.	Group members usually maintain a positive attitude about the task(s) and are energetic and enthusiastic throughout most of the process.	Group members sometimes maintain a positive attitude about the task(s) and are energetic and enthusiastic throughout some of the process.	Group members maintain a negative attitude about the task(s) and are not energetic and enthusiastic throughout the process.

Adapted from Rubistar.4teachers.org, rubric ID 1004399 (September 18, 2003). Copyright ALTEC at the University of Kansas (2008).

The self-assessment form in Figure 4.2 should be completed by individual students after engaging in group work to help them reflect on their own interactions. Again, this form should be shared and discussed with students before they begin their collaborative work to help them better understand appropriate behaviors during group work.

Figure 4.2 Student Self-Assessment of Group Participation

My Contribution to Group Work

My group was discussing/solving...
Rate each entry as:
1 - Needs Improving   2 - Satisfactory   3 - Excellent

Please also provide an example for each of the following questions.

1. I shared my ideas and offered suggestions. Example:	1	2	3
2. I spoke clearly and slowly enough. Example:	1	2	3
3. I answered others' questions. Example:	1	2	3
4. I remained on topic and helped the group stay focused. Example:	1	2	3
5. I encouraged others to participate. Example:	1	2	3
6. I disagreed without hurting others' feelings. Example:	1	2	3
7. I summarized or repeated my ideas when necessary. Example:	1	2	3
8. I gave reasons for my opinions. Example:	1	2	3
9. I listened courteously and effectively. Example:	1	2	3
10. I tried to understand and extend the suggestions of others. Example:	1	2	3

11. My most important contribution to the discussion was

12. I would like to improve _____ the next time we meet.

13. My plan for improvement is

Adapted from Saskatchewan Education (1996).

Taping as an Engagement and Management Technique for Group Work

One technique we have found to be particularly helpful in teaching and managing expectations of group work is the use of a recording. There are many tools available online for taping and videoing students. In addition to providing a monitor of the work, it also validates the importance of the work to the teacher if the students get feedback on what was heard or seen.

Implementing This Tool

First, begin by introducing the method for recording. Explain to the students that this tool will be used to help you better understand where they are in their learning, to monitor their progress, and to listen to their conversations that you are unable to hear when you are working with another group. Explain to them that they will also have an opportunity to listen to their conversations.

Before using the audiotape to record conversations, have a discussion with the students about how the recording device works and how students might feel the first couple of times they are being recorded. Model the process for the students, then give students time to "play around" with the audiotape for a few minutes and allow them to practice using it. We found that this practice eliminates some of the silliness and uneasiness that sometimes goes along with being recorded.

Next, select a group to record for a collaborative activity. An inner-outer circle could be used for this part of the demonstration. This group work activity is described more completely later in this chapter. Make sure the students understand that they need to speak clearly and into the microphone (if there is one). Once they begin the activity, you will have more time to spend with the other groups, as you will be able to go back to the taped group and analyze their work later.

Analyzing the Conversations

Try to listen to the audiotape as soon as possible. In this way, you may quickly address any learning misunderstandings or inappropriate group work behaviors immediately. After you have listened, you can share the examples of effective group work and of times when students were not as effective so that students understand clearly how to make the groups run smoothly.

For example, one teacher could uncover and consequently address an ongoing problem one literature circle group was experiencing. The audiotape allowed her to listen to this group's entire conversation and analyze what was happening about group dynamics. Without being able to do so, it is unlikely she would have uncovered what was happening in this group. In this case, one student dominated the conversation, and because he was so outspoken, all group members listened to him, agreed with him, and even changed their views. Because the teacher only listened to small pieces of the group's conversation during the class, she assumed that the vocal student understood the text and could clarify any confusion his group members had. Unfortunately, this student communicated his *misunderstandings* of the text to the other students.

Because the teacher could take a deeper look at this group via the audiotape, she could address these issues the following day.

The teacher also had these students listen to their conversation and asked them to reflect on the dynamics of their group. The outspoken student immediately realized he had dominated the conversation and commented, "I never realized how much I talked. I guess I should work on giving other people a chance to talk, too." This group came up with a plan to help one another take turns talking and, consequently, had much more interactive, effective discussions in the future.

> *The students remarked that the audiotape had the effect of keeping them on task, as they knew the teacher was going to be listening to their entire conversation.*

Unexpected Outcome

The students also remarked that the audiotape had the effect of keeping them on task, as they knew the teacher was going to be listening to their entire conversation at some point. The teacher found that she had to spend less time dealing with discipline issues with the group that was using the audiotape. The students seemed to like using the audiotape, as they felt that it helped them to stay more focused and eliminated some of the off-task behaviors groups experienced when a teacher wasn't working with them.

Partner Work

Effective partner work provides us with many of the benefits of group work. Partner work is really group work, but the size of the group is only two people. Most of the components noted above are important components for groups as small as two people. Teachers who are new to group work often begin with partner work before moving on to groups of three, four, or five. One strategy unique to partner work is processing partners.

Higher-Order Thinking Using Processing Partners

It is often helpful for students to discuss their responses to higher-order questions with a partner. Doing so enables them to build upon one another's thinking, thereby producing high-level answers. One strategy teachers use to get students to effectively process questions with a partner is processing partners.[9] In this strategy, students quickly discuss a higher-level (or any) question with a partner and then quickly return to their seats to join a general discussion. Teachers create a partner sheet using terms they want the students to learn through repetition. In the following example, the generals from the Civil War are used. The students then follow the instructions below to get one partner for each blank line.

The instructions given to the students are as follows:

1. When the teacher gives the direction, find one class partner for each of the generals noted below.

2. Be certain that, for any space in which you have the name of a classmate, your classmate has your name in the same space. For example, if you have John Doe's name in your Stonewall Jackson space, then John Doe should have your name in his Stonewall Jackson space.

3. You may not have any partners who sit at your table (or sit at a contiguous desk).

4. You may not have a partner more than once.

5. Fill as many slots as you can in the five minutes given. Don't worry if you don't fill them all. We will help you to do so after the five minutes are up.

After the five minutes have passed, students are asked to return to their seats. Now the teacher asks, "Who does not have a Robert E. Lee?" If an even number of students raises their hands, then the teacher has them take each other's names to fill that slot on their sheets. If some students still have blanks, it is fine to bend the rules at this point and let students partner with someone at their table or someone they already have had as a partner. If there are an odd number of students with a blank slot, the teacher pairs up as many as possible and assigns the one remaining student the name "wild card." The teacher completes this process for all the spaces on the sheet. When it comes time to share, the "wild card" student partners with someone whose partner is absent or is assigned as a third person joining a pair of partners.

The teacher is now ready to ask a higher-order thinking question, and he or she tells the students to find their partners for a category. For example, the teacher might say, "Pair up with your Stonewall Jackson partner." Once the students are sitting with their partners, the teacher then asks the higher-order thinking question for the pairs to discuss. After the students finish discussing the higher-order thinking question in pairs, they return to their original seats and either share their answers orally or write them in their response journals.[10]

Civil War General Processing Partners

Robert E. Lee _____

Ulysses S. Grant _____

Stonewall Jackson _____

George Meade _____

William T. Sherman _____

Joseph Johnston _____

Joseph Hooker _____

Pierre Beauregard _____

William Hayes _____

Alfred Sully _____

John Jones _____

James Longstreet _____

---

9 The use of processing partners is also an excellent strategy to use with recall and comprehension questions when teachers want to firmly embed information.

10 The following sample is for a high school history class. Teachers in other disciplines have used terms such as *the being verbs, poets of the 19th century, titles of Shakespeare plays, elements from the periodic table, the continents, words that are difficult to spell*, etc. A partner sheet can be made from any list of content-related terms a teacher wishes to have students frequently review.

Homework Routines

Homework has an especially important function socially and emotionally because managing homework supports the self-management skills of students. Homework requires using social-emotional skills no matter the age of the student. The challenges to homework completion include getting the materials and assignments home, setting goals, and implementing them in the midst of an afternoon and evening full of "alluring distractions, enticing temptations, or competing personal strivings" (Como, 2004, quoted by Xu, 2013). From playing outside to cell phones, navigating homework assignments requires "arranging the environment, managing time, handling distractions, monitoring motivation, and controlling emotion" based on Xu's research.

> *The challenges to homework completion include getting ... assignments home, setting and implementing goals in the midst of an afternoon and evening full of "alluring distractions, enticing temptations, or competing personal strivings."*

Thus, in addition to the work that may need to be completed, homework entails daily consistent organization, motivation, and determination on the part of students and involves the teacher as well as parents if students are to learn this important self-management skill.

As a component of academics, homework's impact has been in question for years. Some researchers go so far as saying that homework makes no difference in academic achievement. However, research suggests that homework does increase family involvement in the children's education, and this involvement results in more positive attitudes toward school and higher achievement later in school (Hampshire, Butera, and Hourcade, 2014). In addition, it does help develop important social-emotional, self-management, and motivational skills. In helping to be successful in doing their homework, teachers have two major responsibilities: 1) to provide meaningful, engaging practice and 2) to help students learn through developing routines in class that show how to navigate the distractions at home and return their work to school successfully.

Researchers have found that practicing a skill that students know that they will apply can make the assignment meaningful. For example, most early elementary students have reading or practicing mathematical fluency as their daily homework assignment. By becoming more fluent in math and reading, students can see the meaningfulness of the work. In addition, teachers must help students understand why they have this responsibility.

The At-Home Factors

Families can provide positive influence which, based on research, is needed from the earliest years through high school. Students continue to need parental/guardian support to develop self-management and to create a good place and time for doing the work as the amount of time spent and the complexity of the work increases.

The recommended time from most experts is 10 minutes per grade level, maxing out at 80 minutes for middle school and two hours for high school. Beyond that amount of time, homework does not have an appreciable positive impact on academics and may result in a negative attitude toward school (Xu, 2013, pp. 97–100). Families need to help their children select a good time and prioritize their after-school activities as they help them determine whether they do their work after a brief snack when they arrive home or after dinner or if they study in a quiet room or at the kitchen table in the midst of the rest of the family.

Maintaining and Monitoring Motivation

To maintain focus and motivation, students may resort to "self-consequenting," that is, promising themselves a reward if they finish the work. A family member might help the homeworker by suggesting that he will play a video game with him once he finishes. Or, the student may use "self-talk" to stay in focus and encourage themselves about their ability to do the work (Xu, 2013, p. 101). Some middle and high school students have formal or informal (over the phone) study groups because they provide a positive social component to homework, though, if not chosen carefully, the group could be more of a distraction.

Despite its character-building importance, homework is a routine with which both teachers and students struggle at times. For example, if a teacher gives a reading assignment and plans her lesson on that assignment, those who have not done the work will not profit from nor contribute to the discussion. Some teachers see this lack of preparation as contributing to reduced academic success for that student.

Homework is perhaps the most difficult routine

to establish well in a classroom because the teacher does not have any control over the environment surrounding the completion of the work. The teacher cannot follow the student home and sit with the student to ensure the homework is adequately completed. Yet, teachers can act proactively at the beginning of the year to increase students' success with homework by teaching them the routine of effectively completing homework during the first three weeks of school. Students will then know what good homework looks like, what the directions mean, and how to deal with homework that is too challenging.

The amount of time needed to teach the homework routine may vary, depending on grade level and the school population. In addition, teachers need to remember that students may face many challenges in their homes. For example, they may have no family support to monitor or assist with homework. In one school in which we worked, 20 percent of the students lived in homeless shelters; they had few opportunities to get homework assistance nor to find a distraction-free space. Even in cases when a parent or guardian is home, some parents are unable to assist because of language barriers, a lack of formal education, or even a lack of familiarity with a new programs' methods. Thus, as one high school teacher told us, "You need to teach your homework routine with the assumption that no one is at home to help."— and assign work that way

Deborah Meier, in her work with students in New York City public schools, found that "a sizable number of students didn't really know how to do the homework, or at least how to do it well enough to get any satisfaction from it. [Another] group just couldn't or didn't plan" (2006, pp. 8–9). To deal with this problem, the staff ensured that students knew how to do the homework before the end of each class. The staff also provided direct instruction to students throughout the school year.

Before establishing a homework routine, it is necessary for the teacher to think about his or her own beliefs about homework. Questions for the teacher to consider when establishing a homework policy and routine include the following:

- **What is the purpose of homework?** Some teachers use homework to extend the learning from the class and to try new concepts in preparation for the next day's lesson. Homework can also be used as a review of the day's lesson and as an opportunity to practice what is presented in class.

- **What is the definition of homework for this classroom?** Is homework a written assignment, a reading assignment, a long-term project, or a combination of two or more of these? Explaining at the beginning of the year what constitutes homework gives students a more concrete idea of what will be expected of them.

- **How often will you assign homework?** Some teachers assign homework every night. Others choose to assign homework four nights per week, opting to give students a reprieve on the weekend. Best practice would say to assign homework only when it is meaningful and useful for teaching and learning.

- **How much does homework count?** And how does it count? Is its purpose to practice and to be an opportunity to learn content as well as self-management skills?

- **What does an "acceptable" homework assignment look like?** Just as it is good practice to share model essays with students so that they know what is acceptable and what is not, it is also good practice to show students what passes as acceptable for a homework assignment.

- **What do you expect when a student does not understand a portion of the homework?** Because homework is an opportunity for students to practice what they have learned in class, they may have occasional difficulty completing the assignment at home without help.

- **What kind of help is appropriate?** How much help is too much?

- **What is the routine for collecting homework?** Some teachers prefer to collect homework at the beginning of the class to ensure that students aren't scurrying to complete it during class time. Others prefer to give students an opportunity to modify their homework as it is reviewed in class.

- **What happens when a student does not complete homework?** High school students have many competing interests, such as work, extracurricular activities, other schoolwork, etc. Inevitably, there will be students who do not complete homework. Teachers need to have a plan in place to work with such students. Phone calls or emails home and after-school sessions are two ways by which teachers address this problem. How does it impact the student's grade? Keep in mind that even the best plan is ineffective unless there is support, consistency, and follow-through in the plan's implementation.

The "**flipped classroom**" is seen by some educators as a comprehensive change in teaching. Others see it as a new way to think about what teachers do in class and what teachers assign for homework.

In the flipped classroom, teachers record lectures, have students watch videos, or use other avenues in which the students learn content at home. When they come to school, class time is used to delve into the knowledge with greater depth. Sams and Bergman (2013, pp. 16–20), who are experts in "flipping," tell us that flipping is not for every classroom nor for every topic. Teachers must be sure that the media used is available to all students since some students lack adequate technology at home. Most of the homework issues we discussed above still exist with flipping. These must be resolved with careful planning and teaching such as that discussed above and in the following section.

According to Nancy Frey and Douglas Fisher (2011), homework should serve as practice with skills/content that students already know how to do rather than a time to introduce new material. When students are not prepared to work on new material or material that they have not yet mastered, their responses may fall into four categories. In each case, students come to class without having mastered the material. At times,

Homework should serve as practice with skills/content that students already know how to do rather than a time to introduce new material.

1. parents have done the bulk of the work
2. the student did not do the work by choice or because of external circumstances
3. the work has many errors, indicating that the student does not understand
4. students use other students' work as if it is their own

In each of these cases, the teacher is left with little accurate information about the work that students could complete independently or about students' level of mastery. The causes may be out of a student's control—for example, being homeless, living in a chaotic home, having the responsibility of taking care of their siblings. If a student merely decided to ignore the homework, a teacher may need to investigate why there is a lack of interest or motivation. Finally, a student may be having difficulty with the work because of an undiagnosed learning difficulty or because of a problem that may be resolved with targeted support in the classroom.

Frey and Fisher sum up their findings this way:

In reality, schools and classrooms are filled with a mix of all … types of students, which likely contributes to the lack of consistent evidence of the effect of homework on student learning.… [W]hat educators need to figure out is how to ensure that students understand the homework that they are assigned so they actually complete it. To change a maxim, only perfect practice makes perfect.

Homework can be one of the most difficult routines to establish effectively in a classroom.

Therefore, it is important that teachers devote adequate time at the start of the year to establish classroom homework routines. Teachers also must be ready to reteach the routine when they find the quality and quantity of the homework they receive beginning to diminish.

Lesson Plans for Teaching Routines

In this section of the chapter, we have provided sample lesson plans for teaching routines. As noted earlier, routines must be taught and modeled not "told." Effective teaching of classroom management expectations, and these important self-regulation skills, requires as much planning as the effective teaching of the curriculum content and skills. The first two lessons below are sample plans for teaching the homework routine.

Plan for Teaching Homework Routines to Upper Elementary Students

What do I want students to know and be able to do by the end of the lesson? By the end of the lesson on homework, the students will be able to

1. Copy the assignment each day at the start of class, exactly as written on the board, in their homework notebook. Make sure they understand the directions.
2. Complete the homework by the start of the next day's class using appropriate forms.

3. Complete homework independently to the best of his/her ability. (The homework will demonstrate a level of quality like that of work completed in class and accepted by the teacher as the student's best work. Only use parents or guardians (older siblings, etc.) to assist as a last resort. Students will solicit parent support only upon the following conditions:

   a. The student attempted the assignment independently without success.

   b. The student reviewed the classroom notes and/or textbook pages explaining the concepts required in the homework.

   c. The student attempted the assignment independently at least one additional time without success.

4. Bring their homework notebook and all necessary materials home each night.

Teachers' Assessment of Students' Level of Mastery

1. I will review the homework completed in class during the instruction phase of teaching the students how to do homework.

2. I will keep the homework examples completed in class as a benchmark for the quality of homework completed at home.

3. I will record the quality and quantity of the homework completed by each student during the Do Now.

What are the activities and the sequence of the activities?

1. The expectations noted above in the criteria for success section will be taught during the first week of school.

2. The students will be given copies of examples saved from previous years.

3. The homework expectations will be posted on the wall. (See the sample below.)

4. Students will complete all homework assignments in class during the first three weeks of school. The teacher will closely monitor students' adherence to the expectations to ensure that all students understand and successfully follow the expectations.

5. A homework packet containing a letter describing the homework procedures, homework expectations, and ideas for setting up an area conducive for doing homework will be sent to parents during the first week of school. (See the sample below.)

6. The homework expectations (particularly the one about help from parents as a "last resort") will be explained on parents' night.

7. Students' homework during the first three weeks of school will be to bring home the homework assignments they completed in school for parent review and signature. Parents should be encouraged to write back with any questions they have about the homework procedure. Homework is the one routine that requires training the parents as well as the students!

The following pages contain sample letters and checklists that might be sent home to parents. It includes a specific list of the homework expectations referred to previously.

Letter Home About Homework in the First Two Weeks of School

September 4, 2017

Dear Parents and/or Guardians,

As we work to become more responsive to the needs of our students, I have developed the following approach to "teaching" homework. For the first three weeks of school, time will be devoted each day to clearly defining my expectations of good work and to teaching students how to successfully complete homework. We will discuss the following: how to become an organized student, how to prioritize assignments, how to get started on homework assignments, what to do when an assignment is difficult, and how to set up a space at home conducive to fostering good study habits.

Please note that all written work will be completed in class for the first three weeks of school.

During the first three weeks, your child's homework will be completed at school and brought home to share and explain these assignments with you. This task will reinforce the learning that took place during the school day. In addition, all students are expected to read for at least fifteen minutes each night. Students will receive specific directions in class about at-home reading assignments.

After you and your student understand what good homework looks like, I will be sending home another letter that clearly outlines the classroom policy on homework and provides our classroom website where I will post homework assignments daily. If you have any questions, please contact me by email or by phone.

Please sign this letter below and have your child return it to me.

Sincerely,

Mrs. Deane

mdeane@bestschool.k12.school.us

(617)-987-1234

Parent/Guardian Signature: _____

Provided by Dr. Jennifer Deane, Director of STEM Westborough, Massachusetts, Public Schools

Letter Home About Homework Policies

Dear Parents/Guardians,

I believe homework is important because it is a valuable aid in helping students make the most of their experience in school. Homework is given because it is useful in reinforcing what has been learned in class, prepares students for upcoming lessons, extends and generalizes concepts, teaches responsibility, and helps students develop positive study habits.

Fifth graders will be given homework Monday through Thursday nights. Homework should take students no longer than 40–50 minutes each night, not including studying for tests and working on long-term projects. A mathematical problem of the week will be given each Monday, and students are expected to turn this assignment in on Friday.

Students are expected to do their best on homework. Since homework reflects what a student is learning, generally, it can be done independently. If your child has difficulty with an assignment, s/he should ask for help only after giving his or her best effort. Please contact me if your child consistently needs help with homework. All homework assignments will be posted on the class website at www.BESTSCHOOL.K12.school.us.

All homework will be checked, and sometimes they will be graded. I will not always announce when I will be grading homework. Therefore, it is important for each child to be well-prepared.

If students consistently choose not to complete their homework, I will ask that parents begin checking and signing their child's assignment notebook each night. If students still choose not to complete their work, they also choose to lose certain privileges. If students choose to make up their homework the next day, their homework will be accepted.

Please be assured that if there is a legitimate reason a student is not able to finish homework, I will make exceptions. Please send a note to me on the day the assignment is due.

I feel that parents and guardians play an important role in making homework a positive experience for children. Therefore, I ask parents and guardians to make homework a priority. You can do this by providing necessary supplies and a quiet work environment, setting a daily homework time, providing support and encouragement, and not allowing children to avoid homework. I encourage you to contact me if there is a problem or concern.

Please read and discuss this policy with your child and sign and return the bottom portion of this letter to me. Thank you for your cooperation. I look forward to working with you and your child.

Sincerely,
Mrs. Deane
mdeane@bestschool.k12.ma.us

I have read the homework policy and discussed it with my child, _____.

Comments:_____

Parent Signature: _____

Homework Expectations

- All homework should have your name, the date, and the subject on the top of the page.
- All math homework should be completed in pencil.
- All other written homework should be completed in one color of pen or on your tablet.
- All work should be done in your neatest handwriting or word-processed if appropriate.
- All work should be carefully proofread and edited.
- No cross-outs.
- Paper should not be torn from a spiral notebook and should not have jagged edges.
- Homework should be clean and unwrinkled.
- Homework should be turned in on time.
- Remember to always do your best.

Helpful Homework Hints

Work Area
- clean
- quiet
- all supplies available

Time—Make a Plan For
- homework time
- break/snack time

Supplies
- pens, pencils
- erasers
- crayons, markers
- glue
- lined paper
- scissors
- ruler
- dictionary
- thesaurus

Prioritize your assignments. Assignments that are due the next day should be completed first. Map out a schedule for long-term assignments so that they are not left until the last minute.

Provided by Dr. Jennifer Deane, Director of STEM Westborough, Massachusetts, Public Schools

When implementing this homework policy, teachers found this strategy to be well received by the parents and students alike. Parents and guardians commented that it really taught the students good study habits and gave them an opportunity to practice them with guidance. It also concretized what good study habits look like and how to develop them.

Teachers found that it reduced the number of missing and incomplete homework assignments, as the expectations were laid out and practiced at the beginning of the year before bad habits were established. Although this strategy does take time during the first few weeks of school, we feel it is an invaluable process and ultimately saves time over the course of the year.

Sample Plan for Teaching Homework Routines to Middle School[11] Students

Dear Student,

Welcome to Grade 9 English. I am looking forward to working with you this year and helping you to meet your full potential as a student. While we will complete much of our work together in class, it is necessary that you work independently at home to extend your learning and practice the skills presented in class. In order to assist you, all homework assignments will be posted on the classroom website.

To help you understand what I expect from you in terms of homework, I have addressed a number of common questions.

Frequently Asked Questions about Homework

- **What is the purpose of homework?** In this class, homework will be an opportunity to practice and apply what we have learned in the day's class. Homework can take the form of reading a selection from a novel, a written assignment, or a long-term project.

- **How often will homework be assigned and how long will it take to complete?** Expect to receive homework assignments Monday through Friday. It should take you about 30–45 minutes each night to complete your homework assignments. Keep in mind that studying for a test will require more time (and should be spread over several nights).

(continued on next page)

---

11 Teachers of sixth- and seventh-grade students may find the elementary plan preferable for their grade level.

- **How much does homework count?** Homework will count for 15% of your term grade. Most homework assignments will be checked off if they are complete. More formal writing assignments may be subject to counting as a quiz or test grade. In cases in which homework counts as a quiz or test grade, I will let you know that ahead of time.
- **What does an "acceptable" homework assignment look like?** I will show you examples of acceptable homework assignments so that you have a clear idea of what your homework should look like. If you still have questions about expectations for the assignment, please ask me after class, and I will be happy to go over the assignment with you.
- **What if I get home, look at the assignment, and have trouble understanding it?** While you may not understand the whole assignment, you are expected to do as much as possible of the assignment. For example, if I assign a set of questions and you understand only three of the five, I expect that you answer the three that you know and make an attempt at those you don't. In cases in which you don't know where to begin, you need to explain in complete sentences exactly what is causing the confusion (e.g., vocabulary, comprehension of the reading passage, etc.) and what I can do to help you.
- **What is the routine for collecting homework?** I will collect homework at the beginning of the class. Homework that is not turned in at that time will be considered late and will receive half credit.
- **What if I am absent?** We will choose homework buddies during our first week of class. Students who are absent are expected to call their buddies to find out what the assignment is and make an attempt at completing the homework. Students who are out sick have one additional day to catch up on the homework they have missed.
- **What happens if I don't complete homework?** Late homework will receive no more than 50% credit. I will call your parent(s) if you have a chronic habit of not completing homework. Together with your parent(s), we will work on a plan to remedy the situation.

Additional Homework Expectations

- All homework should have your name, date, class, and assignment written at the top of the page.
- Homework should be written legibly or word-processed. Please skip a line between questions.
- Homework should be turned in on time.

If you have any problems associated with the completion of homework, you are expected to advocate for yourself and let me know about the issue.

I have read the above information related to homework expectations, and I understand what is expected of me.

Student name _____ Signature _____

Date_____

Parent/guardian signature _____ Daytime phone number _____

Comments or questions related to homework

_____

_____

_____

Note: Teachers, students, and parents/guardians should all have a copy of the above letter. Students' copies should be kept in their binders. A copy of the policy should be posted in the classroom next to other important information, such as the class grading policy.

Plan for Teaching Homework Routine to High School Students

What Will Students Know and Be Able to Do by the End of the Lesson?

By the end of the lesson, students will be able to

1. Describe what to do if absent from class.

2. Describe what an acceptable homework assignment looks like.

3. Describe the consequences of not completing homework.

4. Have homework complete at the beginning of the class when it is collected.

5. Complete homework that follows the format outlined in the policy.

6. When having difficulty with a portion of the homework, complete the portion they understand and articulate in complete sentences what they do and do not understand about the rest of the assignment; they will also outline what type of help they need to complete the assignment.

7. Complete homework on a nightly basis.

How Will I Formatively and Summatively Assess Students' Level of Mastery?

1. Oral question-and-answer sessions

2. Ungraded quiz at the end of the presentation

What Are the Activities and Sequence of the Activities?

1. The teacher will take time during the first week of school to review homework expectations with the class.

2. The teacher will provide several examples of homework assignments to students.

3. Students will examine the samples and then determine which samples meet the criteria of an acceptable homework assignment. For examples that do not meet the criteria, students will identify the problem areas. Examples presented during this activity will include an incomplete assignment, an assignment with which a student had difficulty, an exemplary assignment, an assignment without the proper setup, and a late assignment.

4. The teacher will ensure that each student has a copy of the policy in his/her binder. In addition, the teacher will provide a copy for the parent and post a copy in a prominent place in the classroom.

5. The teacher will allow students to begin homework in class for the first two weeks of school. During this time, in addition to grading the content of the assignment, the teacher will comment on the setup of the assignment and adherence to the expectations.

6. During the first two weeks of teaching the routine, the teacher will contact parents of students who are having trouble with following the routine.

7. The students will self-assess their level of mastery for completing the homework routine.

Plan for Teaching Classroom Routines to Middle School Students

Below is a plan created to teach middle school science students the routine for cleaning up after a lab.

What Will Students Know and Be Able to Do by the End of the Lesson?

By the end of this lesson, the students will be able to

1. Clean up their lab areas so areas are ready for the next class.
2. Have all equipment returned to its proper location and have their lab areas ready for the next class within five minutes of being given the direction to clean up.
3. Wipe all fluids from the microscope, dry the microscope thoroughly, and place the microscope on the shelf that corresponds with the number on the microscope (Partner 1).
4. Return the specimens to their containers and to the appropriate shelf and then wipe down the lab area and discard all disposable materials (Partner 2).
5. Check his/her partner's work to ensure it meets the criteria.
6. Leave the lab area with no sign that there was a lab.

How Will I Formatively and Summatively Assess Students' Level of Mastery?

1. During the instruction phase of teaching the routine, I will time each attempt at lab cleanup.
2. Throughout the year, I will begin the clean-up time by placing the timer on the SmartBoard counting down from the number of minutes allotted for cleanup.

What Are the Activities and the Sequence of the Activities?

1. I will explain this routine and explain why it is important at the end of the next science class, prior to the next lab.
2. At the start of the next class, I will explain the steps for correctly cleaning up and post the steps on a chart paper.
3. I will set up a lab area and have a pair of students demonstrate the procedure.
4. At the end of the next lab period, I will have the group that finishes first walk through the steps while I describe them to the class.
5. I will structure the lesson so there is more than the typical amount time at the end for cleanup. I will plan my time so I am free to monitor and coach the groups during the cleanup.
6. Guided Practice: In the next lab period, I will review the steps and keep myself free to coach, but I will require the independent completion of the cleanup in ten minutes.
7. In each subsequent lab, I will slightly decrease the cleanup time until the targeted time is achieved.

Sample Plan for Teaching Classroom Routines to High School Students

Below is a plan created to teach high school students in an English class the routine for peer-editing drafts of each other's essays.

What Will Students Know and Be Able to Do by the End of the Lesson?

By the end of the lesson, the students will be able to utilize already-created rubrics to peer edit the rough drafts of four to five other students in the class.

Expectations:

1. Students must place their own rough drafts on their desks along with a blank rubric.
2. Students will all stand up and find new seats where they will read and edit the rough draft of another student in the class.
3. Students will offer detailed comments on the blank rubric form.
4. Upon completing this task, students will go to the front of the classroom to pick up a second blank rubric form.
5. Students will then choose a second peer's rough draft to edit and peer review using the blank rubric.
6. Students will repeat this process until they have read and edited the drafts of four to five of their peers.

How Will I Formatively and Summatively Assess Students' Level of Mastery?

1. I will circulate around the room and observe students' work.
2. I will randomly select one-third of the student papers at the end of the class and check the comments written on the papers.

What Are the Activities and Sequence of the Activities?

1. I will first explain this routine in general terms when initially discussing the due date of students' rough drafts to emphasize the importance of having one's draft in school on the day on which feedback will be solicited from peers.
2. I will explain that the purpose is to support each other in producing high-quality final drafts and to practice catching spelling and grammatical errors.
3. I will explain the steps of this routine in detail at the beginning of the class period in which students bring their drafts to be peer edited.
4. I will ask the students to read and edit four to five of their peers' rough drafts by doing the following:
    -   I will first ask students to clear their desks of all materials except for their rough drafts and rubrics.
    -   Next, I will ask students to stand up and find new seats within the classroom.
    -   Next, I will read through the various components of the rubric with my students.
    -   Next, I will describe to students the procedure for acquiring a new rubric and finding a new rough draft to edit upon completing their edits of the rough draft currently in front of them.
    -   Finally, I will remind students of the expectation that they edit four to five of their peers' rough drafts within the specified time.
5. I will float around the classroom, guiding students on the next steps to take as they complete their edits of the first manuscript: namely, acquiring a new rubric and finding a new peer's rough draft to edit and review.

Guided Practice: The second time that students bring in their rough drafts to be read and edited by peers, I will have them complete the peer edit routine independently. I will keep myself available to reinforce and re-explain the routine as needed.

The SEL and Academic Purposes of Group Work

Getting students to work effectively in groups requires careful planning, but it is worth the organizing because group work can result in both social-emotional learning as well as effective academic learning. A variety of group work protocols and their social-emotional connections is below.

The social learning theories connect student talk directly to student learning. The adage, "The person who talks the most, learns the most" reflects the importance of talk in the learning process. At times, the person talking the most is the teacher. Group work provides opportunities for students to learn together academically and socially. Lev Vygotsky's (1962) research on cognition found that people learn best when they interact with teachers, peers, and experts. Thus, discussion, collaborative groups, conferencing, and feedback support learning. Vygotsky argued, "that language is the main tool that promotes thinking, develops reasoning, and supports cultural activities like reading and writing" (Vygotsky, 1978). So, group work such as jig saw and Socratic seminars discussed below as well as other instructional strategies in which students work collaboratively on research, share their results, and perform or produce a final project help to create a collaborative community of learners (quoted by Neff Vygotsky, 1978, p. 102).

The first section on group work describes the way in which group work can foster both academic growth and the social-emotional skill of relationship management in a gradual process.

Social-Emotional Skills Developed by Group Work

Group participation including whole-class discussions require social-emotional skills. Below are several examples of group configurations that can be used for a variety of purposes.

The following SEL skills are called upon in each activity that follows.

Self-Management. Set individual goals, work toward them, monitor progress, control my behavior

Relationship Management. Work toward group goals, communicate my ideas effectively, engage with people, show leadership skills, work with a team cooperatively, prevent interpersonal conflict, resist inappropriate social pressures

Responsible Decision-Making. Identify problems, analyze situations, solve problems, evaluate ideas, reflect on my actions and thinking, be ethical and fair

Accountable Group Work

Group size and group time can vary from one minute in a turn-and-talk partnership to a few days of teamwork as four teams of five students prepare for a team-based Socratic seminar. At times getting students to work together can be a problem at the beginning of the year.

Example of Group Work Used to Decrease Classroom Conflict

When I began teaching a group of sophomores, I realized that I had two distinct and not socially tolerant groups. I always use a lot of group work in my classroom because it supports my high expectations, allows for effective practice, and engages everyone in reading, writing, speaking, listening, and presenting. Seeing that this group was almost antagonistic with one another, I began using processing partners, that is groups of two, but groups that I could change many times during a block. (See "Civil War General Processing Partners" in this chapter as an example of processing partners.) Each student had 10 different partners. I had them work in two's at least three times during a class, but each of the meeting of the partners was extremely brief, only one or two minutes to finish the tasks and they returned to their seats.

The English class was reading short texts, and the partners would have to figure out a question relating to the text, then return to their seats to discuss the passage as a class. I was teaching them "accountable talk," using sentence starters or sentence frames requiring one per processing partner meeting. A sentence starter might be focused on listening and summarizing what the other person said, so the sentence frame would be, "I heard you say that…" or "Building on what I heard you say…"

Gradually, as September went on, the tasks and sentence frames became more complicated when students were asked to critique one another's claim, evidence, and analysis, and they used evaluative feedback such as, "I am confused by…" or "Your evidence is not clear," or "I don't understand your analysis. Could you explain it to me." However, I kept changing the groups at least twice a class as the length of the discussion extended to up to 10 minutes.

Once I determined that students could work with "anyone" without a problem, I then began to increase the length of the tasks and their complexity. I had to stay focused all of the time and provide clear feedback about how well they listened, whether they used accountable talk, and how well they accomplished their task. I had a clipboard to write notes about my observations and gave each student a large note card for self-assessment. On the front of the card, they self-assessed. On the back, I commented, sometimes during the class, sometimes after the class was over. I had to work more carefully than I had ever worked before. As we began each new level of group work and moved to three and then four, I used a fishbowl with the class around the three or four group members as they modeled the new procedure or process. Initially, I did the modeling with the students. As the year progressed, the students became far more able to model appropriate group behavior and accountable talk. The process stayed labor-intensive, but the class was learning academically and socially.

Twosomes: Think-Pair-Share, Think-Pair-Square, and Snowballing

Think-Pair-Share. First, all students are asked to "think" and write what they are thinking, then each student finds a partner using the processing partners protocol (pair), and then they orally exchange ideas (share). This group work can last two minutes or longer depending on the complexity of the task This activity provides time for students to process the material that the class is doing thoughtfully and allows them to move from their seats. It can be used in any class.

Think-Pair-Square. The square is made of two pairs from the "Think-Pair-Share" who have already shared. The two pairs become a foursome (a square) and they then share. This addition of another twosome allows further sharing and deepening of the ideas. This gradual incremental growth gives shyer students an opportunity to share their ideas twice before they may be asked to give whole class feedback. Once more, it is about adding depth to ideas, stimulating debate, and collaborative thinking.

Snowballing can be the third step after the "Think-Pair-Square." The groups of four (square) could become a group of eight. Like the "square" approach mentioned in think-pair-square, the snowballing activity is another simple but very effective way of building on ideas by starting with small groups and expanding the groups in a structured way. To keep this larger group organized, the teacher may ask students to do a "whip around" asking for each student to contribute for 30 seconds in sequence around the circle that the group forms. Then the entire class can assemble in a large circle and the teacher can facilitate discussion.

Jigsaw

This group process requires accountability from every student. A text is divided among three or four groups. Each group becomes an expert in one section of the text. Then the groups remix so that there is an expert from each section in each group. The jigsaw (from Aronsen, 1978) is an excellent strategy for helping students to learn a large volume of information in an efficient and effective manner.

The steps to the jigsaw are as follows:

1. The teacher divides the information to be learned into equitable chunks. The number of chunks depends on the number of students in class. For example, if there are 25 to 28 students in the class then, five chunks is a good number. If there are 30 to 35 students, then the teacher may wish to break the information into six chunks.

2. The teacher creates several groups that are equal to the number of chunks. For example, if there are five chunks of information and 28 students, then the teacher would make five groups with five or six students in each group.

3. Each group is assigned one chunk of information about which they must become "expert" enough to explain to the others.

4. The teacher provides enough time for the individuals in each group to learn the information and for the group to develop a presentation that is given to the other groups. It is recommended that the teacher give a time range for the length of the presentation. For example, each group may need to keep their presentation to between two and three minutes. The teacher should also give the groups a fixed amount of time to learn the information and prepare their presentation.

5. The leader ensures the task is completed. The gopher keeps track of the preparation time to ensure the group finishes the task on time. As the presentation is created, the scribe writes presentation notes that can be used for the presentation of the information to the other groups. When the presentation is complete, the reporter gives it to his/her own group as a "practice run." During the practice run, each of the group members writes his/her own set of presentation notes, so every member of the group has a set of notes to use in the presentation. The scribe's notes can be used as a guide for the other group members when writing their presentation notes.

6. Once each group has its presentation completed and all members have their notes, the teacher regroups the class. Every student in each group is assigned a number. For example, if there are five people in the group and five groups, each student in the group is assigned a number one to five. Once all the numbers are assigned to all the groups, the class is regrouped. All the ones make a new group, all the twos make a new group, etc. For those groups that have six members (when there will only be five new groups), two students are assigned the same number. Those two students jointly present to the new group.

7. Once the new groups are made, the teacher indicates the person who is to give the first presentation. The teacher instructs the group that once the first person finishes, then the next person to present is the person to the left of the first person. This continues until all the students have presented. Thirty seconds before each presentation time is up, the teacher should give a 30-second warning, so students know it is time to finish up the presentation.

Note: This process can be shortened after step 6. Each "expert group" can report out to the rest of the class.

Carousel (or Museum Walk)

This group process encourages ongoing evaluative conversation among small group members and ends with a full-group sharing.

The carousel is an efficient and effective technique for brainstorming ideas or answers to questions. In addition, it can be used as an evaluation or feedback process.

A science example in a unit on energy is described below:

1. The science teacher broke her class of 29 into four groups of six students and one group of five students. On the whiteboard was the statement "List everything in the universe that has (or gives off) energy."

2. Each group made a list with a marker on a large sheet of chart paper. The leader led the work, the scribe wrote on the chart paper, and the gopher watched the time.

3. The teacher gave the groups five minutes to brainstorm.

4. The lists were then placed on top of each group's table (or grouped desks).

5. The teacher then instructed the groups to stand up together, rotate one group, and read the list of the group next to them. At the signal, the groups then moved on to read the next list, until all the groups had a chance to read all the lists.

6. During the "carousel," the scribe noted any questions the group had about any of the lists.

7. After the groups returned to their own tables, the teacher and class generated a list of things that give off energy and those that do not. Each group then had to come up with a generalization about energy.

Note: Other variations: student work can be posted and two-person teams can give feedback beneath the posted work about an essay, lab report, art work, etc. The class can regroup and discuss after the carousel— for example, effective narratives, good lab conclusions, effective pastel paintings.

Take a Sip

This group work asks students to select something in an article that speaks to them, to reflect on this and share it. This is a good introductory exercise to a new and complex subject. The following protocol is a slight adaptation of the Take a Sip protocol developed by Jennifer Fischer Mueller and named by Ms. Carol Daddazio.

The Protocol

1. If possible, participants receive the text before the meeting and are asked to read the text in preparation for the meeting.

2. The What: Each participant reviews the text for five minutes to identify a piece (word, phrase,

sentence, or group of sentences) of the text that resonates with her or him. They highlight or circle this piece in the text. This is *The What*.

3. The So What: Each participant takes two minutes to write why that piece resonates with her or him. They answer the question: What does it mean to you? This is the *So What*.
4. The Now What: Each participant takes two minutes to write what she or he will commit to because of this new learning. This is the *Now What*.
5. In small groups, each participant has two minutes to share her or his responses to steps two through four with the group members.

Debriefing the Protocol

Possible debriefing questions include:

- What was it like to explore the general idea of a text in this way?
- Was this a useful way to explore the general idea of a text? If so, why? If not, why not?
- How did looking at the text this way expand your understanding of the topic?

Scaffolded Socratic Seminar

Teachers gradually support students through the expectations of the seminar step-by-step. They provide incrementally fewer supports as students learn to discuss independently. Initially, the teacher may provide a structure—for example, to make sure that each student contributes, the teacher may require each student to develop two quotations or two ideas and must contribute both by the end of the discussion. Or, the class might watch a brief video of a Socratic seminar as part of their introduction. Also, the class may be divided into four teams that initially study and prepare for the Socratic seminar with a specific, assigned aspect of the topic. Initially, one member of each team represents that team and the four carry on the discussion in the center of the room. Other team members eventually take the center seats and replace the first representative. The team supports the speaker and provides notes and research. The focus could originate in any content area in any area students could research and discuss—from should the US have dropped atomic bombs on Japan during World War II to the ethics of genetic engineering to interpretations of literature, art, or primary sources.

Literature Circles in a Socratic Seminar Format

This is a small group seminar. This **protocol** fosters a deeper understanding of text through a close reading and analysis of a piece of writing. Through questioning and discussion, participants analyze, interpret, and discuss the specific piece of text they have read.

1. Students face one another in their group.
2. Students should have read the text prior to meeting. (The text itself must contain some ambiguity and be challenging, yet not beyond the students.)
3. Both teacher and students should prepare open-ended questions regarding the text to pose during the session.
4. Teacher sets norms for the class (or group), or teacher and students together set norms.
5. Students (or teacher) may begin the process by posing a question.
6. Students take charge of the discussion and questioning. The teacher serves as a facilitator to guide the process if necessary.
7. Teacher may pose the final question, whereby students may draw from their own experience and connect to the text or opinions voiced in the seminar.

Debriefing and Reflecting on the Protocol

Teacher-posed questions serve to help students debrief the process and assess the value in understanding the text at a deeper level. Additionally, the students may debrief the process itself and how well participants adhered to the norms.

Socratic Seminar

The ultimate goal for the Socratic seminar is for students to lead academic discussions. However, students need to learn the protocol gradually. These whole-class dialogues explore ideas, values, and issues drawn from readings or works of art chosen for their richness. Student leaders help participants make sense of a text and of their own thinking by asking questions about reasoning, evidence, connections, examples, and other aspects of sound thinking. A good seminar is devoted to making meaning rather than mastering information. Participants are actively engaged in rigorous critical thought. To be worthwhile, they should involve a relatively short text, a piece of art, etc., that is controversial or difficult to interpret. After the seminar, students often reflect about its impact on their thinking and are asked to determine its name based upon the qualities and objects that they see in it.

Conclusion: Academics and SEL Working Hand-in-Hand

Successful group work provides both academic and social-emotional learning. At its simplest when two students turn and discuss their thinking, students are processing and beginning to deepen their learning at the same time as they are developing SEL skills and language. Students learn to take turns and listen carefully, using self-management skills. They build on the ideas of their partner and give their partner credit for their thinking, using relationship-management skills. As group work progresses and becomes more academically and socially-emotionally demanding and complex, and as group sizes increase and tasks become more complex, students grow both academically and socially-emotionally.

This chapter also provided a method for breaking down barriers within the social makeup of the classroom in the example of group work that decreased classroom conflict. Thus, these academically effective activities provide what Durlak et al found in successful SEL programs. They provide:

- a safe, caring classroom climate that improves students' SEL skills.
- student participation in collaborative and group learning that increases student achievement and student engagement providing students have adequate SEL skills to work with others.
- a decrease in high-risk behaviors when students are working with teachers and with peers who have learned these social skills, and their attitude toward school becomes more positive.

As in the entire book, the techniques described support teachers as they develop classrooms that provide emotional safety, respectful relationships, and worthy tasks with high expectations that support both SEL growth and academic achievement (Durlak et al., 2011, p. 417).

Discussion Questions for Reflection

Chapter 4

1. This chapter offers a strong assortment of strategies that will facilitate classroom routines and the creation of classroom community. **Select a passage that resonates with you and relate it to your practice.**

   I appreciated the comprehensive list of classroom routines and to think how to break down the tasks/expectations of each into observable behaviors then model/practice effective/ineffective examples.

2. **Why is the creation of classroom routines and expectations something that must be explicitly taught at the beginning of a school year? Why should a review of these strategies be revisited during the year?**

   Routines help manage expectations/behavior; allow for effective time on learning; minimize the need for the teacher to discipline; teach SEL skills like self-awareness self discipline, resp. dec. mkg.

3. Most students have difficulty in staying organized with long-term assignments. In addition, students who have executive functioning disorder often have a more difficult time. **What strategies would you implement when working with this challenge for most students, for students who have particular difficulties?**

   Break down tasks to smaller chunks w/ associated due dates

   checklists

   Exemplars of each task

Discussion questions continue on next page

4. The use of modeling of desired routines and examples of quality work are emphasized in this chapter. **How might you employ some of these strategies to help a class learn the art of organizing a course notebook? Cleaning out a locker? Doing a research project?**

> ex. Locker - have class working on indep. work while teacher brings small groups to lockers for modeling/organizing

5. Sometimes, teachers need to be out of school for a variety of reasons. **If a teacher has not adequately organized his or her classroom and work expectations, how might that impact what happens during his or her absence? Which of the routines discussed would be helpful to provide for a substitute teacher?**

> Students should understand work/behavior expectations hold regardless of who is teaching - sub, student teacher, volunteer.
>
> Some important routines to consider in this:
> see p. 81-82

6. **How would you scaffold the use of a "cooperative learning jobs" grid with English language learners or a student with a nonverbal learning disability?**

> ○ assign jobs on random qualifications (i.e. person w/ fewest sibling is the leader. Provide sentence stems/dialog/picture cards to communicate
> ○ use students w/ particular strengths in particular jobs to help model/role play effective group work
> ○ Make sure groups have a procedure to follow when they are finished to allow for teacher work w/ specific groups

7. The use of a timer can be very useful in helping students stay on task and be aware of the actual time that is passing. **Although an educator may not need to utilize this tool for every instructional period, when would you find it most effective? What strategy would you take when a student becomes overly anxious about time limitations (e.g., rehearse the strategy)?**

Allowing partners or groups time to discuss a question/complete a task to report out to whole class. Give updates of time elapsed/remaining.

If student is anxious make sure they understand that there will be time to complete what is needed

8. Reflect upon a time when you were having some difficulty with the facilitation of group work. **What strategy or strategies mentioned in this chapter might have been particularly useful?**

- videotaping

9. Imagine that you will implement one of the strategies mentioned in this chapter to increase class discussions. **What lesson would you be teaching and how would you utilize the strategy?**

socratic seminar - soc. studies

Engaging Students

Obtaining, Maintaining, and Regaining Student Attention and Its Implications For SEL Support

Defining Engagement: A Cautionary Tale

I remember when my district decided to focus on student engagement. I was responsible for teaching and learning as the assistant superintendent and, as a group of administrators and teacher leaders, we struggled to describe precisely what engagement meant. Were students engaged when all students were looking at the teacher and taking notes as the teacher led the class? Was it defined by students who did exactly what the teacher asked and were "on task"? **We decided that a quiet, compliant, student may have been appropriate at times when teachers were directly teaching, but when students were working independently or in groups, we agreed that we wanted to see far more than silent, often passive, attention. We wanted to see interest, engagement, and activity** although it might look different if the students were engaged in a whole class discussion or lecture, individual work, or group work.

The three types of "look fors" are whole class discussion or lecture, individual work, and group work, listed in the left column in Figure 5.1 (on the following page). Within each activity are two ways of looking at students' engagement, both as the student's apparent focus or concentration on the activity and as commitment to the task. In addition to the students' behavior, the conditions of the classroom are described. Thus, if students seemed engaged (both focused and committed) and the classroom was highly engaging, the observers would rank each of the three categories on the high end of the continuum with an upward pointing arrow or an exclamation point.

On the other hand, if engagement and involvement was low and the task was not engaging, each category would be ranked in the low levels of engagement (a 0 or a downward pointing arrow). The "look fors" that we included in our classroom visits described both behaviors and attitudes or emotions of the students (involved, questioning, contributing, listening) as well as the level of engagement of the classroom environment or task. Chapter 6 provides further details about student engagement.

We found that creating engaging classrooms included these elements:

1. Active, engaging learning activities that may include group work and student active participation as described in Chapter 2 of this book
2. A challenging academic climate with high expectations as described in Chapter 8 of this book
3. A classroom with positive relationships and with connections to the students' life and with real life as described in Chapters 2 and 8 of this book

The research validates the three areas for engagement that we found in our local look at classrooms. The area with the greatest impact, according to Findley, is the third—relationships—which has an impact seven hundred times greater than the others. Findley says, "**The power of connective instruction comes from the instructor helping students see the curriculum as critical to their current lives, their future, and their culture**" (Findley, 2015). Engagement had seemed so simple, but we found defining it necessitated a look at active participation, a challenging classroom, and a safe and welcoming place.—*Deb Brady*

Figure 5.1 Engaging Classroom Checklist and Self-Assessment

Observer_____ Date_____ Time: from_____ to_____ Initial: _____

The unshaded areas require looking at the students.

The shaded areas require looking at the conditions and environment of the work.

For each type of activity observed, whole class, individual work, or group work, select from one of four levels observed from Lacking to High.

Activity Type Please check at least one activity and fill out the level of engagement.	Specific Behavior	Lacking 0	Low ↓	Solid ↑	High !
☐ **Whole Class Discussion/ Lecture**	Focused on discussion				
	Seriously involved in discussion				
	Discussion is engaging, lively				
☐ **Individual Work**	Focused on completing task				
	Seriously involved in completing task				
	Work is challenging and engaging				
☐ **Group Work**	Focused on group work and role				
	Seriously involved in group work				
	Work is challenging, engaging, and roles are accountable				

Gaining Students' Attention

A component of gaining and maintaining student engagement involves the ways that teachers gain that attention and how they respond to students' positive or negative behaviors. Peter Johnson said that the language that teachers use can signal both an academic and social-emotional classroom culture: **authoritarian, cooperative,** or **collaborative**. From praise to direct teaching to feedback, teachers' words create the classroom culture throughout every class.

Teachers use a wide variety of strategies for signaling to students that it is time to be quiet. An article in the *Responsive Classroom Newsletter* (Farnsworth and McErlane, 2002) categorizes these as **visual attention strategies** and **auditory attention strategies**. Visual strategies include hand signals, specific teacher posture (e.g., hands on hips), closing our eyes, and other teacher behaviors the students know mean it is time to be quiet. The second category of signals discussed in the article is auditory strategies. Auditory strategies include chimes, a bell, playing notes on a musical instrument, and other sounds that signal to

the students that it is time to be quiet. It is important for teachers to have a large repertoire of strategies to gain student attention. If our voices are the only strategy we use to gain student attention, students soon learn to tune it out.

These cues support a positive classroom that is orderly and runs smoothly. By using signals, the teacher makes students aware of their social responsibility within the class and indicates that self-management skills are needed to respond appropriately within the classroom culture.

The following steps establish the effective use of signals for getting students to be quiet:

1. Choose signals that are easily noticed.
   In group work a visual signal may not be seen by everyone because some students may have their back to you. With group work it is important that those who see you also echo the signal for others so that those who are looking at them receive the signal as well. As discussed earlier, when teaching teams use the same signals. It makes it easier for students to respond successfully and for the class to run smoothly.

2. Teach and practice the signals with the students before expecting students to use them.

3. Always use the designated signals to achieve quiet. This consistency is important for all students. It is particularly important for students with certain disabilities.

4. Expect everyone, even adults who enter your room, to adhere to the signal.

5. Don't begin talking until you have everyone's attention.

6. If it is taking too long to get everyone's attention, then it is probably time to re-teach the signal.

7. Use frequent and specific positive praise and appreciation with the class and with individuals who demonstrate timely adherence to the signal.

8. Have clearly defined warnings and consequences for those students who do not respond.

9. Remember that the goal of the signal is to gain the children's attention. If everyone is paying attention, it is okay to start talking.

Auditory Strategies for Gaining Attention

- bell
- whistle—often used by coaches and by teachers in large group situations (One physical education teacher uses different whistles to indicate different behaviors. For example, a single loud whistle can mean *everyone freeze and be quiet*. Two short whistles can mean *continue with the activity but stop talking and listen for instructions*.)
- speaking softly—teachers who do this will give a direction in a voice volume that would allow all the students to hear the direction if no one was talking. The teacher gives the first two or three sentences of the direction knowing full well that few, if any, students hear the direction. He or she then repeats those sentences in the same soft voice as often as needed until all the students are listening. When the teacher starts talking, some students notice the teacher is talking and try to listen. When they cannot hear, they quiet down the other students so they can hear what the teacher is saying. When we speak softly, the student noise typically stops because students are curious to hear what the teacher is saying.
- piano notes (or other instrument notes)
- chime
- alarm or buzzer from a timer when it reaches the set end time of a group or partner discussion activity
- humorous comment (please note that educators make a distinction between humor and sarcasm). Humor is something that is appropriately funny that does not make one of the students the target of the humor. Sarcasm, though at times causing laughter, may have an impact on the self-image of the target student and/or generate fear among other students that they may be the next target student. Sarcasm makes a classroom unsafe for students.
- clapping hands to a familiar rhythm
- humming or singing a specific tune
- asking students to stop talking
- playing music as a signal that it is time to stop talking
- counting down (5, 4, 3, 2...) or counting up (1, 2, 3, 4...)
- telling students they may have or do something they all would like only when everyone is listening (this strategy places peer pressure on those still not listening).
- saying "Excuse me" in a firm but calm voice and repeating "Excuse me" in a softer and softer voice until room is silent
- saying "Excuse me, Mark" to a student who is speaking
- making instructional statements that raise the students' curiosity (for example, one high school social studies teacher starts his classes by singing a humorous song that was popular with adolescents during the period they are studying)
- Teacher-student responses such as "One two three, look at me." The children respond, "One, two, eyes on you."

Visual Strategies for Gaining Attention

- flash the lights (this strategy may cause problems for some autistic students)
- hand signal
- hands on head
- hand in the air (a variation of this used by some teachers when students are working in pairs or groups is to allow the students to put up one finger to request an additional minute to finish their conversation)
- hold up two fingers as a peace sign
- close eyes
- point to or hold up a *"Quiet, please"* sign
- place a single finger over lips
- humorous activity
- wave arms dramatically and humorously to signal for attention

- stand quietly in the front of the room until all students are quiet
- use a "Yacker Tracker," a device that looks like a stoplight with green, yellow, and red lights and is sensitive to noise levels in the room. When the noise is at an appropriate level, the green light is on. If the noise nears the maximum appropriate level, the yellow light goes on. If the noise exceeds the appropriate level, the red light goes on.
- signal for quiet and then hold up a stopwatch to gauge how many seconds it takes for the room to fall completely silent (compliment students on a job well done or note the need for improvement if a quiet classroom took too much time to achieve. Some teachers make this a game by providing a point each time the class quiets down in a predetermined amount of time. The points can then be redeemed for incentives.)
- marble jar—Each time the class quiets down in the predetermined time, a marble goes into the jar. Once the jar is filled, the class receives a reward. In both examples, keeping the jar or score visible helps serve as a visual reminder to students.
- dramatize (for example, one middle school social studies teacher frequently greets students in an outfit from the period they are studying)
- inanimate objects—chime, music, lights

Some high school and middle school teachers who use inanimate objects, such as the chime, music, and/or flashing lights, report that students who are displeased with the need to be quiet, associate their displeasure with the object rather than the teacher. They report statements from students such as "that darn chime," rather than indicating displeasure with the teacher. Although we can find no research that supports or refutes this, these teachers report that it helps them maintain their positive relationships with the students.

Strategies for Getting the Attention of Students Who Don't Respond to the Group Signal

- using the *hairy eyeball* (this is a stern look and stare teachers give to those students who are not yet adhering to the signal for quiet)
- turning squarely to face the student, making eye contact, and saying that student's name in a calm but firm voice
- moving next to the student or students who are still talking

- praising those students who are quiet
- rewarding the students who are quiet (for example, you may allow these students to present their ideas first or leave for lunch first, etc.)
- asking those students who are talking to stop
- putting the name of the student who is talking on the board as a warning that there will be a consequence
- giving the student a *warning card* (the warning card indicates to the student that if the talking does not stop immediately, s/he will get a consequence)
- giving the student a *consequence card*
- startling the students with a loud noise or surprise behavior

Deciding to Use Negative or Positive Strategies

The strategies above may also be categorized along a continuum of negative, neutral, and positive responses. Those that directly identify a student who is not giving attention or provide a consequence for students not exhibiting the desired behavior are *negative*. Those that affirm or reward appropriate behavior are *positive*. Still others, such as a chime, are *neutral*. We identify attention strategies along a continuum to highlight the impact of relationships on classroom management. Every teacher must consider that his or her decision to choose a specific strategy to gain student attention has an impact on the culture of the classroom, the self-image of individual students, the relationship between the teacher and the students, and the relationship among the students.

As discussed above, sarcasm may effectively obtain student attention; however, the negative impact on student self-image outweighs its value in gaining attention. Another example of an impact on students' self-image is the constant use of peer pressure after the teacher finds that certain students are always the ones who cause the class to miss some opportunity (e.g., go to recess late in elementary school or go to the pep rally late in high school). This response may undermine the classroom community or make the student angry with the teacher and, as a consequence, result in acting-out behavior and might lead the teacher to use this strategy less often than some of the more positive strategies (e.g., rewarding those who are ready to go first or complimenting those who are ready).

Table 5.1 How Teacher Language Creates Classroom Culture

Type of culture	Teacher language examples	Possible consequences of using this language for individual students and for the whole class
Authoritarian	"Get back to work right now or you'll miss recess."	Students must comply with teacher because she's the boss. Work is done to avoid punishment.
Cooperative	"Keep your voices small; remember, some people can't concentrate with too much noise."	Students become aware of the impact of their behavior on others. This can be an opportunity for SEL in self-management.
Collaborative	"I can see that your groups look a bit discombobulated. What's the problem, and how can we solve it so that we can figure out…"	Students are considered thinkers who, along with the teacher, can solve problems in the class.

Adapted from Johnston, P. 2004, pp. 100–110.

Transitions

The easiest way to regain students' attention is never to lose it. As discussed earlier in this chapter, transitions between activities are a time when many teachers lose students' attention. Well-planned transitions help maintain student attention as we shift from one activity to the next. One technique for ensuring quick transitions from teacher-directed work to student group work is the cooperative learning jobs grid. Both processing partners and cooperative learning grids provide efficient ways for maintaining attention as students make transitions from teacher-directed to pair and group work. Both techniques are covered thoroughly in Chapter 4, Tables 4.4 and 4.5, under Partner Work.

The Impact of Negative Strategies

Almost all strategies discussed previously may be appropriate in certain situations. It is important to be aware, however, that disproportionate use of negative strategies or peer pressure instead of positive strategies may undermine some of the teacher's long-term goals, such as raising students' self-image, building a supportive classroom community among the students, and building trust and supportive relationships between the teacher and the students.

Conclusion

This chapter covers the moves that teachers use to obtain, maintain and regain student attention, which range from simple, quiet gestures to more elaborate strategies including providing praise or using negative strategies. A teacher can quietly gain attention with a raised hand and wait until all students have stopped talking. To maintain attention, a teacher can stand next to students who are talking. Signaling concern, teachers can use the "hairy eyeball." In addition, teachers can praise or reprimand. **Each of these gestures and words contribute to the social-emotional culture of the classroom.** These often quick responses signal to students the expectations for the quality of their engagement and their role in the class. A teacher may remark shortly, "Because I say so," or, may say, "I can see that your groups look a bit discombobulated. What's the problem, and how can we solve it so that we can figure out a solution?" The words clearly indicate to students either that they need to do as they're told or that they are part of a community in which they're expected to employ social-emotional skills by self-monitoring their participation in a group and by solving the problem of how the group became confused (see Table 5.1). Although negative responses may become the only alternative in some circumstances, their impact may have a long-term negative impact on the class culture or on an individual student's social-emotional growth.

Chapter 8 goes more deeply into the critically important area of student engagement and disengagement. The chapter provides more techniques for teachers to use further engagement in the classroom with positive student-to-teacher relationships, enthusiasm, passion, and supportive feedback.

Discussion Questions for Reflection

Chapter 5

1. Chapter 5 focuses on engaging students and obtaining and maintaining attention. A variety of methods, both auditory and visual, were provided. **Select a passage that resonates with you and relate it to your practice.**

   • "The easiest way to regain students' attention is never to lose it"
   - have several attention-getting strateg[ies]
     - auditory & visual
   - teach/practice strategies; be consist[ent]
   - strategies have an effect on the culture of the classroom & the relatio[n]ships w/ and among students (eit[her] positive or negative - CHOOSE CAREFULLY)

2. "As a guideline, some research suggests using a child's age as a general starting point for the number of minutes a child can attend to a single assigned task ... so 5 minutes for a 5 year old, 7 minutes for a 7 year old, etc." Children with Attention Deficit Disorder or Attention Deficit Hyperactivity Disorder will need more support in this area. In the article, "Exercise Is ADHD Medication" (Hamblin, James, Atlantic, Sept. 29, 2014) research is showing that "physical movement improves mental focus, memory and cognitive flexibility." **What are some strategies that you might employ to increase attention for a student with this profile? How could you incorporate physical movement into your lesson planning?**

   Flexible seating - yoga balls, cushions, standing desks...
   group work - move to different groups
   Go Noodle breaks
   Hands on activities

6

Habits of Successful Students
Student Self-Assessment for
Social-Emotional and Academic Learning

Self-regulating strategies support both academic and self-management goals. According to Bloom, "Setting realistic but challenging goals and monitoring progress result in a greater sense of self-efficacy and a higher level of motivation in learning." (Bloom, 2013, p. 50.)

When students set and self-assess their goals, particularly when the teacher is coach, they begin to see their strengths and weaknesses more clearly, become more reflective about their learning and make changes to achieve their goals. When students begin to see that changes in their behavior result in accomplishing their goals, their confidence, motivation, and willingness to persevere increase (Zimmerman, 1990).

Goal Setting and Reflection

A technique for supporting self-management and self-monitoring is student goal setting, which can begin as early as kindergarten. As I worked with a group of special educators who wanted to look at students' work habits, we developed a rubric, listed in Table 6.1, that they called "Habits of a Successful Learner." The criteria include the social-emotional skills that are necessary for students in every classroom. Please note that this comprehensive rubric has many descriptors of each behavior. The rubric can be simplified for younger students or modified to reflect the focus in specific classrooms. For example, self-management includes the following SEL behaviors through which a student can demonstrate this SEL skill. A student can:

- Set goals, work toward them, and monitor progress
- Seek out help when needed (self-advocacy)
- Control my impulses

- Display grit, determination, perseverance
- Exhibit positive emotions: hope, optimism, motivation
- Manage my stress
- Control my behavior
- Motivate myself
- Organize my day

A specific grade level or course may select one or more of these very specific behaviors as a focus for self-management. In addition to using the rubric to set high standards, the middle school special educators decided to use the rubric as a resource for goal-setting by individual students who selected one, or perhaps two, of these SEL descriptors as their goal for a quarter or semester. Each student self-assessed progress reflected every week based on classroom-based evidence as pictured in Table 6.2. Students conferenced with their teacher about their own and their teacher's assessment of the progress on their goals every month.

For example, if self-management is the area that the student and teacher see as a priority, then this student might select only one or two of these descriptors as the focus for their goal setting. Thus, a student who has occasional outbursts might select "Control my impulses," or a student with organizational concerns might decide to "Organize my day." By specifying and measuring a behavior and seeing the impact of working toward a goal of their choice, students can grow in SEL skills, and, if they see positive change, can develop a sense of self-efficacy and confidence in their self-management skills.

In Chapter 2, the goal-setting focused on seeking support (self-advocacy) in mathematics. In Table 2.1, the student decided that homework completion, attendance, and effective effort—that is working with focus and using effective strategies—were the most important habits of successful students for them to monitor. In addition, the student had an opportunity to reflect upon his or her successes and challenges.— *Deb Brady*

Table 6.1 Habits of a Successful Student—Rubric for Student Self-Assessment

Self-Assessment of Habits of Effective Students **Directions.** You may use all five of the habits: Self-Awareness, Self-Management, Social Awareness, Relationship Management, and Responsible Decision-Making with each descriptor in bulleted lists, or you may choose to focus on one or two habits and one or two descriptors. Rank each with a 4, 3, 2, or 1 for the level of your behavior from 1 (Not Yet Meeting the Standard) to the highest level 4 (Exceeding the Standard).	4 Exceeding the Standard I CAN ALWAYS	3 Meeting Standard I CAN GENERALLY	2 Approaching Standard I CAN SOMETIMES	1 Not Yet Meeting Standard I CAN OCCASIONALLY
Self-Awareness	• Identify my emotions, needs and values • Accurately understand my reasons or triggers for doing/saying things • Recognize my strengths • Be self-confident • Make a difference by what I do (self-efficacy)				
Self-Management	• Set goals, work toward them, and monitor progress • Seek out help when needed (self-advocacy) • Control my impulses • Display grit, determination, perseverance • Exhibit positive emotions: hope, optimism, motivation • Manage my stress • Control my behavior • I can motivate myself • Organize my day				
Social Awareness	• Recognize social cues from others • Listen closely and accurately • Look at things from others' points of view • Feel empathy for others • Appreciate diversity and differences among people • Respect others' feelings and reactions				
Relationship Management	• Communicate my ideas and feelings effectively • Engage with people, make friends • Show leadership skills • Build relationships, help others • Work with a team, cooperatively • Work toward group goals • Prevent interpersonal conflict • Resist inappropriate social pressures				
Responsible Decision-Making	• Identify problems • Analyze situations • Solve problems • Use strategies to resist peer pressure • Evaluate ideas • Reflect on my actions and thinking • Be ethical and fair				

Table 6.2 **Goal-Setting: Weekly Reflection**

	4-always	3-usually	2-sometimes	1-occasionally
Directions: Rate yourself on Friday each week and place your self-assessment in your file.				
1. How are you doing?	4	3	2	1
Assignment Completion (Self-Management)				
Attendance and Tardiness (Self-Management)				
Effective Effort (Self-Awareness)				
2. What are your one or two goals for this term?				
Select 1, 2, 3, or 4 for your progress on the goal this week.	4	3	2	1
Goal 1:				
Goal 2:				

Reflection

3. What was something you found difficult or challenging this week? What did you do (or could have done) to help solve this difficult task or situation?

4. What was something you found you were successful with this week? Why do you think you were successful with this?

5. Do you have any missing assignments (homework, tests, projects, etc.)?

List the class, the assignment, the due date, and your plan for making up this work below:

Class	Assignment Missing	Due Date	Plan to Make Up

Research is well established about the importance of student performance and feedback (Andrade, 2011). Student performance increases when students receive accurate descriptive feedback on their work.

Rubrics can support SEL development at the same time that they support high and clear goals. These rubrics clearly define and measure both the quality and degree of a student's progress. Because rubrics define a skill in progressively higher levels, students see what the next step in their academic or social progress looks like. When used consistently and provided at the beginning of a year or unit, rubrics serve as a concrete reminder of what proficiency and the highest levels of performance look like. In this way, rubrics support high expectations and what they look like.

As Andrade notes, students can be taught to formatively and summatively assess their own performance from an early age. For this to happen, students must be taught how to assess their own work, with clear criteria, rubrics, and models, and to act on their self-assessment to revise their work.

In the same way, students can improve their

Rubrics can support SEL development at the same time that they support high and clear goals.

behavior given clear expectations clearly taught, and periodically self-assessed by students. Tables 6.3 and 6.4 are two samples of student self-assessments used by a high school teacher and a middle school teacher, respectively.

Getting Started With Student Self-Assessment

If your students have had no experience with self-assessment, start small. Use a self-assessment form with two or three areas. Initially, the teacher should give frequent feedback to help the students learn to accurately assess themselves. Frequent monitoring and feedback will help students determine their level of success accurately. Below is a modified version of a self-assessment used to introduce self-assessment at the beginning of the year. As the year progresses and students' self-assessment competency increases, more specific descriptors can be added. The Self-Assessment in Science (Table 6.4) is one that should be used only with students who have been taught to self-assess.

Mid-Quarter 1: Self-Assessment in Science

Middle School Science

This self-assessment is an opportunity to think about your actions since the beginning of the year. The worksheet in Table 6.3 includes questions on academic performance, class behavior, organizational skills, use of your agenda book, preparation for class, responsibility with homework, and ability to work in groups. Based on your self-assessment, you will design a plan to continue to build your strengths and to address areas that need more effort. You'll create your own action plan for success in this course. We'll discuss your plan in a conference within the next week.

Table 6.3 **Weekly Science Checklist**

Name: _____   Period: _____

	On time: ☐ Yes ☐ No +1 Yes	Prepared with: ☐ Writing utensil ☐ Notebook ☐ Homework +1 for each	Student comment Goal: To ask or answer at least one question +1	Teacher comment Maximum of 5 per day
Monday	+1	+2 *Forgot homework*	+1	*+4 for the day*
Tuesday				
Wednesday				
Thursday				
Friday				
Total for week				Total of Totals Maximum 25

Table 6.4 Science Self-Assessment

Directions: Rate yourself using the scale below as the first step in creating your action plan for success in science class. We'll conference about this self-assessment within the next week.

		1 Needs a Lot of Work	2 Needs Some Work	3 Achieved Near-Mastery	4 Achieved Mastery
Homework	My homework assignments are completed on time.				
	I check my work before I decide my homework is done.				
	If I'm absent, I go directly to the absent homework folder for my block.				
	I always have my agenda book for every class.				
	I have my HW assignments written down before the teacher reminds the class to do so.				
Class Behavior	I understand what I wrote in my agenda book when I get home.				
	The first thing I do when I come into class is look at the whiteboard.				
	I always come to class with a pencil and pen/marker.				
	My Science Journal (binder) is organized. I am not missing anything that I should have.				
	I am always ready to start class when the teacher is.				
	I do my best in every task.				
	I always raise my hand when I would like to speak.				
	I actively listen to what my classmates say during class discussion.				
	I don't talk out of turn.				
	When the teacher makes transitions between class activities, I don't take that opportunity to talk.				
	When other students try to distract me, I ignore them or tell them to stop.				
	I don't distract other students from being successful in class.				
	I effectively communicate my ideas during class discussion.				

Do lab activities help you understand the textbook and concepts discussed in class? Explain your reasoning.

Does your lab grade reflect your effort? Explain your reasoning.

What is your best work so far in this class? Why do you take pride in it?

Does your homework grade reflect your effort? Explain your reasoning.

Does your quiz/test grade reflect your understanding of the material? Explain your reasoning.

What areas do you feel are your priorities for focus during the next semester of science?

List three goals for your action plan based on your analysis above:
1.

2.

3.

How can I help you in executing your plan for success?

Reprinted with the permission of Mitzi Sales, a teacher in Rye, New York.

Conclusion

Social-emotional habits of work can support a student's SEL development and awareness. When students can regulate behavior, their academic and social growth increases. Self-reflection and self-monitoring connects students to a metacognitive awareness of how their actions and strategies have worked to support their success in the classroom with peers, academics, their teacher, and themselves.

Discussion Questions for Reflection

Chapter 6

1. Chapter 6 focuses on habits of successful students. Various rubrics are provided to enable the student to examine his or her own habits with regard to goal setting, self-awareness, self-management, social awareness, relationship management, and responsible decision making. **Select a passage that resonates with you and relate it to your practice.**

   • student self-monitoring & goal-setting can begin as early as kindergarten
   • student performance ↑ when they receive accurate, descriptive (timely?) feedback on their work.
   • Students must be taught how to assess their own work, w/ clear criteria, rubrics, + models, & to act on their self-assessment to revise their work.

2. Imagine you have a student who is struggling with the issue of bullying. The student may be the instigator or the recipient of the bullying. **Using some of the recommended strategies from this chapter, what action(s) might you employ to address each situation?**

   work on goal setting in the area(s) of social awareness + relationship bldg. (Habits of successful students)

3. Imagine you have a student who is struggling with social awareness. This student may require explicit instruction and practice with recognizing social cues from others and understanding someone else's point of view, etc. **What kinds of dialogues might you set up between you and the student and between the student and other students?**

use social stories/videos to observe facial expressions/body language/tone of voice... Practice w/ peers teacher in a structured way

4. A student with time management difficulty and organizational issues has expressed a desire to improve his/her productivity. He or she needs to work on these goals at a different pace than a typical student. **How would you prioritize the student's goal setting (e.g., mapping out their schedule, starting homework during the day)? How might you limit the focus of the rubric in the chapter so it is specific to that student's schedule?**

7

Restorative Discipline
Consequences With Long-Term Positive Results for Inappropriate Behavior

Restorative Discipline

This chapter keeps the focus on preventive and restorative approaches to behavior in the classroom and continues to support a safe, supportive, accepting environment that strengthens the connections and relationships among peers and with the teacher. At times, educators need to seek out the support of school administrators and counselors, along with other specialists when addressing challenging behaviors. Recent research has found that when empathy and trust-building become part of the disciplinary approach of the entire school, relationships improve and suspensions drop by as much as half in some schools. (Okonofua, J.A. et al., 2016)

In previous chapters, we identified a number of the social-emotional skills that we can encourage, model, and support by creating a safe, orderly classroom with positive and respectful relationships among all members of the class. Frequent positive and authentic responses to students' positive behavior (for example, the use of accountable talk by "building on the ideas" of another student or "respectfully disagreeing" with another student), support both social-emotional and academic growth in the classroom.

Recent research has found that when empathy and trust-building become part of the disciplinary approach of the entire school, relationships improve and suspensions drop by as much as half in some schools.

The Matching Law

The matching law provides guidelines for a teacher's response to students' positive or negative behaviors. Walker, Ramsey, and Gresham (2004, p. 2) describe the law, first described by Herrnstein in 1961, this way:

The rate of any given behavior matches the rate of reinforcement for that behavior. For example, if aggressive behavior is reinforced once every three times it occurs (e.g., by a parent giving in to a temper tantrum) and **pro-social behavior** is reinforced once every fifteen times it occurs (e.g., by praising a polite request), then the Matching Law would predict that, on average, aggressive behavior will be chosen five times more frequently than pro-social behavior.

In other words, teachers should respond positively to students' positive behaviors and should avoid giving attention to negative behaviors and thereby "rewarding" a student with attention to the behavior. Subsequent research (Snyder, 2002) has shown that behavior closely follows the matching law.

Often our intuitive responses to behaviors make our punishments ineffective, according to Minahan in *The Behavior Code: A Practical Guide to Understanding and Teaching the Most Challenging Students*. For example, a seriously misbehaving student may feel that being sent out of the classroom is a reward, not a punishment, as a teacher may believe. For this reason, Minahan recommends that educators put less emphasis on rewards and consequences of behavior and increase emphasis on "building the skills students need to exhibit appropriate behavior" (2012 Kindle Location 101).

She also recommends that educators build a positive classroom by proactively teaching pro-social

Table 7.1 How Teacher Language Creates Classroom Culture

Type of culture	Teacher language examples	Possible consequences of using this language for individual students and whole class
Authoritarian	"Get back to work right now or you'll miss recess."	Students must comply with teacher because he or she is the boss. Work is done to avoid punishment. Sometimes students do not feel safe.
Cooperative	"Keep your voices small; remember some people can't concentrate with too much noise."	Students become aware of the impact of their behavior on others. This can be an opportunity for SEL in self-management.
Collaborative	"I can see that your groups look a bit discombobulated. What's the problem, and how can we solve it so that we can figure out…"	Students are considered thinkers, who, along with the teacher, can solve problems in the class.

Adapted from Johnston, P., 2004, pp. 100–110.

skills. For example, as addressed in Chapter 4, routines prevent misbehaviors and do not "reactively" respond with anger, but instead use informed and calm responses. Another example is when a student puts her head down instead of doing her work resulted in remarks that reflected irritation from the teacher. However, after discussing this students' learning needs with a colleague, the teacher realized that the student disconnected from the class only if she felt incapable of doing the work. The teacher then made sure that the student understood the task and saw this "misbehavior" as a way of communicating not disrespect or rebellion, but her feeling of inadequacy of doing the task. Instead of reprimanding her behavior, the teacher supported the student's academic and social-emotional learning, and the "misbehavior" stopped. Often the causes of students' behaviors are complex and may require enlisting the assistance of the school's and district's experts or the development of a contingency plan, addressed later in this chapter.

Effective Praise

Perhaps surprisingly, praise is not uniformly a positive reward. Walker, Ramsey, and Gresham (2004, p. 4) describe effective praise as genuine, immediate, frequent, enthusiastic, descriptive, varied, and involving

In each example, the teacher is asking students to be quiet; yet, the way language is used, beyond maintaining a quiet class, sends additional messages about the students' role.

eye contact. They suggest that teachers use praise at least four times as often as criticism and more often, if possible. They also found that teachers tend to praise those students who regularly exhibit good behavior, but tend not to seize opportunities to praise the more disruptive students when they are behaving well.

Language in the Classroom

Peter Johnston, in *Opening Minds: How Our Language Affects Children's Learning*, describes three different classroom cultures embedded in the everyday language of teaching and learning. Table 7.1 shows examples of each and the consequences to the learner.

In each example, the teacher is asking students to be quiet; yet, the way in which language is used, beyond maintaining a quiet class focused on work, sends additional messages about the students' role as: 1) compliant rule-followers in the authoritarian classroom; 2) responsible members of a group in the cooperative classroom; or 3) thinkers who can solve problems along with the teacher and contribute to the learning in the class.

In the same way, positive responses can send messages beyond "the answer is correct."

On the surface, responding to students who have demonstrated an appropriate behavior or have given a correct answer seems significantly easier than responding to students who have answered or behaved

Table 7.2 Specific Praises Connected to Social-Emotional Skills

Skill	Sample of Specific Praise
Self-Awareness Accurately recognize own strengths and limitations	Group one resolved their disagreement about the correct answer by having everyone give their reason for their answer before deciding the best answer.
Self-Management Display grit, determination, or perseverance	I can see that you continued to work on this problem using different strategies until you were satisfied with this clearly developed sketch for your project.
Relationship Skills Provide help to those who need it	I saw that your group made sure that everyone had a chance to respond to the question and to create this chart about the main claims of each primary source.
Social Awareness Respect others	Thank you for picking up the papers in the hallway so the custodian did not need to do it. It sends a message that everyone in the school is a valued member of our community.

incorrectly; however, this is not always the case. A college professor of ours had the habit of responding, "Well done!" in a bright, enthusiastic tone to virtually every comment a student made. Initially, students in the class beamed at this enthusiastic praise, but after a few weeks, it became apparent that virtually every correct response received a "Well done!" in that same enthusiastic tone. In short, the praise lost its luster through overuse.

There was much that this college professor was doing correctly when it came to responding to correct behavior and answers. Perhaps most importantly, his tone conveyed warmth and enthusiasm. This educator's method also serves as a cautionary tale, however, in that he came to rely too heavily on one phrase. Whether we realize it or not, students are paying close attention to our every move, and that includes the ways in which we offer praise. Thus, we must consciously work to diversify the ways in which we praise student responses.

Whether we realize it or not, students are paying close attention to our every move, and that includes the ways in which we offer praise.

Tone

A teacher's tone of voice also lends meaning to his or her words. A tone of sarcasm can contradict positive words. An enthusiastic response is more likely to gain the attention of other students in the room. It also increases their desire to obtain praise. However, simply wanting the approval of a teacher is not teaching the social-emotional skill of student agency for doing a job effectively.

Be Specific About What Is Praiseworthy

Praise can be categorized as general or specific. Frequent use of general, enthusiastic praise does typically make the student feel good. It also causes others in the room to seek the praise. However, praising with specificity provides higher levels of instruction than general praise (see Table 7.2).

Teacher: What do you consider to be the start of the Cold War?

Student: I think the Cold War was getting started even before World War II ended. I think that President Truman began to see Russia as a future competitor, and some historians say that Truman dropped the atomic bomb on Hiroshima to intimidate Stalin.

Teacher: Your answer brings up an interesting proposition, that the US's act in Japan had a motivation that included sending a message to Stalin.

As may be seen in this dialogue, the teacher's acknowledgement goes beyond simply "That's a great contribution." Rather, the teacher explicitly notes what the student contributed to the class's discussion. Such praise acknowledges that the students are being more accurate and authentic and increases their knowledge about the content being taught as well as about this student's efficacy as a student. The feedback from the teacher also makes a statement that learning effectively is important in the class.

The same is true for behavior. Frequent praise makes it easier for all the students to replicate the behavior. In the table below are examples of how specific praise can be used to support social-emotional growth.

Facing a student, nodding or smiling as he or she is speaking, remaining focused on his or her words—rather than taking attendance, or reading your email on your cell phone, or turning away—communicates either respectful listening or its opposite.

Praise Student Effort

We often praise student achievement. It is a natural tendency to see success and then praise the accomplishment. Instead, in giving feedback, we need to make praising *effort* and perseverance at solving problems the primary method of positive feedback because often students believe that if they were "smart," the answer would come to them immediately. Instead, they need to understand that the struggle is a part of learning in all content areas.

The students who made the greatest growth toward incremental growth mindset thinking were those who were recognized for their effort or strategies with statements or questions, such as the following:

"You really tried hard. I saw you revising your paragraph, and you've added vivid details."

"You found a way to do it."

"You found more than one way to do it."

"You kept trying even when you didn't get it right the first time."

"You've tried it that way and it didn't work. What is another way you might try to solve this problem?"

"You really put the time in to make this work pay off."

"The three drafts really showed your effort. The final piece of writing is well-organized and your claims and evidence have solid analysis."

"You were determined to turn this into a really excellent piece of work." (Dweck, 2000, p. 112-113).

Don't Repeat the Correct Response That Is Praiseworthy

Craig and Cairo (2006) observe that, after asking students a question and then listening to a student's response, many teachers instinctively repeat that re-

> *The students who made the greatest growth toward incremental growth mindset thinking were those who were recognized for their effort or strategies with statements or questions.*

sponse for the benefit of the rest of the class. However, Craig and Cairo report that when teachers refrain from repeating their students' responses, studies have found that "students pay greater attention to and show increased respect for their classmates' responses" (p. 2). In other words, when students know that their teacher is *not* going to repeat a classmate's words, they pay more attention to what their classmate is saying in the first place.

Sincerity of Praise

Cognitive scientist Daniel Willingham explained in a 2006 article that another key to effective praise is sincerity. According to Willingham (2006, p. 2), "To motivate students—especially older students who are more discerning and better able to appreciate the differences between what is said and what is meant—teachers need to avoid praise that is not truthful, is designed to control behavior, or has not been earned."

Interestingly, he found that students react particularly negatively to praise that gives and criticizes simultaneously. For example, imagine a teacher who offers the following "praise" to a student: "Good job answering that question; you should do your homework every night!" While the teacher who offers this statement is simply trying to make the point that doing one's homework yields good results in class, students tend to hear such a statement not as praise, but as a reprimand. In other words, the students focus less on the "good job" and more on the "you *should* do your homework every night."

An example of this related to social-emotional learning is "you are *finally* learning to wait your turn;" rather than, "your patience is showing clearly as you waited your turn."

Summary of Characteristics of Effective Praise

___	diverse phrases
___	warm tone
___	attentive body language
___	specific praise connected to the student's work or behavior
___	direct praise
___	effort and perseverance are recognized
___	sincere and authentic

Table 7.3 **Comparison Between Punishments and Consequences**

Punishments	Consequences
Use an angry tone.	Use a calm and matter-of-fact tone.
Are not related to the behavior.	Are logical outcomes of the behavior.
Leave child believing he/she is the problem.	Leave child believing the behavior is the problem.
Use fear as an external motivator of change.	Help child understand the negative impact on self and others, thereby intrinsically motivating change.

Rewards and Consequences

In addition to praise, teachers often use other rewards to reinforce appropriate behavior. In some instances, these are individual rewards and, in others, they are group rewards. An example of an individual reward in an elementary school is to provide those students who exhibit appropriate behavior over a period of time with the opportunity to enjoy extra computer time or an opportunity to help in another classroom with younger students. In middle and high schools, an individual reward might be the privilege to go to the library during study hall or to leave class first for the bus, so the student may acquire that coveted back seat. A note home or phone call to a parent commending the student's good behavior has been found to be an effective reward for students on all levels.

A classroom management plan with clearly taught and consistently followed expectations coupled with ample positive reinforcement and a system of rewards will eliminate most disruptive behavior; however, there will be times when we need to give students consequences for not following our expectations.

Robert Marzano, in his book *Classroom Management that Works* (2003, pp. 28–32), tells us that the most effective plan for classroom management contains consequences as well as rewards. Consequences are not the same as punishment, as described in Table 7.3. In their book *Rules in School* (2003, p. 89), Brady, Forton, Porter, and Wood draw a clear distinction between consequences and punishments. Some of the characteristics of punishment are that it has an angry tone, is not related to the behavior, leaves the child feeling he or she is the problem rather than his or her behavior, uses fear as an external motivator for stopping the behavior, and leaves the child feeling shamed. Consequences, on the other hand, are as-

A classroom management plan with clearly taught and consistently followed expectations coupled with ample positive reinforcement and a system of rewards will eliminate most disruptive behavior.

signed using a calm and matter-of-fact voice, are a logical outcome of the behavior, help the child understand the negative impact of the behavior on himself/herself and others, leave the child believing the behavior is the problem (not him or her), and build an intrinsic desire to use more appropriate behaviors. In their book *Engaging Troubling Students* (2005, p. 116), Scott Danforth and Terry Jo Smith tell us that "even when the teacher is confronting a student about a specific behavior or incident, the message within and throughout should be that even this incident does not diminish the student in the teacher's eyes."

Group Rewards and Consequences

Walker, Ramsey, and Gresham (2004, pp. 9–10) explain the appropriate and inappropriate uses of group rewards and consequences for classroom management. **Group reinforcement** (the authors refer to it as **group reinforcement contingencies**) involves the group receiving a reward as the result of meeting a measurable behavior goal. It is important that the group reward that teachers choose is one that they, their teammates, and the building administration feel is appropriate. For example, if a lab group completes science lab cleanup in the time allotted (self-management), it can earn a point toward leaving for lunch five minutes early one day. In elementary school, students can earn points toward extra recess time. Some teachers and/or administrators disagree with "free time" incentives. In those cases, reward points may be used toward time when the class will play an educational game like Jeopardy or for an extra point on a quiz.

Group reinforcements have been found to be quite successful when used as part of the overall behavior plan; however, it is important to note that

Walker, Ramsey, and Gresham warn that the group contingency should never be a group consequence. The distinction here is that the failure to obtain an additional benefit (such as extra recess) is appropriate; however, a group consequence, such as the class losing five minutes of recess should never be applied to the group because of the behavior of some or even most of the students. Consequences should be applied only to those individuals who fail to meet the behavior requirements. A consequence for all for the actions of some can undermine the social-emotional development in the students causing the consequences as well as those innocently having to accept the consequence of the actions of others. For the offending students, it can undermine their ability to make friends (relationship skills) as others shun them. It can make them the object of peer criticism thereby lowering self-esteem (self-awareness) and sends them deeper into the cycle of deficit mindset described in Chapter 1. It also may push those innocently caught in the punishment to exhibit behaviors of retribution against the offenders.

> *When students can take another's perspective, reflect on their own actions or feelings, and work with others to achieve goals, then restorative techniques can work.*

Clear expectations, fair consequences, and restorative conversations, as described in Chapter 2, Peer Conflict Resolution Protocol, work only when students have self-regulation, emotion knowledge, and social skills—competencies taught through social-emotional learning. When students can take another's perspective, reflect on their own actions or feelings, and work with others to achieve goals, then restorative techniques can work because a student who hurts another can empathize with that person and can see that their behavior could have done harm (Elias, 2016).

Up to this point, we have looked at the various components that make up a successful classroom management plan and those actions that can enhance or detract from social-emotional learning. Even the best classroom management plan may fail to cause some students to respect the routines and norms of the classroom. We may have students in our class who have experienced the trauma of a parent's death or who are the victims of verbal, physical, or sexual abuse. We may have students in our class who have been the victims of repression in their native countries, or who experience daily the results of of their parents' contentious divorce or of their alcohol or drug abuse. We have students who have chemical or brain abnormalities that are unrelated to their environment but can cause unprovoked outbursts. According to Walker, Ramsey, and Gresham (2004, p. 4) research indicates that troubled students may actually be between 2 percent and 16 percent of the general population, yet only about 1 percent of the school population has been identified with emotional disorders through the special education process.

Most students can be accommodated by a well-constructed classroom management plan; however, for one percent to five percent of the classroom population, our classroom management plan will not be sufficient. For these students, we will need to have *individual contingencies* within our classroom management plan. The goal of these individual contingencies is to decrease the negative behaviors and limit their impact on the learning environment. It is hoped that the individual contingencies will bridge the gap between what these students need to be productive and socially and emotionally comfortable and safe members of the class and the routines and expectations in the classroom.

Individual contingencies are most effective when the student, teacher, parent, and a third party in the school (assistant principal, special education teacher, school psychologist, etc.) collaboratively develop and agree to the strategies of the plan. Individual contingencies should include both incentives and consequences. Effective incentives may vary from student to student, so it is important that you choose incentives that truly are valued by the students. They may be incentives given by the school or incentives given by the parent(s) [provided the parent(s) will follow through consistently with the incentives].

Some school-given incentives include:

a. a note home to the parent
b. a phone call home to the parent
c. lunch with the teacher, principal, or group of friends
d. a gift certificate to a favorite ice cream shop or fast food restaurant (my apologies to the Department of Education and their efforts to limit obesity)
e. a pass to a school dance or sporting event
f. a pass from doing homework
g. the privilege of a preferred activity (e.g., listening to music, drawing, computer, reading)
h. a magazine on a topic of interest to the student (cars, sports, wrestling, fashion)
i. stickers, pencils, or candy/food if appropriate
j. baseball cards or other collectibles

k. the privilege of borrowing an electronic device
l. time with a favorite/previous teacher
m. time assisting a teacher with a class of younger students

Some parent-provided incentives include:

a. additional TV time
b. staying up an extra half hour
c. a play date or sleepover with a special friend
d. extra Nintendo time
e. a trip to a sporting or other enjoyable event
f. extra computer time or other technology opportunities
g. a pass from needing to complete a home chore
h. extra time with a preferred activity (e.g., playing the guitar)
i. a trip to the mall
j. special time alone with a parent

It is still important to have a plan specific to these students when proactive responses are either not feasible or do not have the desired result.

At the high school level, most individual contingency plans are developed by counselors, special education teachers, or assistant principals, with input from the classroom teachers. A meeting with the counselor, teacher, student, and parent(s) may be helpful so that all parties are aware of the plan and the efforts being made to help the student succeed. Searle (2013, pp. 130–131) and Caltha Crowe (2011, p.2) discuss the importance of **understanding triggers to counterproductive behavior** for these students when beginning to construct an individual contingency plan. By doing so, we can be more proactive than reactive in our interactions with this student and limit the times the behavior is triggered. Green (2011, p. 27) tells us, "All too often, intervention for behaviorally challenged students occurs in the heat of the moment or immediately thereafter. ... Solving problems before they occur is far preferable and more productive." We are not suggesting that understanding all the triggers and avoiding them will eliminate all the inappropriate behaviors. It is still important to have a plan specific to these students when proactive responses are either not feasible or do not have the desired result.

To begin, the teacher needs to disassociate this student from the group incentive system so that student's behavior does not inhibit the class's ability to earn an incentive. Instead, the teacher and others in the support system meet with the student to develop an individual incentive system for that student. They determine incentives, perhaps time on Friday for a choice activity. Whenever possible, engage parents/guardians to provide an incentive at home, extra time on the computer, more phone time, or more frequent opportunities to borrow the car. The ultimate goal is for the teacher to develop a relationship with this student that results in a joint decision by the teacher and the student to rejoin the group incentive system. Below is a sample of an individual contingency plan for a high school senior.

Robert Condon Individual Contingency Plan

Robert has difficulty staying seated, remaining still, and paying attention. He also may distract other students. To keep Robert on track for a successful senior year, the following behavior plan has been agreed to by Robert, his mother, and all of his teachers.

Contingency Plan Expectations

- Robert will not ask to leave class, short of a medical emergency.
- Robert must have a pass if he is scheduled to see the school psychologist, nurse, guidance counselor, or another teacher for extra help. He agrees not to wander the hallways.
- He will use the nurse's bathroom before homeroom, between classes, specifically during the 9:22–9:28 AM break, and during his lunchtime.
- He will not be in the cafeteria except for his lunch.
- If Robert does need to leave class, his pass will include a five-minute time limit to get to where he is going and return to class. Robert may leave his study hall only once per period and only for five minutes unless he has a pass to that location.
- Robert will not touch anyone by hugging, patting, hitting, etc. If he does, the staff member who observes this behavior will warn him about this behavior. This behavior will be documented and checked regularly to determine the number of warnings Robert has received.

If Robert is disruptive in a class, for example, he makes inappropriate comments, interrupts a lesson, gets up without asking, the teacher will use the following language with him:

- ○ **First warning:** "Robert, you are interfering with my teaching."
- ○ **Second warning:** "Robert, this is the second time today that I've told you that you're interfering with my teaching."
- ○ **Third time:** "Please go to Mr. Sanchez's office." He will then receive a detention, which he will serve on that same day.

If Robert demonstrates a need to go to the nurse or psychologist, and a teacher gives him permission to go, the teacher should call the nurse or psychologist to let him or her know Robert is on his way.

Suggestions for Success

1. Robert may be helpful with classroom chores that involve movement: writing on the board, collecting papers; however, these activities are privileges that may be revoked if not successful or they're distracting to other students.
2. Help Robert to reflect about why he made a bad decision and what to do for the next time.
3. Use calm, clear, and consistent language to communicate desirable and undesirable behaviors.
4. Provide positive feedback for appropriate and on-task behaviors.
5. Make consequences clear and consistent. Good communication among staff is important. Please see Mr. Sanchez immediately with any problems or concerns.

Incentive: Robert will receive one point for each class in which he remains for the entire period. He will receive two points for any class when he does not receive any warnings. Mr. Sanchez will email Mrs. Condon each Friday with a report on the number of points Robert earned during that week. Robert may use his points to "purchase" time using Mrs. Condon's car. Robert will be permitted to use the car for one hour for every ten points he earns.

We agree to the following behavior plan.

_____　　　　_____
Robert Condon　　　　　　　　　　　　　Mr. Sanchez

_____
Mrs. Condon

Sample Individual Contingency Plan

For the student who may have difficulty following the norms of the classroom, it may be necessary to develop an **individual contingency plan**. The following steps may be used to create a plan for a student having difficulty in meeting expectations.

a. Identify areas of concern[1]
  i. Is the student disruptive during whole-class instruction?
  ii. Is the student disruptive during independent work?
  iii. Does the student have difficulty working collaboratively?
  iv. Does the student have difficulty completing class and/or home assignments?
  v. Does the student have difficulty during lunch and/or recess?
  vi. Is the student disrespectful to other students and/or adults?

  Once the areas of concern have been identified, the teacher sets up a chart in which each area of concern is stated positively. When a student can meet each expectation, the student will earn a point. For an example, see Table 7.4.

b. Determine and explain to the student how points will be earned. We have found it to be extremely important to separate the school day into a morning session and an afternoon session. In this way, the student who is having a difficult morning has an opportunity to start over in the afternoon.
c. Determine with the student what will happen when the student earns a certain number of points. It is important that the incentive is something that is meaningful for the student.
d. Be sure to involve the parents, as well as any other adult who will be working closely with this student.
e. Contact previous teachers to get information regarding which techniques worked well and which were not particularly helpful for this student.
f. Determine a specific time at which you and the student will go over the chart together.

Table 7.4 Sample Contingency Plan Behavior Chart

	Monday	Tuesday	Wednesday	Thursday	Friday
I worked well independently.	AM: PM:	AM: PM:	AM: PM:	AM: PM:	AM: PM:
I worked well during group work.	AM: PM:	AM: PM:	AM: PM:	AM: PM:	AM: PM:
I completed my class assignments.	AM: PM:	AM: PM:	AM: PM:	AM: PM:	AM: PM:
I completed home assignments.					
Total Points:					

---

1 These questions are often best answered when a colleague observes in our classroom to gather specific, objective data about a student's behavior.

A unique method of earning back demerit behavior points in one high school is through mindfulness. As part of a school-wide initiative in social-emotional skills and mindfulness, volunteer teachers piloted inviting students to engage in a minute of mindfulness before the first bell in some classrooms. Teachers also offered voluntary workshops in which students learn to understand mindfulness and to recognize the damaging effects of stress and the healing effects of intentional self-calming and deep breathing. Students who have demerits from tardiness or lateness to class can earn back demerits by voluntarily participating in these activities.[2]

Some teachers have wondered if rewards are fair. "These students get a reward for doing the same thing the other students must do without a reward?" If other students are concerned, teachers can respond by explaining that being fair means that *people get what they need to succeed*. Not everyone needs the same things to succeed, but they all get the support that they need (sitting close to the front of the class to see the board, extra time to finish work, etc.). In the same way, *fairness* applies to behavior. Many teachers find they can keep individual contingency reward plans a private matter between the adults in the students' lives and the students involved. The students involved often prefer this arrangement.

Rewards can be a very powerful motivator of appropriate behavior; however, they do not always achieve the desired results. In these cases, consequences (as defined earlier) will be needed. Some **logical consequences** in school may be:

a. not allowing a student to attend an extracurricular activity.
b. notifying parents/guardians of the misbehavior. For some this may by prior agreement, accompanied by a consequence at home.
c. losing points that are accumulating toward an incentive.
d. spending time after class or after school.
e. changing a student's seat.
f. sending a student from the class to a prearranged time-out area (office, in-school suspension room, etc.)[3] in extreme cases when the previous interventions do not work.
g. keeping a student after class to discuss the disruptive behavior.
h. asking a student to take a walk for five minutes and to come back when he or she is ready to work.
i. sending a student into another teacher's classroom with work to complete silently.
j. calling in parents for a conference to discuss the disruptive behavior.
k. providing a space in the classroom for a student to voluntarily take a time out.

Conclusion

The effective use of praise, rewards, and consequences can support the development of social-emotional learning. Implementing effective versus ineffective strategies takes no extra time for the teacher (or parent) since praise, rewards and consequences are part of a typical day in school or at home.

---

3   It is important to note that students should not be sent without supervision unless the teacher is certain that the student will report to the designated and supervised area. This consequence is most productive if students can be sent with class work or another productive activity; however, this may not be possible, given the students' emotional state at the time they are sent from class.

---

2   Provided by Jason Gilmartin, Quabbin Middle and High School

Discussion Questions for Reflection

Chapter 7

1. Chapter 7 focuses on restorative discipline and consequences with long-term positive results for inappropriate behavior. **Select a passage that resonates with you and relate it to your practice.**

   Authoritarian v. Cooperative v. Collaborative
   - the use of teacher
   language in the
   classroom (p. 132)
   i would like to learn more about this
   in terms of Responsive Classroom

2. Dealing with behavioral issues for students with special needs can be especially challenging because often the student's disability can be the cause of some very challenging behaviors. **For example, does the student create a disturbance every time the teacher asks the class to "take out your reading book?" What might the teacher do to redirect this reaction?**

   In some situations, if the student's behavior is outside the realm of typical interventions, the services of a behavioral consultant will be used to do a functional behavioral assessment (FBA) to determine the cause of a behavior or a pattern that may occur around a certain activity. Once the FBA is done, a behavior intervention plan (BIP) can be implemented.

3. While teachers are trained to praise students for academic performance, commenting on effort and perseverance may yield more positive results for social-emotional learning. **What are examples of feedback you can give that will be most beneficial for students with a learning challenge and typical students?**

   base praise on use of different
   strategies, time spent on a problem
   learning from/recognizing mistakes
   progress over time...

4. Mr. Smith "praised" one of his students by saying, "Nice job on that test. What a difference it makes when you actually crack a book open!" Mr. Smith was surprised that the student did not seem happy with this comment. **Reword this statement to reflect a more positive approach to this feedback and that provides a comment that specifies what is good.**

    Great job on the test! What study strategy did you use that was helpful? Maybe you could share your suggestion w/ the class!

5. "I'm sorry to inform you that our class will be unable to attend the field day today because John did not...." This group consequence statement will be counter-productive to creating a SEL classroom. **What approach would employ a group incentive, but not a group consequence?**

    If the group meets objectives, they all earn reward. If some don't meet obj, maybe it takes longer to reach reward & those who are eligible get to participate.

8

Engaging Teaching

Connecting Academics and Social-Emotional Learning

Create an Engaging Classroom

According to a recent Gallup Poll survey, engagement in school decreases as students progress from pre-school through high school—from 75% in kindergarten to 32% in grade 11, when it is at its lowest. Thus, the task of supporting positive student engagement is an essential skill for all teachers.

In Chapter 7, we discussed the ways students can demonstrate engagement or lack of engagement as they work individually, in groups, or as part of a class lesson. This chapter shifts focus from relationships to the classroom environment and how teachers can make their classroom conducive to engagement. It focuses particularly on self-awareness and self-management skills for students as they recognize the impact of their emotions, needs and values on their engagement in their learning. In addition, the chapter addresses relationship management as the teacher's relationship with students becomes a factor in engagement as the teacher uses enthusiasm, passion, and positive feedback to engender and improve students' engagement in the work.

When students are disengaged, they may become passive and withdraw or, in the most extreme form, disengaged students may become disruptive.

When students are disengaged, they may become passive and withdraw or, in the most extreme form, disengaged students may become disruptive. Phillip Schlechty in *Shaking Up the Schoolhouse: How to Support and Sustain Educational Innovation* describes five levels of student engagement, with the lowest level acting out behavior in the Rebellion level:

1. Authentic Engagement
2. Strategic Compliance
3. Ritual Compliance
4. Retreatism
5. Rebellion

Only the highest level in Schlechty's model fully involves the whole student "authentically;" that is, the student demonstrates both high attention and high commitment to the goal. Students are focused on attaining the goals of the work and display grit, determination, and perseverance. Their attitude toward the work is positive because they see it as worthy and meaningful. Students learn the most at this level because the task has meaning; students persevere through difficulties because of their commitment. In the elementary and secondary Socratic seminar example below, students who are authentically engaged would have high commitment—that is they would be involved and persist in the work, and they would show high attention and involvement. In the examples below, the elementary unit's focus on friendship and the secondary focus on American values connect to the student's concerns in their everyday life. Their high commitment and high attention of **authentic engagement** would be reflected throughout the project from the research to the group work to the discussion to the final summation. To engender engagement, their teachers would need to begin their units by connecting to each student's experience with the topic: friends or success or greatness in America.

If students' involvement in the class falls below the level of full, authentic engagement to **strategic compliance**, they learn less than at the authentic engagement level. Students at strategic compliance willingly pay attention and comply with the task, but they are not deeply committed to the goal. To ramp up this level of engagement to a higher level, a teacher could focus on the student's low commitment to the work's value to them. To increase a student's perception of the value of the work, the teacher needs to help students see the usefulness of the learning and to see that knowing about friendship or the American Dream is worthwhile and relevant to their world. The teacher would need to help students see connections to their lives and values. "Did you ever wonder if someone was a true friend? Can you have many good friends?" or "What are your goals in life? Would they be part of what all Americans dream of? If the Constitution guarantees the pursuit of happiness, how does that relate to your life?"

If students don't know how to be successful or if the work has no meaning, students may be frustrated or bored.

In **strategic compliance**, the level below full engagement, students go through the motions and do the work lacking enthusiasm in passive compliance. Although students may do as they are asked, because they are not convinced that this work is connected to their lives, they go along, but do not deeply engage in the work. To help students become more engaged, the teacher needs to work not only on the connections to students' lives, as in strategic compliance, but they also need to help students become more energized by the task to go beyond their passive compliance. To do this, the teacher needs to convince students of the value of doing the work at a high level of quality. At times, examples of finished projects that demonstrate insight, for example, by illustrating the many kinds of friendships or the many American dreams in unique and engaging ways, can entice students to attend to the quality of the work.

A level below strategic compliance is **ritual compliance**. Students are more disengaged, and demonstrate both low attention and low commitment. The student only uses enough effort to avoid "getting in trouble," but sees no value in the work. At this level of disengagement, students do their work without energy or enthusiasm. If most of the class demonstrates this level of disengagement, the teacher can intervene with the whole class or only with students who are disengaged. The elementary teacher might work on commitment and attention by letting students see the engaging work by others in the class by doing a

processing partners exercise (see Chapter 10) and by asking each student to share their in-progress work. The teacher could then gather the class together to ask provocative questions about real friendship.

At the next lower level, **retreatism**, students disengage from the activities of the classroom. These students do not act out, but they do not work with classmates or with the teacher. A student who is retreating from the work may put his head on his desk, but will not cause disruption in the class. These students require individual work with the teacher to determine the cause, which may be the content or activity but may have other outside sources. In the conversation, the teacher would need to connect the student to the importance of the question or provide supports to help the student engage with the work.

Finally, the least engaged students at the **rebellion** level are so disengaged that they distract others and pull other students away from the task. When students are retreating or rebelling, clearly, they are not learning. Interventions are necessary to support students' successful completion of the work. To address the rebelling student would require an individual conference in which the teacher would try to determine the cause and to then build attention and commitment to the work. If, for example, the student is in rebellion because she believes she cannot do the work, the teacher might do a check-in daily at the beginning of class to make sure she understands the assignment and get her started on her work.

Frustrated and Bored Students

If students don't know how to be successful or if the work has no meaning, students may be frustrated or bored. Frustrated students either shut down or act out. Students who are not challenged either shut down or act out. Bored students either shut down or act out. In her book, *Causes and Cures in the Classroom: Getting to the Root of Academic and Behavioral Problems* (2013, p. 129), Margaret Searle tells us, "When students feel discouraged, bored, left out, or mistreated, they are likely to learn less and misbehave more."

Without direct teacher intervention, students may stay in the self-perpetuating cycle of deficit perspective discussed in Chapter 1 throughout the year to their academic and social detriment. Interventions may connect students to the meaningfulness and worthwhileness of the work.

The Frustrated Student. This is the student for whom the teaching has not been sufficiently differentiated to enable him or her to successfully master the concepts. A student who does not feel successful in learning the content of the course often feels unable to do the work. The student who feels this way typically responds either by shutting down or acting out. Students who shut down may doodle, put their heads down, daydream, or ask to go the bathroom. These students are not disruptive to the class, but they are also not learning. Students who act out are often doing so to hide their embarrassment at not being able to do the work. They are sending the message *This is not important so I don't need to learn it.* They are also looking to mask their failure by shifting the way people see them from being thought of as "stupid" to being "funny" or "bad." When frustration makes a student choose between being perceived by his or her peers as either "bad" or "stupid," the student will almost always choose to be bad. This attitude can activate the Cycle of Low Motivation and the Impact of Deficit Mindset on Student Behavior described in more depth in Chapter 1.

The Bored Student. Students who master the information and skills in the lesson quickly and are not further challenged often behave in a similar way to those who are frustrated. They will either shut down or act out. Boredom causes these students to look for ways to entertain themselves. Some students entertain themselves in ways that are not disruptive, such as reading, drawing, daydreaming, going to the bathroom, etc. Others entertain themselves with disruptive behaviors such as talking to their classmates or inappropriately performing for their classmates.

For some students, the information is at the correct level of challenge, but the instruction is not engaging. To make the class more engaging, teachers can provide opportunities for student choice, or add movement through pair and group work. In addition, they can use learning activities such as Museum Walks, or Get the Gist, described in detail at the end of Chapters 4 and 10. Also, teachers can vary their materials or use technology to engage students. They

Bored students, like frustrated students or students who are not challenged, may act out or shut down, and, consequently, not learn.

can engage students as detailed in the Socratic seminar described later in this chapter. Boredom can come from a lack of challenge or a lack of energy in the classroom.

Motivating and Engaging All Students

It is important that a teacher models enthusiasm for the information and skills being taught in the lesson. In her book, *Increasing Student Motivation: Strategies for Middle and High School Teachers* (2006, p. 26), Margaret Theobald writes, "Students watch their teachers. If we cannot be excited about teaching and learning, then we cannot expect the students to be excited." Bored students, like frustrated students or students who are not challenged, may act out or shut down and, consequently, do not learn (see Table 8.1).

Six Classroom Conditions for Creating an Engaging Classroom

Research finds that there are six essential classroom conditions (Ribas, Brady, Tamerat, Deane, Greer, and Billings, 2017) for creating an engaging classroom as reflected in the Essential Conditions for Student Engagement listed below. Engaging classrooms need a thoughtfully planned and meaningful curriculum. The skills and content of the curriculum are taught by an energetic teacher who makes the goal clear: mastery of skills and content rather than grades. Knowing that their success is completely supported by their teacher, engaged students respond to these conditions by seeing their progress and work as worth the struggle and they persevere to achieve these tasks.

Essential Conditions for Student Engagement

1. **Connecting the curriculum to the students' world and lives helps students see the work as engaging.** The scaffolded Socratic seminar described below provides elementary and secondary examples of connecting the curriculum to the students' world and develops student self-awareness and student management.

2. **Teaching with enthusiasm** and passion for the learning engages students because the teacher's attitude communicates the importance of the

Table 8.1 Levels of Engagement and Possible Interventions

Level	Definition	How to Improve
Authentic Engagement	The highest level of authentic engagement, which fully involves the whole student "authentically," which indicates both high attention from the student as well as high commitment to the goal. Students are focused on attaining the goals of the work and display grit, determination, and perseverance.	There is no need to improve, only to sustain the high level of attention and commitment
Strategic Compliance	Students go through the motions and do the work lacking enthusiasm in passive compliance. Although students may do as they are asked, because they are not convinced that this work is connected to their lives, they go along, but do not deeply engage in the work.	• Connect to students' lives • Help student become more energized by the task to go beyond their passive compliance • Convince students of the value of doing the work at a high level of quality. • Show students examples of finished projects that demonstrate insight or that show their knowledge in a particularly clear, interesting, or unique way.
Ritual Compliance	Students are more disengaged, and demonstrate both low attention and low commitment. The student uses only enough effort to avoid "getting in trouble," but sees no value in the work. At this level of disengagement, students do their work without energy or enthusiasm.	• If most of the class demonstrates this level of disengagement, the teacher can intervene with the whole class or only with students who are disengaged. The elementary teacher in the scaffolded Socratic seminar described below might work on commitment and attention by letting students see the engaging work that others in the class are engaged in by doing a processing partners exercise and by asking each student to share their in-progress work.
Retreatism	At the next lower level, **retreatism**, students disengage from the activities of the classroom. These students do not act out, but they do not work with classmates or with the teacher. A student who is retreating from the work may put his head on his desk, but will not cause disruption in the class.	• These students require individual work with the teacher to determine the cause, which may be the content or activity but may have other outside sources. In the conversation, the teacher would need to connect the student to the importance of the question or provide supports to help the student engage with the work.
Rebellion	Finally, the least engaged students at the **rebellion** level are so disengaged that they distract others and pull other students away from the task. When students are retreating or rebelling, clearly, they are not learning.	• Interventions are necessary to support students' successful completion of the work. To address the rebelling student requires an individual conference in which the teacher would try to determine the cause and to then build attention and commitment to the work. • If, for example, the student is in rebellion because she believes she cannot do the work, the teacher might do a check-in daily at the beginning of class to make sure the student understands the assignment and to get her started on her work.

ideas and helps students see the work as important and see their struggle as they learn as worth the effort. Teachers' words of encouragement that emphasize mastery and recognize that learning requires struggle are important interventions along with scaffolds and differentiating options.

3. **Engaging teaching** provides students with a clear pathway to mastery and success. Engaging teaching helps students develop positive attitudes toward themselves and the work so that they feel able to succeed and are willing to struggle and persist to finish classroom tasks.

4. **Differentiating instruction** lets teachers communicate their commitment to each student's success by providing different pathways and alternative ways of demonstrating knowledge in content, product or process. In addition, alternatives include supportive interventions and supports from step-by-step instructions and examples to rubrics. Finally, effective individual feedback can support discouraged students and build confidence, or connect the disengaged student to the challenge of doing quality work. These techniques are shown below in both an elementary and secondary example of a Socratic seminar.

5. **Interpersonal relationships** with students help teachers engage students. As discussed in Chapter 2, students feel a sense of relatedness when they perceive that their teachers like, value, and respect them. In addition, positive peer relationships facilitate relationship management and social awareness skills to work with classmates on shared goals, to work together in groups, and to assess peers' contributions to group work.

6. **Teacher and student beliefs** about the nature of intelligence are expressed in teacher and peer feedback and discussions. These beliefs need to be clearly modeled by teachers to support a growth mindset, the belief that students can be successful at mastering the concepts and skills. Chapter 1 discusses the growth mindset in more detail. This positive mindset supports a students' focus on mastery orientation and on their own competence as they strive toward independence in the application of skills and concepts. Teacher and peer feedback that is carefully provided to express that students are a welcome and accepted member of a learning community with high expectations for work and social-emotional relationships. This community provides a variety of ways in which students are supported from clear, supportive feedback: "This work clearly provides a claim, and your next step is to develop evidence to support this claim." Peers, too, respond to one another with supportive responses. For example, "Building on Jon's ideas" gives credit to others and welcomes others' ideas in the discussion. With this orientation, students believe they can be successful and can master the skills and concepts and ideas taught, not just pass the course or get a good grade or a better grade than other students. Thus, student engagement and positive student behavior work hand in hand. **The scaffolded Socratic seminar described below provides elementary and secondary examples of how a growth mindset can be supported at all grade levels.**

Scaffolded Socratic Seminar as an Example of Engaging Work

The Launch: Teacher Enthusiasm and Passion

The attitude of the teacher toward the work is critically important. When a teacher shows passion for the content as well as for the students' mastery, students see the level of the expectations as attainable and know that they will be supported in every step of the learning process. In addition, the launch of a unit needs to clearly define the destination, the expectations, and the steps that students will need to take to be successful. In this example, a checklist and a rubric are used to support students' self-management.

- **Elementary Launch; Engaging, Enthusiastic Teaching:** To engage students, the teacher shares a story about her best friend in the fifth grade who continues to be her best friend now 10 years later. During Classroom Meeting time, described more fully in Chapter 10, she "launches" the unit on friendship and engages students in the topic by having them share with a partner one example of how someone shows friendship. She then tells them that they are going to read *Charlotte's Web* and see parts of the two movie adaptations to figure out what a friend is, what a friend does, and how stories describe friendships such as the one between a spider and a pig. The teacher shows a short clip of the first time that Charlotte and Homer meet and asks them to take notes with a partner about what is said and what is done that might be what a friend does. Students share their answers by passing their notes to the right and writing a comment, then giving the answer back. The teacher then asks the students to begin to create a chart of what friends do and what friends do not do.

- **Secondary Launch; Engaging, Enthusiastic Teaching:** To engage the students in the *Gatsby* unit, the teacher asks students to decide exactly how great Gatsby was and to rank him as a "1" (not at all great) to a "10" (the greatest). Then, the students find one passage that they could use to defend that ranking. The students then "Vote with their Feet," which is described more fully in Chapter 10, and select their chosen rank for Gatsby along a number-line posted along the classroom wall. They then share their selected passages with their fellow 10's or 8's or 1's. The teacher asks them to decide as a 1 or 10 what quality they based their greatness on in their selected passage. These qualities—for example, financially successful, a true romantic, or a person who would give up his life for love—are noted on chart paper. Next, the teacher has the students stand in line—still based on their rankings—and tells the 5's to walk in a ranked line to stand with the 1's and to pair up. Each student would have a partner whose opinion was quite different. The teacher paired those who had 1's with those who had 5's, the 2's with the 6's, the 3's with the 7's, the 4's with the 8's, and the 5's with the 9's or 10's. Each pair shares their rationale and their selected passages so that each pair could see Gatsby from at least one perspective that differs from theirs. The teacher then shows Gatsby's party scene from the four adaptations of Gatsby and asks what "greatness" was portrayed at this party and if, based on their rankings, they thought these examples were examples of greatness.

- **The Launch; Differentiating Instruction:** Both the elementary and secondary teachers provides a step-by-step checklist for the unit and a rubric that describes the criteria for assessing their mastery of the task. The checklist provides specific resources as well as choices for demonstrating their mastery at the end of the unit. In both the elementary and secondary classrooms, students have a final culminating synthesis that provides a choice of how they demonstrated their knowledge unit in process, product and content. For example:

  - ○ **Elementary** students could define friendship using a poster, an essay, or a PowerPoint that shows at least three examples of friendship from *Charlotte's Web* and explains how these words from the text or actions show friendship.
  - ○ **Secondary** students could write an argument with claims, evidence, counterclaims, and analysis, but present the argument as a formal essay, as a PowerPoint, or as a visual and illustrated display on chart paper. Debate?

- **The Launch and Throughout the Process; Interpersonal Relationships:** The teacher's relationship to students as well as to their engagement and mastery are demonstrated throughout the process. From individual feedback that tells students that they are capable to clear descriptions of where they are and what their next step is: "You have three clear examples of friendship. Now you can explain why this quote or action shows friendship." More examples are included below.

> *The teacher's relationship to students as well as to their engagement and mastery are demonstrated throughout the process.*

The Connection to Students' Lives

The seminar's topic is a crucial choice for teachers and needs to be based on their knowledge of the class that may have been gleaned from earlier successful work, from individual surveys about student interests and from teacher-to-student discussions (positive student-teacher relationships). The topic needs to be connected to important curricular and student areas, which vary by course. Here are examples of a connected seminar:

Elementary: What is a good friend? Base your answer on both the book and on the two movies of *Charlotte's Web*? Can a friend sometimes do hurtful things to another friend? Can a friend be more like a parent and give advice? These questions connect to students' everyday life.

Secondary: What is Fitzgerald's tone in *The Great Gatsby*? What is his attitude toward American values as it plays out in his attitude toward Gatsby, the narrator, and the main characters? How accurately have the movie adaptations reflected this tone? The glitzy world of the roaring twenties is distant enough for students to see flaws in American ideas and is close enough for them to have insights into their own lives and values.

These themes support self and social awareness in their discussions of friendship and the American Dream and connect to students' social-emotional lives at their age level. Analysis of these themes will provide students with self-awareness about their own friendships or American values.

Differentiating and Supporting All Learners in Positive Teacher-Student Relationships

To support all learners, the seminar was organized into four teams of mixed abilities. supported by the teacher's feedback on their work as they researched and organized information with note cards and references before the seminar. The step-by-step checklist and rubric oriented students to the sequence and destination of the task. The teacher had students check with her at specific junctures in their learning, called milestones below, to make sure all students understood and were moving forward.

Elementary: Each team researches a character and finds passages where that character is a friend or is not a true friend.

- **Milestone**: The teacher wants to make sure that students understand what they are doing with the idea of friendships. At the end of the class, students could be asked to pass in their best example of a character and passage with a clear explanation of how this passage relates to friendship. Students who are having difficulty are called together as a group or individually to work with the teacher.

- **Milestone**: The teacher checks in with every group to make sure they know what they will say in the discussion and how their note cards can support their participation. The teacher informally asks each group what are you going to say? She works with each group so that each student knows his or her part and what to say.

- **Milestone**: This is a check to be sure each portion of the work is completed and to high quality. The students create a final product outline, and peers assess the checklist and rubric with one another's work. Peers use rubric on the drafts and assess the quality of the work. Students who are having difficulty meet with the teacher individually as they put their final draft together.

Secondary: Each team researches in the text and in one of the four Gatsby movies, one character and connects that character to American values.

- **Milestones:** Check to make sure students are making progress. Every day each student fills out an exit slip that summarizes the day's progress on their film and character. Students who are having difficulty meet either as a group or individually with the teacher depending on the level of need.

- **Milestone:** The teacher checks on the group's readiness for the discussion by having a verbal, informal group check each day to see the progress. The teacher works with each group to make sure each will be successful.

- **Milestone:** Final product checks before the final work is given to the teacher. Peers review the checklist with one another and use the rubric on the draft of the final summary. The teacher monitors the progress of each student and conferences with those who are having difficulty.

- **Group work:** Students' learning is supported by group work on research. The groups collect specific examples from the text that connect the character to the question with either quotes or summaries from the work studied. Peers work together on the collaborative goal of presenting a character and that character's representation of the American Dream. The class is divided into four teams; the initial discussion will be among four students, with one representative from each team discussing in turn.

- This activity supports the social-emotional skill of **social awareness and relationship management** in its group work. The group members share a team goal, **collaborate** in their work preparing for the discussion, and develop positive peer relationships in group work that has clearly defined norms that are respected when peers achieve common goals.

- Each student in sequence represents the team over the course of the seminar.
   - **Elementary and secondary**: Students prepare for the seminar by creating note cards as a group addressing their question. The person who is representing the team at the time has the note cards while the rest of the team takes notes and prepares for their turn in the discussion.

- Each student is responsible for presenting, which supports the development of the self-awareness skills of competence and independence, and it supports relationship management as they must share group goals in this collaboration.

Using a clear rubric provided as the seminar project began (as shown in mastery orientation), the teacher assesses the seminar, and the students assess their own and their group's participation (mastery orientation).

- A **mastery orientation** of valuing the demonstration of understanding is underscored by using rubrics. The teacher provides an assessment of the students' behaviors and students assess their peers and themselves. They don't focus on grades, but on the degree of mastery that they have attained both as a member of a team and as an individual reader and analyst.

Secondary and Elementary Mastery is validated through the rubric introduced during the launch. Independently, in a poster for elementary students and in a formal argument for secondary students, all students summarize what they have learned from the seminar, which supports their mastery orientation. The rubric is based upon levels of mastery that underscore the sequential successes social-emotionally and academically of each learner throughout the unit and the **mastery orientation** of their work.

Mastery Learning and Transfer

According to Nicolas Pino-James in "Golden Rules for Engaging Students in Learning Activities," two conditions blend academics with students: 1) the academic work needs to be meaningful and because of that, students see the time and work worthwhile; 2) the purpose of the academic skills and knowledge must be mastery, not good grades or out-performing other students.

Growth mindset is another way of saying mastery mindset. With it, students believe that they can master ideas and skills and that their work and effort can make them "smarter" as discussed in Chapter 1.

Grant Wiggins, in his article *How Good Is Good Enough?* (2013, p.4), defines mastery:

Mastery is effective transfer of learning in authentic and worthy performance. Students have mastered a subject when they are fluent, even creative, in using their knowledge, skills, and understanding in key performance challenges and contexts at the heart of that subject, as measured against valid and high standards.

Level of mastery is the degree to which students have acquired the knowledge and skills identified in the standards on path toward mastery.

Understanding how to develop an orientation toward mastery begins with clearly understanding the phases that students go through as they learn and move through each **Level of Mastery**. Ribas et al. (2017) define the levels of mastery as follows:

1. The first level is **introduction** or **exposure** level of mastery. A student is at the introduction level immediately after the knowledge or skill in the standard has been presented for the first time. At this level, there is no expectation that the student will be able to demonstrate mastery of the standard.

2. The second level is **guided practice** level of mastery. At this level, the student can demonstrate the knowledge or skill only with prompting from the teacher or another person who has mastered the standard.

3. The third level is **immediate mastery** level of mastery. At this level, the student can demonstrate the knowledge or skill of the standard independently, shortly after the teacher has presented the knowledge or skill of the standard.

4. **Immediate application mastery** occurs when the student can use the knowledge and skill in an unfamiliar setting shortly after the presentation of the concept.

5. **Mastery** is achieved when the student can demonstrate the knowledge or skill after a period has passed since the standard was taught.

6. **Application mastery** is the level at which the student can demonstrate mastery after a period, in an unfamiliar situation

Figure 8.1 shows the typical progression students follow as they learn new knowledge and skills. It is important to note the following two factors that make teaching so complex:

1. **All students *do not* follow the same path to application mastery.**
2. **All students *do not* move through these steps at the same pace** (Ribas et al., 2017).

Figure 8.1 **Mastery Levels of Learning**

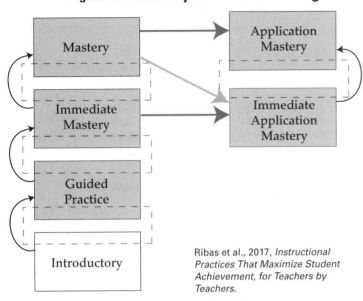

Ribas et al., 2017, *Instructional Practices That Maximize Student Achievement, for Teachers by Teachers.*

You will note the dotted-line boxes that connect the levels of mastery in Figure 8.1. They represent the fact that the levels of mastery flow into one another, instead of being distinct lines that are crossed among the levels. For example, a student moving from guided practice to immediate mastery does so by straddling the two levels, not by taking a step across a line. Upon entering the guided-practice stage, a student may need a very high level of teacher guidance. As his or her mastery progresses, the level of guidance needed decreases until the student can perform the skill or apply the concept independently (immediate mastery). In some cases, a student can complete the skill independently but needs the reassurance that the teacher is readily accessible before attempting the skill independently. Some people would consider this student at the immediate mastery level, while others would consider the student still at the upper end of guided practice.

Example of Progression Through Application Mastery for Two-Digit Multiplication

1. **Introductory Level:** If the standard that is to be mastered is "Students will be able to successfully complete a two-digit multiplication problem using clusters." The students begin at the *introduction level of mastery,* when the teacher first presented the steps for completing a two-digit multiplication example using clusters.

2. **Guided Practice**: Often, the next step in teaching this concept is to have the students complete one or more examples. Those students who can correctly complete an example with one or more prompts from the teacher or with the assistance of a peer are at the **guided practice level of mastery**.

3. **Immediate Mastery:** Those students who can correctly complete the example independently are at the **immediate mastery** level.

4. **Immediate Application Mastery:** Those students who can complete the assigned problem and the two-digit multiplication story, which is not just made up of numbers, but which is a word problem that asks students to determine the largest classroom on the corridor based on their ability to do two-digit calculations for the area of each classroom are at the **immediate application mastery** level.

5. **Mastery:** Those students who can complete a two-digit multiplication algorithm two weeks[1] later are at the **mastery** level.

6. **Application Mastery:** Finally, those students who can create and solve their own two-digit multiplication story problem based on designing a new classroom and needing to calculate the area of the rug, the area of the rest of the tiled floor, and to determine how many tables can fit into the tiled area, thus using a real-world setting, are at the **application mastery**[2] level.

Example of Progression Through Application Mastery to Identify the Author's Craft

1. **Introductory Level:** If the standard that is to be mastered is "Students will be able to identify the author's craft based on the standard for Grade 4: CC.4.RL.6. Compare and contrast the point of view from which different stories are narrated, including the difference between first- and third-person narration (Massachusetts Curriculum Frameworks, 2011, p. 16).

---

1   We use two weeks for this example only. Differing periods of time may be more appropriate for various knowledge and skills.

2   Application mastery is like what Grant Wiggins and Jay McTighe refer to as transfer in teaching *for understanding* (Wiggins and McTighe, 2011).

2. The students begin at the **introductory level** of mastery, when the teacher first presented the concept of author's craft in point of view in *Charlotte's Web*. At this stage, students know that the first-person point of view is a story told by a narrator who calls himself "I." If the story is told in a third-person point of view, all the characters are described as he or she. The author crafts a point of view because of the way the author wants the reader to experience the story. If the author uses an "I," only the details the narrator sees and experiences are told in the story. If the author uses third person, the details of the story can be what any or all the character sees. *Charlotte's Web* is told in the third person because the reader can read about the family, listen to the conversations of the animals and even of a spider.

3. **Guided Practice:** Often, the next step in teaching this concept is to have the students complete one or more examples. Students read different dialogues from the novel and identify that the point of view is third person because all characters are he or she (no I's). In addition, they explain the perspective of each character because often point of view in common language means in my opinion. The teacher guides the students as they identify the point of view of the dialogues among people, the farm animals, the hero (Homer), and a spider. The teacher can prompt, "Is one person in these conversations? Why didn't the author have one I tell this story?" The answer is that the first-person point of view limits the scene to where the "I" is.

4. **Immediate Mastery:** Those students who can correctly complete the example independently and identify third-person point of view and accurately explain that character's perspective is at the immediate mastery level.

5. **Immediate Application Mastery:** When new examples from other short stories that students have heard in read-alouds are given to the class, those students who can identify the point of view and describe each character's perspective are at the *immediate* application mastery level.

6. **Mastery:** On the next day or later in the year, when students are given a first-person point of view and can describe character perspectives accurately, those students who can identify first person and describe the perspectives accurately later are at the **mastery level**.

7. **Application Mastery:** Finally, those students who can identify the point of view, the perspectives of characters in independent reading as well as in any story they read independently are at the application mastery[3] level. These students are building a very concrete understanding of how an author "crafts" a story. Thus, identifying the point of view is the first step, but application mastery means that the student understands why the point of view was chosen.

Developing a Mastery Orientation

When students' individually set goals are focused on grades or competition with their peers, they have a performance orientation; they want recognition through honor rolls, grade point averages, and Advanced Placement test scores. On the other hand, students with a mastery orientation or mastery mindset:

> have learning goals—they are concerned with increasing their competence and abilities while mastering new tasks over time. (Snipes, Fancsali and Stoker, 2012, p. 3)

Goal setting provides a focus on mastery for students. As described in Chapter 6, students select one or two behaviors to self-assess for the term. Their weekly assessment of progress looks at developing their competence, and so does not focus on grades, but mastery.

Delale-O'Connor et al. (2012) found three general strategies for developing a mastery orientation:

- Provide meaningful tasks
- Provide challenging but attainable tasks
- Focus on the value of learning (Delale-OConnnor et al., 2012, p. 5)

The first two strategies often take place in classrooms in which students work on worthwhile tasks that are sufficiently challenging so that all students are learning, yet not so challenging that they are outside the students' capacity. These attainable tasks are created by the teacher, but the focus on the value of learning is a function of teacher feedback. The teacher needs to describe: 1) the quality of the work at this moment, and 2) the next step for improving it. She could say, "This first paragraph could capture the reader's attention more effectively

---

3   Application mastery is like what Grant Wiggins and Jay McTighe refer to as transfer in teaching *for understanding* (Wiggins and McTighe 2011).

with an example." The feedback demonstrates the teacher's focus on the student's mastery, not on grades. This revision shows your work on finding a good example for the first paragraph," shows the student that the teacher is responding to that student's learning, not just on grades.

On the other hand, although a high grade indicates success, and great work is certainly positive, if a teacher says, "A 92! Great work!" a student would not walk away knowing his strengths or next steps toward mastery. How can he get an A+? If, instead, the teacher said, "This paper is a solid paper, and if you want to improve further, work on your analysis statements. They are clear, but could go further and connect to the major claim of the paper." This shift from grades to the personal gain in learning makes students want to learn, not just to get a good grade.

Students need to know where they are in the learning process. A checklist of steps provides structure. Milestones provide clear feedback as students work through the unit. A clear rubric provides the level of performance that is expected. Examples make the expectation of quality even clearer. Using both a checklist and a rubric, students can gauge where they are in terms of the process and the quality of their work at every step in the process. This knowledge gives students a sense that they have control over the mastery of the unit or project. These supports give students help in self-management and self-awareness.

> *Students need to know where they are in the learning process... Milestones provide clear feedback as students work through the unit.*

Sample Checklist and Rubric with Milestones for Secondary Socratic Seminar

What Is the American Dream? Is Gatsby an American Dreamer or an American Failure?

The final expectation for the unit is your argument about the American Dream. You can write a traditional paper, write a film and literature review that could be submitted online to Rotten Tomatoes, create a more visual argument with technology (PowerPoint) or illustrate and write using chart paper. As the rubric describes, you need to have a claim, provide evidence from the text or films, and analyze your evidence.

Below are the dates and the expectations of the major milestones for this unit.

- **Milestone 1:** Daily exit slips that summarize the day's progress as you begin research on your character and film. Your progress and an evolving possible thesis is to be passed in daily.

- **Milestone 2:** Before the Socratic seminar, the group will develop an outline of their argument with specific examples and quotes and will review it with the teacher during class time.

- **Milestone 3:** Self-assess your participation in the Socratic seminar using the rubric and assess your group's work. (See Chapter 6 for an example of a group participation rubric.)

- **Milestone 4:** Final product checks. Before you pass in your final paper, use this sheet and the rubric with a peer and review the checklist with one another and use the rubric on the draft of the final project. Pass the checklist and rubric in at the end of that session.

- **Final Milestone:** On the due date, this checklist, the argument rubric signed by a peer, the draft and the final paper are due.

Table 8.2 Grades 3–11 Reading and Argument Writing Rubric

	Score of 4	Score of 3	Score of 2	Score of 1
Reading/Research X ___ = ___	The writing – • makes effective use of available resources • skillfully/effectively supports an opinion with relevant and sufficient facts and details from resources with accuracy • uses credible sources	The writing – • makes adequate use of available resources • supports an opinion with relevant and sufficient facts and details from resources with accuracy • uses credible sources	The writing – • makes limited use of available resources • inconsistently supports an opinion with relevant and sufficient facts and details from resources with accuracy • inconsistently uses credible sources	The writing – • makes inadequate use of available resources • fails to support an opinion with relevant and sufficient facts and details from resources with accuracy • attempts to use credible sources
Development X ___ = ___	The writing – • addresses all aspects of the writing task with a tightly focused response • skillfully develops the claim(s) and counterclaims fairly, supplying sufficient and relevant evidence for each while pointing out the strengths and limitations of both in a manner that anticipates the audience's knowledge level and concerns	The writing – • addresses the writing task with a focused response • develops the claim(s) and counterclaims fairly, supplying sufficient and relevant evidence for each while pointing out the strengths and limitations of both in a manner that anticipates the audience's knowledge level and concerns	The writing – • addresses the writing task with an inconsistent focus • inconsistently develops the claim(s) and counterclaims fairly, supplying sufficient and relevant evidence for each while pointing out the strengths and limitations of both in a manner that anticipates the audience's knowledge level and concerns	The writing – • attempts to address the writing task but lacks focus • attempts to establish a claim or proposal • supports claim(s) using evidence that is insufficient and/or irrelevant
Organization X ___ = ___	The writing – • effectively introduces precise claim(s); distinguishes the claim(s) from alternate or opposing claims • effectively creates an organization that establishes clear relationships among claim(s), counterclaim(s), reasons, and evidence • skillfully uses words, phrases, and/or clauses to link the major sections of the text, create cohesion, and clarify the relationships between claim(s) and reasons, between reasons and evidence, and between claim(s) and counterclaims • provides an effective concluding statement or section that follows from and skillfully supports the argument presented	The writing – • introduces precise claim(s); distinguishes the claim(s) from alternate or opposing claims • creates an organization that establishes clear relationships among claim(s), counterclaim(s), reasons, and evidence • uses words, phrases, and/or clauses to link the major sections of the text, creates cohesion, and clarifies the relationships between claim(s) and reasons, between reasons and evidence, and between claim(s) and counterclaims • provides a concluding statement or section that follows from and supports the argument presented	The writing – • introduces the claim(s); however, may fail to distinguish the claim(s) from alternate or opposing claim(s) • has a progression of ideas that may lack cohesion (ideas may be rambling and/or repetitive) • inconsistently uses words, phrases, and/or clauses to link the major sections of the text, creates cohesion, and clarifies the relationships between claim(s) and reasons, between reasons and evidence, and between claim(s) and counterclaims • provides a sense of closure	The writing – • identifies the claim(s) • has little or no evidence of purposeful organization

	Score of 4	Score of 3	Score of 2	Score of 1
Language/Conventions	**The writing –** • demonstrates an exemplary command of standard English conventions • skillfully employs language and tone appropriate to audience and purpose • has sentences that are skillfully constructed with appropriate variety in length and structure • follows standard format for citation with few errors*	**The writing –** • demonstrates a command of standard English conventions; errors do not interfere with understanding • employs language and tone appropriate to audience and purpose • has sentences that are generally complete with sufficient variety in length and structure • follows standard format for citation with few errors*	**The writing –** • demonstrates a limited and/or inconsistent command of standard English conventions; errors may interfere with understanding • inconsistently employs language and tone appropriate to audience and purpose • has some sentence formation errors and/or a lack of sentence variety • follows standard format for citation with several errors*	**The writing –** • demonstrates a weak command of standard English conventions; errors interfere with understanding • employs language and tone that are inappropriate to audience and purpose • has frequent and severe sentence formation errors and/or a lack of sentence variety • follows standard format for citation with significant errors*

Argumentation/Opinion Text-Based Writing Rubric Grades 9–10. Delaware Department of Education.
file:///C:/Users/dbrad/Downloads/Gr11-12_Argument_2-13.pdf

Student engagement requires far more than teaching the content at the appropriate level of mastery for each student. Appropriate pacing moves through the content quickly enough to keep students engaged, but does not move so quickly that students are lost or overwhelmed. Some of the factors that contribute to correct pacing are giving clear and concise directions, using effective questioning techniques, classroom routines, attention signals, and sufficiently provisioning materials discussed more fully in Chapters 4 and 5.

Conclusion

Social-emotional skills play an essential role in student engagement. Students need to be aware of their attitudes, manage their emotions, work with the teacher and peers, and make good decisions to maintain a strong connection to their learning. The student's relationship with the teacher as described in Chapter 2 can support a student's engagement. Students need a sense of belonging to succeed academically. A good relationship between the student and the teacher is a strong motivator for positive behavior and academic achievement. Without that critically important rela-

tionship, and without the trusted support for the students' success, students can disengage.

This chapter details two major interventions that support student engagement. Teachers need to create engaging classrooms and support a motivating, positive growth mindset so that their students do not become disengaged or, far worse, become defiant. Two measures are essential. First, students need to believe they are capable and supported. Second, students need to be motivated by a passionate, enthusiastic teacher so that they see the work as worthwhile and meaningful.

To provide this positive mindset of confidence and competence, students need assurance that their teachers will support their success throughout the learning process. Their teacher needs to provide clear feedback, differentiate instruction, and scaffold the tasks so that each student can learn effectively through every milestone, through every step of the journey in the student's growth toward mastery. For students to see the worthiness of the work, the teacher's passion and enthusiasm are essential. Students need to use their social-emotional skills to truly engage in the classroom and see their work through the lens of a mastery mindset and see that not grades, but *their own learning* is the destination.

Discussion Questions for Reflection

Chapter 8

1. Chapter 8 concerns itself with connecting academics and social-emotional learning. **Select a passage that resonates with you and relate it to your practice.**

   Mastery v. Good grades: students work on 1-2 goals/term and their mastery is determined by their learning/application - not grades, competition, comparison

2. In ideal circumstances, all of your students are authentically engaged in learning. In real life, you will find that in an inclusive classroom of diverse learners, students may fluctuate in their ability and desire to attend. Students who may stall at the "ritual compliance" stage will need more assistance in getting back to engagement. Students who have entered into the lower levels of engagement may struggle with self-esteem or a self-defeatist attitude. **Name one strategy that would move a student at the ritual compliance stage to strategic compliance stage.**

   Foster enthusiasm - allow partner sharing

3. **How do you demonstrate enthusiasm in your teaching? Think of an example of how you encouraged students to develop a positive attitude toward themselves and their work.**

9

The Classroom Management Plan
Social, Emotional, and Academic Learning

This is a how-to chapter. It provides two specific Classroom Management Plans (CMPs) for elementary and secondary classrooms and and some concrete first steps in planning and establishing a classroom that supports both academics and social-emotional skills throughout the school year.

An effective CMP supports the development of social-emotional learning skills all day each day without detracting from important learning time. All five of the skills, self-management, self-awareness, social awareness, relationship management, and responsible problem solving are addressed in the elementary and secondary CMP. The specific CMP activities are described and linked to social-emotional skills at the end of this chapter.

If anything, the SEL considerations enhance the quality of learning and do not take away from the academic needs of students. These two Classroom Management Plans explicitly make social-emotional learning an integral part of everyday learning that does not reduce academic time but rather reinforce academics and academic skills and learning.

Chapter 10 is also a "how to" chapter for establishing a classroom meeting, which provides a variety of activities that teachers can use and modify to develop a classroom community that works well together and that is focused on learning.

The areas discussed in Chapters 1 through 9

> *By using these learning-focused techniques and recommendations, social-emotional learning becomes a part of all learning instead of a separate program or curriculum.*

can be used in an effective Classroom Management Plan. By using these learning-focused techniques and recommendations, social-emotional learning becomes a part of all learning instead of a separate program or curriculum. In addition, Chapter 10, Elementary Classroom Meetings and Secondary Advisories: Blending Academics, Social-Emotional Skills, and Community, provides an optional way to add designated periods during the day or week that can be used to support community, SEL skills, and academics.

The Classroom Management Plan gives teachers an opportunity to think through the ways they will structure their classroom time, space, and climate—from organizing the routines to supporting a growth mindset. In creating this Classroom Management Plan, teachers will need to craft their introduction of norms, routines, and activities as carefully as they craft academic lessons. This SEL planning will support academic achievement, the development of a classroom culture, and social-emotional development.

Typically, the Classroom Management Plan applies to all students, although occasionally a student may need an additional plan with individual modifications to support social and academic success. These individual contingency plans for difficult behavioral concerns were addressed in Chapter 7.

Developing Your Socially, Emotionally, Academically Supported CMP

The following questions based upon the contents in the first nine chapters can serve as a guide for your SEL Classroom Management Plan. Specific examples of an elementary and secondary plan follow these questions. The questions are organized by the book's chapters from one to nine.

Chapter 1

1. Have I incorporated all five SEL skills: self-management, cultural awareness, self-awareness, social awareness, and problem solving?
2. How will I support a growth (mastery orientation) mindset by emphasizing the value of mastering meaningful, challenging tasks instead of basing learning on performance and grades?
3. How will I address the different needs of students: low motivation students, boys, girls, English learners, special education students, and students who have experienced trauma?

Chapter 2

1. How will I support and develop positive relationships with my students?
2. How will I support and develop positive relationships between and among peers?
3. How will I use the nine recommendations of the Measures to Develop Positive Relationships with Students, for example, in communicating positive expectations, calling on students equitably, using wait time, communicating caring and acceptance, and reducing stress?
4. How will I use goal setting and the Habits of Successful Students to support SEL and academic growth?
5. How will I model, develop, and assess group work skills: roles, attentive listening, appropriate commenting, and respect?
6. Will I need to introduce the Peer Conflict Resolution Protocol as part of the classroom plan?

Chapter 3

1. How will I create a safe, positive classroom space and climate?
2. How will I organize desks, centers, materials, and technology for the most effective learning environment?
3. How will I support cultural awareness in the classroom to support diversity for all students, for EL students, for special education students, etc.?

Chapter 4

1. In what order will I teach routines and expectations?
2. How will I model, scaffold, and support students for effective group work?
3. How will I model, scaffold, and support student self-assessment, reflection, and accountability?
4. How will I model, scaffold, and support peer assessment?
5. What homework processes and procedures will I establish? What will I include in my letter home? How will I communicate with parents throughout the year?

Chapter 5

1. How will I engage students who are disconnected and uninvolved?
2. How will I develop a collaborative classroom to support respectful and accountable academic talk?
3. How will I develop challenging, meaningful tasks to engage students?

Chapter 6

1. How will students set SEL (Habits of Successful Students) and academic goals?
2. How often will they reflect? What will I use for a form?
3. How often will they conference with me?

Chapter 7

1. What are consequences for inappropriate behavior?
2. How will I develop an individual contingency plan for students who need modifications and additional supports?
3. Have I decided on group rewards that will be an incentive to the class but do not violate my beliefs, those of my team, and/or those of the school culture?
4. Have I developed a coherent and consistent system by which the students and the class may earn the rewards?
5. How will I give effective praise and feedback?
6. How will I use language to assure a cooperative and collaborative classroom? What words will I avoid and ask students to avoid using?

Chapter 8

1. How will I provide an engaging classroom with meaningful, challenging work?
2. How will I teach to and differentiate for the appropriate level of mastery for each student?
3. How will I support students so that they feel competent and supported as they strive toward autonomy?

Sample Elementary Classroom Management Plan

I. Opening Days

I will spend a substantial part of the first two weeks of school modeling and practicing with my students the rules, norms, and social-emotional and academic expectations in my classroom; at the same time I will model and establish a community of trust and concern for others, as well as a community where all voices are respected.

1. Model and Develop Classroom Rules, Norms, and Expectations:
   a. The class will collaboratively brainstorm a list of ideas that students feel are important in helping them achieve their desired goals. Each table group will present its ideas.
   b. In table groups, the class will synthesize these rules into four or five general categories. (Categories may include rules about how we speak to and listen to each other, rules about how we take care of things, rules about how we do our work, and rules about physical and emotional safety issues.)
   c. The rules will be posted in the classroom and will be revisited daily at the end of each class as each student assesses how well we have followed our classroom norms. Students will stick a "red dot" next to any rule that was not followed and a blue dot for all that were followed well. On the next day, we will begin class by discussing the dots and how norms may have been followed or broken. We'll review them until the rules are established, then periodically we'll review—perhaps after vacations or if behavior becomes problematic. Students sign the poster with the list of rules.
   d. The class will discuss, model, and role-play (where appropriate) what adherence to each of these rules looks like.
   e. I will insure that all students not only follow, but that they also understand the importance and purpose of respecting classroom rules, routines, and expectations.

2. Discuss, Model, and Practice Classroom Routines:
   a. In the first two weeks, we will practice morning routines. For example, we will practice morning routines, beginning with unpacking book bags, placing book bags and coats in lockers, making lunch choices, reading the morning news or message and following the directions given in the morning message.
   b. We will also practice quietly lining up and walking down the halls, transitioning from one activity to another—desk to rug, to centers, to line up—and effectively working in groups, as well as many other routines.
   c. I will create a mental (or written) list of questions and praise statements that develop social-emotional learning that support the idea that everyone is both a leader and a learner in this classroom.

3. Assign Clusters of Four Students:
   a. Name tags will inform students of their seats. We will model the skills needed to sit near another student without infringing on one another's personal space or disturbing one another's work, behavior on the rug, in centers, lining up, etc.

4. Build Community:
   a. The class will participate in daily Getting to Know You activities and projects.
   b. Activities such as turn-and-talk, processing partners, scavenger hunt, and an interest survey will be completed independently and shared in the scavenger hunt and in morning meetings. These activities will be incorporated into different subject areas and will provide some review of the curriculum for students. See Chapter 10 for a full description of the scavenger hunt with a student interest survey.

continued on following page

5. Model How to Share Work Before Assigning the Task:
   a. Also, I will model how to respond when others share work using the response to student work self-assessment rubric (see Chapter 4, Tables 4.8 and 4.9 for peer- and self-assessments of collaborative work).
   b. Use a fishbowl and student volunteers to model this process for the class. See Chapter 10 for a full description of the fishbowl.

6. Assign Homework:
   a. The first night's homework assignment will include a questionnaire asking parents to answer a variety of questions about their children and acknowledging the importance of parental involvement and communication.
   b. Students will also be asked to complete a reflection sheet about their first day of school that will provide parents and me with more information about this year's classroom expectations and activities.

7. Model How to Organize Desks, Tablets, Binders:
   a. We will generate a list and use the Peer Assisted Learning (PALS)1 process to have students teach and check one another's organization in a socially positive way.

8. Model Purposes of Reading, Math, and Writing Centers:
   a. To prepare, I'll work with two volunteers for each center who will model the work in their center.
   b. Students will be given opportunities to practice using each of these centers; the two volunteers will "host" their center and will support practice using the PALS approach.

9. Explain the Portfolio System:
   a. Two volunteers will help model peer feedback, self-reflection, editing, revising, and publishing.
   b. We'll post an anchorchart with models, checklists, and rubrics for the portfolio.
   c. As a class, we will decide what types of things should be placed in a portfolio.

---

1 PALS Reading and Math were developed by researchers at Vanderbilt University to help teachers accommodate diverse learners.

II. Building Relationships

1. Initially, I will write a morning message specific to the class every day to acknowledge successes of the class, offer encouragement when it is needed, and ask students to complete a task relevant to the curriculum. As the year progresses, this responsibility will go to one table group a week. In the first weeks, we'll review the dots voting on how well classroom norms were followed.

2. We will begin each morning with a meeting. We'll establish a **greeting or icebreaker** through which everyone is individually included and welcomed into the community. The meetings will also include time for **sharing** so that by the end of the month, everyone has an opportunity to share. We'll do a **community-building or problem-solving** activity, with a read-aloud or an incident that took place in the school. These discussions will establish respectful talk and attentive listening. Each component of the meeting will be introduced and practiced gradually. See Chapter 10 for a more detailed description of the components and purposes of the Classroom Meeting.

3. I will greet students as they come into the classroom each morning as well as in hallways and in the lunchroom.

4. I will use an interest survey during the first weeks of school to learn about each child's interests and use their interests to support student engagement. See Chapter 10 for an example. We will use information from this survey during the morning meeting in a Give-one/Get-one activity and a scavenger hunt for Who Is the Person Who….

5. I will make myself available to work with all students both before and after school.

6. I will attend my students' sporting events and performances when appropriate.

7. I will maintain consistent contact with parents through a classroom website, phone calls, twitter, text messages and quarterly breakfasts to share projects students have completed in class.

8. Students will set social-emotional goals based on the "Habits of Successful Students" (Chapter 4) rubric that I've modified to connect directly to our classroom routines and expectations. Students will evaluate themselves and I will conference with them at least every month. This process will

be modeled until goal setting, charting progress, reflecting on progress, and conferencing are clear for each student and for the class as a whole.

III. Consistent Clear, High, but Appropriate Expectations

I will consistently model all rules and expectations with clear and logical consequences that will be posted on a class goals anchor chart to monitor class progress toward a reward.

1. **Consequences will be logically and restoratively connected to the behavior.**
   For example:
   a. If a student hurts another child's feelings, he/she may "fix" this by writing an apology letter or asking that child to play a special game at recess.
   b. If a student repeatedly chooses not to complete homework, he/she also chooses to lose free choice time to complete the assigned homework.
   c. If a student has become particularly disruptive during group work, a time-out may be necessary. In this situation, the student would remove himself/herself from the group and work independently on the task.
   d. When a conflict between two students becomes problematical to the two students and/or to the class, I will conduct a Peer Conflict Resolution conference to resolve conflicts.as described fully in Chapter 7.

2. **Handle disruptive cases with time-outs and alternative locations.**
   If a student continues to be disruptive, I may ask him or her to work in a separate location, for example, the back of my colleague's classroom. (Author's Note: This arrangement needs to be discussed in advance. This change of scenery can be helpful for some students.) As a last resort, I would send the student to the resource/behavioral room and seek out support from administrators, guidance counselors, or school psychologists. In schools where no such room exists, this may be the point at which the student is sent to the office. If the student appears to be out of control, it may be necessary to escort him or her or to call the resource teacher for additional assistance.

3. **Use loss of privilege as a consequence.**
   In this instance, the student loses an opportunity that he/she might otherwise have had. For example, a student who is consistently talking to a neighbor in class may lose a part of his/her free-choice time. Note: loss of privilege is the consequence in those circumstances in which there is not a readily usable logical consequence.

IV. Group Incentive System

I will use a group incentive system to reward my students for good work and behavior. As a class, students need to earn a total of fifteen points to earn the chosen incentive.

1. The incentive will be decided upon collaboratively. The following incentives will be considered and may change during the year:
   a. Fifteen minutes of extra recess at the end of the day
   b. Fifteen minutes of a team-building activity
   c. Fifteen minutes of an educational game
   d. A special snack
   e. A pizza party during lunch time

2. We will brainstorm and discuss how the class may earn points. We will consider:
   a. Doing something extra to help another class or student
   b. Reducing lost class time through efficient transitions from one subject to another
   c. Achieving a class goal
   d. Doing exemplary collaborative work during literature circles or problem solving during other activities
   e. Hearing from a specialist or substitute teacher that classwork was notably good

We will distinguish between norms and these exceptional acts. Students will brainstorm a list and this will be part of the Class Goals Anchor Chart where the class will keep score during Classroom Meeting every week.

V. Individual Contingency Plans

Individual contingency plans are for those students who are unable to experience success within the classroom management plan. See Chapter 7 for a sample Contingency Plan for a secondary student.

Sample High School Classroom Management Plan

I. Opening Days

I will spend a substantial part of the first two weeks of school modeling and practicing the rules, norms, and social-emotional and academic expectations with students in my classroom; at the same time, I will model and establish a community of trust and concern for others as well as a community where all voices are respected.

1. The class will post its classroom expectations and norms that may be called "Constitution (history)," "What Counts (math)," "Third Block Rules." This chart will contain clear and specific expectations that may be uniquely crafted by the class. For example:

   a. How we talk respectfully and academically: Sentence frames for accountable talk will be modeled, practiced, and posted, for example, "To build on what Monica said,' or "I think you said that… Is that right?" "I respectfully disagree with…"

   b. One person speaks at a time (self-management); while someone is speaking, I listen to the message because I may be asked to restate it (social awareness).

   c. Gain attention and appropriately ask permission before leaving your seat (self-awareness, self-management, social awareness).

   d. Treat everyone in the classroom including visitors with respect (self-management, responsible decision making, relationship skills, social awareness).

2. I will reorganize the seating order daily for the first weeks to let everyone know that they are expected to work effectively with all of the students in the class. Initially, students will sit in assigned seats (alphabetically) to enable me to learn their names more quickly. Initially, to facilitate relationship-building, I will group desks in four sets of four. Each day, for community building and to help everyone learn one others' names, students will line up (no talking) by birth month, by birth date in the month, by first name, by last name, and then they will be seated. This will build community and provide an opportunity for students to get to know one another by working together for relatively short periods initially. Initially, the four-person seating arrangements will enable students to have eye contact with one another and to have face-to-face discussions, which are an essential part of the class. As the year progresses, I will organize the seats in ways that support the activities in the classroom from a circle for classroom meetings (advisories) and Socratic seminars to a horseshoe for presentations, to groups of desks drawn together for groups, or to rows for whole-class discussions and assessments.

3. Students will fill out an interest survey and index cards with information about themselves and their parents[2] both for communication and to build community.

4. I will model and the class will practice routines. At times, students will model the behaviors in a fish bowl, for example, how to enter class, organize materials, and a Do Now, and how to conference about writing with a peer and how to do self-assessment.

5. The first day, I will model the first night's homework assignment: how to set up their binders and notebooks and identifying an appropriate at home homework time, space, and routine. They will have their parents read and sign the letter that summarizes the curriculum or course description, homework and makeup processes as well as the expectations for the quality of the coursework and long-term projects. I will post exemplars and rubrics on the class' website for parents.

6. Students will sign the classroom contract signifying their understanding of the classroom expectations. I will photocopy these contracts and keep them on file. Students will be expected to keep their original copies in the front of their binders.

7. I will explain the Choose Your Own Activity incentive system that we will use throughout the year (explained below).

II. Building Relationships

1. I will always make it clear, both orally and in writing, that I am committed to my students' success

---

2 Whenever *parent* is used, we intend it to mean *parent and/or guardian*.

and that I believe they can all succeed if they are willing to challenge themselves and persevere, as well as seek out help when they need it.

2. I will greet students in hallways and in the lunchroom.

3. I will always make positive comments and clear next steps in their work on students' graded work.

4. I will make myself available to work with all students.

5. I will try to attend my students' sporting events and performances.

6. I will make phone calls, texts, or send emails home to parents for positive results at least as much as I call about concerns.

III. Consistent Expectations

From day one, the class will develop norms and self-assess their adherence by voting with a red dot on norms that are not followed and a blue one for norms that are. The first weeks' Do Now will be to reflect upon the previous day's votes and consciously build a community.

1. Consequences will be logically and restoratively connected to the behavior. For example:
   a. If a student hurts another child's feelings, he/she may address this by writing an apology letter or by being appropriately respectful in some way.
   b. If a student has become particularly disruptive during group work, a time-out may be necessary. In this situation, the student would remove himself/herself from the group and work independently on the task.
   c. When a conflict between two students becomes problematical to the two students and/or to the class, I will conduct a Peer Conflict Resolution conference to resolve conflicts.

2. Time-out in more extreme cases
   If a student continues to be disruptive, I may ask him or her to work in a separate location—for example, the back of my colleague's classroom (needs to be discussed in advance). As a last resort, I would send the student to the resource/behavioral room and seek out support from administrators, guidance counselors, or school psychologists. If the student appears to be out of control, it may be necessary to escort him or

her or to call a resource teacher for additional assistance.

3. Loss of privilege includes loss of opportunities that he/she might otherwise have had.
   a. For example, a student who is consistently talking to a neighbor in class may lose a part of his/her free-choice time.

IV. Classroom Disruptions

1. If a student is disruptive, I will cease instruction, turn to squarely face that student, and say that student's name in a calm but firm voice. If the student returns to work, I will say "Thank you" in a pleasant voice and return to my instruction. I will seek opportunities in the future to reinforce his or her appropriate behavior.

2. If the student continues to be disruptive, I will calmly approach that student's desk and repeat the procedure above (but from a closer proximity).

3. If the student continues to be disruptive, I have several options:
   a. I might ask to speak to that student out in the hallway.
   b. I might return to my instruction, but find a moment to move to my desk, find the index card filled out by that student at the beginning of the school year, and *subtly* place the card on the student's desk (with a *whispered* warning that I am considering making a phone call home).
   c. I might ask the student to take a brief walk around the school with the paraprofessional and return when s/he is ready to learn again.
   d. I might send the student on an invented errand: for example, to go to the library to find some materials. The student and I know from an earlier private conversation that he/she is to return at the end of the period to speak to me in private. It is important in such arrangements that the librarian know about the plan.

4. If (as happens in rare cases) the student refuses to leave, I have several options:
   a. I might call the school security guard or police officer (if they exist) to take the student away.

continued on following page

b. I might tell the student, "Well, if you won't leave, please just sit quietly while I teach the rest of the class, and we'll talk about this at the end of class."

c. If I know of an empty classroom nearby, I might instruct the rest of my class to come with me to another classroom and continue my instruction from there. (Note: This option is dependent upon having a strong relationship with most the students.)

V. Group Incentive System

I will use a group incentive system to reward my students for good work and behavior. The incentive will be an educational game of my students' choosing or another activity that the class has selected to be played on Friday or during a shortened class.

1. The length of time that the game is played is dependent upon my students' behavior during the week.

2. For each day that every student is in his or her seat and has begun the Do Now, two minutes are added to the game on Friday.

3. For each day that every student has his or her binder, notebook, and a pen or pencil with him or her at the start of class, I will give the class two minutes toward a game on Friday.

4. I will also offer the opportunity to gain minutes through efficient, successful completion of various in-class assignments and group work.

5. I will keep track of my students' accumulated minutes on their class' posted chart that tracks the class's earned bonus minutes of recess.

6. If the students can accumulate some number of minutes (say, 15 minutes), they will receive an incentive chosen by the class, for example, a lunchroom pizza party, the typical choice.

Conclusion

The Classroom Management Plans described above deliberately and carefully develop community-building activities, strategically arrange the classroom, model expectations and routines, and provide ongoing practice and feedback. Table 9.1 details the specific activities that are developed from the first day of implementing the CMP and their connection to self-awareness, self-management, social awareness, relationship management, and problem solving.

The first weeks of the implementation of the CMP clearly communicate the consequences and rewards for appropriate and inappropriate behaviors. More important, they engage students immediately in ownership and responsibility in the classroom socially and academically.

Table 9.1 SEL Skills Developed When Implementing the Classroom Management Plan

Social-Emotional Skills	Descriptions	Explicitly Modeled in the Classroom Management Plan
Self-Awareness	• Identify my emotions, needs and values • Accurately understand my reasons or triggers for doing and saying things • Recognize my strengths and needs • Be self-confident • Feel that what I do makes a difference	• First day of school: students reflect on the first day and share with parents.
Self-Management	• Set goals, work toward them, and monitor (measure) progress • Seek out help when I need it (self-advocate) • Control my impulses • Display grit, determination, perseverance • Exhibit positive emotions: hope, optimism, motivation • Manage my stress • Control my behavior • Motivate myself • Organize my day	• Routines are modeled, practiced, and reflected upon. • Norms are modeled, practiced and reflected upon. • How to organize materials is modeled.
Social Awareness	• Recognize social cues from others • Listen closely and accurately • Look at things from others' points of view • Feel empathy for others • Appreciate diversity and differences among people • Respect others feelings and reactions	• The teacher consciously models appropriate responses to others including praise. • "Everyone is a learner and teacher in this classroom." • How to respond to others' work is modeled and practiced. • Respectful ways of talking to one another is modeled in the Classroom Meeting.
Relationship Management	• Communicate my ideas and feelings effectively • Engage with people, make friends • Show leadership skills • Build relationships, help others • Work with a team, cooperatively • Work toward group goals • Prevent interpersonal conflict • Resist inappropriate social pressures	• Community is developed through norm development and the practicing and reflecting on norms and routines. • Getting to Know You activities support the development of a community including interest survey and scavenger hunt (see Chapter 10). • Morning message is eventually the responsibility of a group that communicates an important classroom norm. • Classroom Meetings are held every day in the elementary classroom and on a planned or an as-needed basis on the secondary level depending on time constraints. • The Peer Conflict Resolution conference is modeled (see Chapter 7 for a detailed description).

continued on following page

Social-Emotional Skills	Descriptions	Explicitly Modeled in the Classroom Management Plan
Responsible Decision Making	• Identify problems • Analyze situations • Solve problems • Use strategies to resist peer pressure • Evaluate ideas • Reflect on my actions and thinking • Be ethical and fair	• Classroom norms are developed, synthesized, and assessed by the class. • Classroom responsibilities and consequences are discussed. • Decision making is a major component of the Classroom Meeting described in Chapter 10.

From "Five Overarching Social-Emotional Competencies." Sources: CASEL, 2003; Durlak, Weissberg, Dymnicki, Taylor, and Schellinger, 2011; Elias, 2006; Kress and Elias, 2006; Zins, Payton, Weisberg, and O'Brien, 2007.

Discussion Questions for Reflection

Chapter 9

1. Chapter 9 combines all of the strategies that you have read about and enables you to create an effective SEL Classroom Management Plan. **Select a passage that resonates with you and relate it to your practice.**

   This whole chapter resonated w/ me! I love the sample planning pages and will def. incorporate them into a future position. I also have a better response to my mgt style in an interview

2. **As you create "Getting to Know You" activities, identify how you might utilize this approach in an ELA lesson.**

   Friendship is a common theme in books – what do you look for in a friend?

3. A novice teacher was fearful that she might fall behind in her effort to cover all the curriculum designated by the school system. Within the first week of the school year, she jumped right in to homework and covering course content. She was disappointed when the students seemed to exhibit confusion about requirements and she felt she was dealing with behavioral issues that slowed down the progress of the class. **What routines did she fail to embed within the first weeks of the term that might have improved the productivity and behavior of the group?**

   class goals, rules, consequences, routines, expectations...

10

SEL Classroom Meetings
Blending Skills and Academics K-12

Effective Classroom Meetings can take many forms. Whether elementary students sit in a circle on a rug or pull their desks into a circle in a middle or high school classroom, **the four main components of SEL Classroom Meetings remain the same because the needs for students, whatever their grade, are the same: to develop and sustain a positive educational environment for a community of learners.** The components of the classroom meeting synthesize the essential elements for providing a classroom that supports students' academic and social-emotional growth.

Classroom meetings at all levels originated in early childhood educations' "morning meetings," when preschoolers met to sing, record the weather, and share. More recently, middle and high schools have created their own versions of what this book calls classroom meetings, which take place at different times of day but like the elementary model combine social, emotional, and academic goals.

Classroom Meetings support students' sense of belonging, an essential component for learning academically. In addition, the Classroom Meetings described in this chapter support both academic and social-emotional behaviors through its four components. Below is a list of the essential purposes of a Classroom Meeting:

- to purposefully build a classroom community
- to develop and refine shared goals to which everyone contributes
- to support a safe, respectful place to learn
- to work to develop a collaborative community in which everyone is an expert or leader some of the time and everyone is a learner or follower at other times
- to develop and support social-emotional goals

for the whole class including self-awareness, self-management, social awareness, relationship management, and responsible decision making

- to develop and support academic attitudes and goals that support collaboration, persevering to reinforce the idea that through effort and engagement, students can grow smarter in the major SEL areas: self-awareness, self-management, social awareness, relationship management, and responsible decision making

Dr. Sheldon Berman, as superintendent of the Jefferson County Public Schools in Louisville, Kentucky, implemented a district-wide social-emotional initiative called CARE for Kids. He said:

> 62 percent of our population is on free and reduced lunch. There are a lot of issues at schools where students do their best but still have home environments that make it very difficult for them to be successful in school. And that doesn't mean we give up on academics or we give up on the social skill development. We have to do both rigorously.
>
> **This isn't about being nice. This is serious work. It's serious work to create a sense of community. It's serious work to resolve conflicts. It's serious work to create a positive environment in a classroom. And it's serious work, on the student's part, to be able to manage themselves in a way that is constructive** (Edutopia 2015).

This "serious work" makes a difference both in the behavior and in the academic success of school. As Roger Weissberg, president of CASEL, says, "There's a growing research base that says when you have high-quality social and emotional learning programs, it improves kids' pro-social behavior; it reduces their conduct problems; and it promotes academic engagement, connection to teachers, and academic performance" (Edutopia, 2015).

Organization and Components of Classroom Meetings

Typical components of Classroom Meetings include opportunities for students to use each of the major SEL skills:

- **A greeting or icebreaker** acknowledges everyone individually and welcomes them into the community. This supports self-management, self-awareness, and social-awareness.
- **Sharing** gives everyone in the circle an opportunity to lead and to follow. This activity supports self-management, social-awareness, and relationship management.
- **Community building** activities establish respectful talk. In addition, attentive listening supports social-awareness, relationship management, and effective problem solving.
- **Problem-solving activities** provide a broad range of both academic and social-emotional activities. They support all five of the SEL skills.

These components can be adjusted to be developmentally appropriate for students from early childhood through high school. While earliest Classroom Meetings may begin simply with greeting one another appropriately, in the later grades, advisories often shift toward providing students with opportunities for leadership and independence. An elementary teacher describes the increasing expectations that she has with younger students:

"As the kids get older, you can challenge them a bit more with your expectations," Carr [the elementary teacher] says. Instead of a typical greeting such as, "Good morning, Alli, I hope you have a great day," she might ask them to use an adjective other than great or good, or ask them to ask a question as a part of their greeting. Then, to add another challenge, Carr might have the questioner ask a follow-up question once he or she gets a response to the initial greeting question. "Adding these little tweaks can help promote good listening skills" (Carr, 2000).

At each grade level, the meeting can scale up as

later levels build upon the skills developed in earlier grades in the Classroom Meeting. "Teachers in the higher grades also start incorporating new skills, such as leadership and public speaking, by giving students the opportunity to lead morning meetings either by themselves or with a partner" (Edutopia, 2015).

As a classroom teacher said:

The work accomplished during morning meeting positively supports both social and academic settings in the classroom. Through morning meeting, students are able to practice skills that help support their work during academic periods in the classroom. These skills support the students in becoming more independent and efficient, able to solve problems on their own, thinking critically, respecting fellow students and teachers, and reacting to situations and people with empathy and kindness (Allen-Hughes, 2013).

Allen-Hughes says that, for her as an elementary teacher, the daily Classroom Meeting blended academics and SEL skills and created a "shift" toward a safe and supportive "community of learners" (2013, p. 35). In the Classroom Meeting examples for elementary and secondary students that follow, the clear connection between SEL and learning effectively is provided. In addition, at the end of the chapter, the SEL and academic skills are detailed along with the specific routines of collaborative group work.

Middle schools need a reliable structure to build community, teach social skills, and prepare students for learning each day.

Often secondary schools schedule Classroom Meetings in a variety of ways. Some schools use "home room" time for these meetings while others use flex-blocks or times that are built into the schedule for class meetings, presentations, and advisories.

A middle school adaptation created by Developmental Designs includes what they call the "Circle of Power and Respect" and "Activity Plus" in which students gather for a brief meeting in a circle and then join in middle-school-focused activities, in which the typical morning meeting components are adapted to the needs of middle school students (Bafile, 2009).

In the article, "Morning Meetings in Middle School: An Elementary Ritual Grows Up," Cara Baflie describes the importance of building socially and emotionally safe places for middle school students. **"Middle schools need a reliable structure to build community, teach (rather than assume) social skills, and prepare students for learning each day,"** observes Linda Crawford, executive director of Origins, a nonprofit organization dedicated to fostering learning and community in schools and other educational institutions (Baflie, 2009). Middle schools focus on the SEL skills that support young adolescents' needs for building a sense of independence and competence, getting along in a diverse world, solving problems, and serving the community. A student in New Jersey said that the result of his middle school Classroom Meeting "helped me improve in academics so much, I went from all Cs to As and Bs last term" (Baflie, 2009).

Advisories have been active in high schools since the 1990s, established because of the importance that each student has the support of at least one adult. The New England Association for Secondary Schools and Colleges (NEASC) calls for advisories to support "each student's educational experience." According to Education Northwest in "What the Research Says (Or Doesn't Say): Advisory Programs" (REL Northwest, 2011), research indicates that providing these supports has a positive impact behaviorally and academically on students.

High schools often call their Classroom Meetings advisories and change their focus in each of the four years of high school on the developmental issues that high school students face as they transition into high school and, after four years, exit into colleges and careers.

On elementary and secondary levels, all Classroom Meetings are undergirded by both academic and SEL goals that support high academic and interpersonal expectations. The research on morning meeting at the elementary and middle school level confirms that clearly organized meetings support student achievement (Brock et al., 2008). Research in elementary and middle schools found that classrooms with meetings had improved emotional support for students and improved classroom organization (Responsive Classroom, 2017).

At all levels, these carefully structured Classroom Meetings set a positive tone for social interaction, develop a climate of trust, provide motivation, support a collaborative and more empathetic environment, and support SEL skills (Dabbs, 2013). When SEL is part of the school culture, these skills can effectively enhance student growth **as much as an 11-percentile-point gain in achievement in mathematics and reading** (CASEL, 2011). Research clearly demonstrates that SEL-supported classrooms provide a positive, supportive climate for learning in which less time is spent on management and more on learning

> *These carefully structured classroom meetings set a positive tone for social interaction, develop trust, provide motivation, support a collaborative and empathetic environment, and support SEL skills.*

(Brock 2008, Gardner 2012, Grant and Davis 2012, Gibbs, 2006, Kagan, Robertson, and Kagan, 1995, Rimm-Kaufman 2011).

The Classroom Meeting Through an Author's Eyes

My first experience with holding a Classroom Meeting was as a middle school social studies teacher in 1981. It was my fourth year of teaching and I was two years into working toward my master's degree in guidance and counseling at night. The school was a K-8 school in the White Mountains of New Hampshire with many students from poverty or near poverty. There was not a guidance counselor and so there were no programs for classroom guidance or counseling support in general.

One of the other teachers I worked with was also working on a graduate degree in counseling. Together we began to run a Classroom Meeting once each week during recess. We gathered my homeroom together in a circle and tried to address some of the interpersonal issues that are typical in all middle schools. We both had received training in therapeutic group counseling, but at that time there was no training available for running effective Classroom Meetings. It is difficult to know how much success we had. Since no one was researching results, we had no concrete data to show any impact on student behavior or performance.

The following year, I accepted a fifth-grade teaching job in a very affluent public school in Brookline, Massachusetts. This school was also a K-8 school and had a full-time guidance counselor. The guidance counselor was very good and worked very effectively with students individually and in small groups. She also served as an invaluable resource for classroom teachers as we worked to address students' personal and interpersonal struggles. However, we did not develop a Classroom Meeting model run by teachers. In moving to a new state and school district, my first year was very busy learning the curriculum and focusing on my academic teaching. Since there wasn't an established whole class Classroom Meeting model in the district, I did not run Classroom Meetings. I did, however, run small recess groups when issues would arise. I remember several meetings with a group of six girls who were enduring continuous conflict and verbal bullying.

My second-year teaching fifth grade was 1986, the year of the space shuttle *Challenger* disaster. Since all of us had been watching the lift off and the resulting tragedy, all the students were aware. We were all strongly encouraged to discuss the issue with our students and the counselor moved from classroom to classroom. I used a Classroom Meeting model similar to the one I used in my previous job. I was thankful that I had previous experience to draw on to run the meetings about the disaster. Since the district had not yet adopted Classroom Meetings as a part of the curriculum, I ended the full class meetings and continued with small group meetings on an as-needed basis.

The next year I became the vice principal in the school. I no longer had a homeroom in which to have Classroom Meetings. One of my roles was as the school disciplinarian and my "meetings" were limited to groups of students when there was an issue of a disciplinary nature. I worked closely with the counselor using my counseling skills as the basis of how I addressed discipline throughout the school.

In 1988 I became a principal of a K-5 school. In this book's Introduction, I described my experience in the first school-wide Classroom Meeting in the district. A lesson I learned during those five years was that most of the skills we teach in traditional classrooms can be taught equally well by classroom teachers in the context of their daily classroom management.

Thirty years of experience leaves me believing these two points:

1. There are teachers who effectively achieve that objective with regularly scheduled full-class Classroom Meetings to complement their daily work managing the classroom (as noted in Chapters 1–9).
2. There are teachers who achieve that objective using class meetings on an as-needed basis to address full class issues that are better addressed with the entire class (e.g., death or terminal illness of a classmate or a child's parent).

We continue to be a strong proponents of daily Class Meetings for all preschool and primary grade classrooms. Children at these developmental levels need the daily review of the day's events, instruction and/or reminders about interpersonal interactions (e.g., respecting personal space, dealing with conflict), and activities that lead to greater self-awareness and growth mindset. My preferred arrangement for these meetings is to seat students on a rug or in chairs facing one another in a circle. The circle facilitates student to student conversation.—*Bill Ribas*

As described above, Classroom Meetings and/or advisories have been developed to appropriately support upper elementary, middle school, and high school meetings—though the components are adjusted to the needs of the students at that age group.

Later in this chapter, specific elementary and high school activities are described in detail. Individual classroom teachers may use the elements throughout their week, making sure that they address the community building, SEL skills, and academic skills supported in these groups: deliberate inclusion of everyone in the class as a learner and leader, who participates by respectfully listening to others and offering cogent, supportive responses. When classroom norms seem to have become inconsistent, a teacher may then use class time to reaffirm the importance of learning in a safe and challenging classroom.

The Four Main Components of a SEL Classroom Meeting

The Classroom Meeting shown in Figure 10.1 has a very simple four-part structure, with four activities that can be adjusted for the specific grade level, time availability, and needs of the group. Students assemble in a circle. Kindergarten children may sit on an **X** provided on a rug and secondary students may arrange their desks in a circle, but the important function of the circle is that everyone is included equally and everyone's contribution is respected.

- **A greeting or icebreaker** through which everyone is individually included and welcomed into the community
- **Sharing**—everyone has an opportunity to lead and to follow
- **Community building** activities that establish respectful talk and attentive listening along with both academic and social-emotional **problem-solving activities**
- **The Day's Lesson, News, or Focus** component, which varies each day

The end of this chapter has examples of the activities mentioned above at the early childhood, upper elementary, middle school, and high school levels.

1. Greeting and Ice Breaker Component

The purpose of greetings and ice breakers is to let students know that they *belong to this group*. Teachers may create a special greeting or may model a specific

Figure 10.1 Major Components of Classroom Meetings

way to greet someone: First, you look into the other person's eyes, and you say, "Good morning" and say the other's name in a pleasant voice. The person greeted returns the greeting with a pleasant, "Good morning" and your name. As the year progresses, the greeting or icebreaker may change but making everyone feel welcome is an essential to building community.

The meeting always begins with a greeting to everyone or an ice breaker (see Figures 10.1 and 10.2) for all. The greeting may range from a group hello to a more elaborate series of greetings.

Figure 10.2 Student Survey Ice Breaker

Directions: Please answer every question. The answers may be shared with the rest of the class in a scavenger hunt. I'll use the information also to get to know you as a student.

What I like

1. What is your favorite color? _____
2. What kind of animal would you choose for a pet? _____
3. What is your favorite genre of book (mystery, humorous, fiction, nonfiction)? _____
4. What do you like to do after school? (read, ride my bike, play _____ with friends, etc.) _____
5. What is your favorite ice cream or treat? _____
6. Which is your favorite team? _____
7. Do you have any brothers or sisters? If you do, how many? _____
8. What do you want to do after you have graduated? _____

Table 10.1 Greeting and Icebreaker

Components of Classroom Meeting	Elementary Examples	Middle and High School Examples
Greeting and Icebreaker	Everyone greets the student on their left and right. Scavenger hunt for "The Person who…" based on Interest Survey (See below.) The "Speaking Ball" is tossed to another student. The person tossing the ball must call out that student's name.	For the first weeks, every day the seating plan is organized by last name, then first, then birthday month, birth date, etc. Students introduce one another and do brief tasks that reveal their interests. Students seek out different processing partners to work briefly on answering questions together.

Figure 10.2 Scavenger Hunt Ice Breaker

Below are things some people in our class like: people, activities, food, colors Find someone who likes one of them and ask that person to sign the square. Try to fill all nine squares with different names. Begin by asking, "What do you like on this list?" When you've finished, return to your space.		
GREEN	A PUPPY	S'MORES
SCARY BOOKS	THE RED SOX	MY OLDER BROTHER OR OLDER SISTER
I PLAY JENGA WITH MY BROTHER AFTER SCHOOL	MY BABY SISTER OR BROTHER	I WANT TO BE A FOOTBALL COACH

Table 10.3 Classroom Meeting Sharing

Components of Classroom Meeting	Elementary Examples	Middle and High School Examples
Sharing	**Elementary** Initially the sharing is simple (middle name) and it will become more detailed as the year goes on (give an example of when a student saw a classmate do a random act of kindness)	**Secondary** Using turn-and-talk, initially students share in two's, and the sharing may have a social-emotional component (share your best school day) or an academic component or combine both (what qualities make Gatsby great?)

2. Sharing Component

Sharing, too, is a brief component of the group meeting. The purpose of this component is to have students actively engaged in building relationships with one another. As described in the elementary section of Table 10.3, students might share their middle name or everyone might share their favorite color. This should be a time for everyone to share with at least one partner, not just a single person with the whole group. The sharing can focus on social-emotional awareness as described in the secondary section in Table 10.3 when students share their best day at school or on academic areas when students decide if Gatsby is great and why.

The many group activities discussed below in "Group Work and Classroom Meeting Activities That Support Social, Emotional, and Academic Development" can be used, in addition to the read-aloud, to engage all students in the activity. So, for example, if the read-aloud is *Charlotte's Web* and the passage read-aloud is on being a friend, students can do a Get the Gist activity and summarize the ideas in 10 words or less, or the teacher could have students do an interactive reading in pairs and then share what they've read about friendship on chart paper. These activities are appropriate for secondary students who could read one of four articles in a Jigsaw and then share their expertise in a group.

3. Community Building or Problem-Solving Component

The third component may combine SEL and academics. For example, in the elementary section of Table 10.4, the teacher may select an engaging read-aloud to connect with a topic or concern that the children have. Similarly, the secondary meeting may focus on a brief video, an article, or a situation that will engage the students in understanding one another better or in solving problems.

To get students moving, Agree/Disagree with Your Feet could be used to activate a discussion about mindfulness. The teacher could ask, "How much pressure do you feel from school?" on a scale from 1–10. Those who answer 1 go the back corner; if 5, they go to the middle of the room; and if 10 they go to the front of the room. The teacher could continue with questions such as, "Who would try yoga to de-stress?" Who would try sports?" After each question, students move to different parts of the room. The teacher can ask those who chose similar numbers to explain their reasoning. Academic questions can also be asked in this kind of group work.

The class can also be asked to solve a problem, which could come from a story, a case study, a recent event in the school, or an article from current events, history, or literature. For example, the class could be organized into a fishbowl with the students who will have the first discussion in a small circle in the center of the rest of the class. The problem could be what should be done with cell phones during school time, or for elementary students, how to share the swings, and the center group would begin to discuss the problem. The class would then stop and list the ideas on each side and those in the outside circle could continue the discussion or rank the solutions from the most possible to the least possible. The teacher should make sure the discussion ends on a positive note and that the positive contributions are recognized.

4. The Day's Lesson, News, or Focus Component

The purpose of this component is to send students off with a positive focus, ready to work for the remainder of the day. A lesson could come from the Community Building or a Problem-Solving activity, or it could focus on SEL skills that the students are developing. It could serve as a transition to the next

Table 10.4 Community Building and/or Problem-Solving Activity

Components of Classroom Meeting	Elementary Examples	Middle and High School Examples
Community Building and/or Problem Solving	**Elementary** The teacher may do a read-aloud that connects with a school or classroom concern or with an academic theme that is engaging for the students. Students may solve problems for characters in the story or for their community.	**Secondary** Initially the teacher may bring in an article, story, picture, or even a short video to inspire a conversation that connects to the class. For example, if cultural awareness was a focus or needed to be one, the documentary called "God Grew Tired of Us" about the Lost Boys of Sudan with questions from the National Geographic Xpeditions lessons, or "God Grew Tired of Us: Migration and Cultural Interaction" or "God Grew Tired of Us: Culture Clash and Community-Building" could be shown to discuss points of view of looking at American culture as a newcomer and as a long-time person sees it.

Table 10.5 The Day's Lesson, News, or Focus

Components of Classroom Meeting	Elementary Examples	Middle and High School Examples
The Day's Lesson, News, or Focus	A thought of the day, a school activity that week, a saying. Over time, students may create this focus individually or as groups.	A quotation from something the class is studying, a school activity for their class that week, a saying. Over time, students may create this lesson, news or focus individually or as groups.

activity that the class will work on. Table 10.5 shows some examples.

Below are the steps for setting up a variety of group activities that are appropriate for this Classroom Meeting as well as for academics throughout the day.

Setting Norms for Secondary Classrooms

Secondary Classroom Meetings that are not part of the regular school day (as they are in elementary schools), may need to develop norms since the group gathers solely for the purpose of having the meeting. (Chapter 4 provides examples of norm-setting for a general classroom.) The areas that the advisory needs to consider may include:

- the inclusiveness of the meeting; everyone is invited to be part of the conversation.
- the importance that everyone is an equal part and that nobody should "take over" the meeting and do all the talking.

- how to listen respectfully (described in terms of visual behaviors—looks at the speaker, nods or asks appropriate questions).
- how to disagree in a respectful manner.
- how to include everyone in the discussion.
- how to move to a new grouping or arrangement of furniture.
- the role of facilitator (teacher or peer).

The first meeting of an advisory would need to work collaboratively to develop appropriate norms. The language for how to agree, give another credit for an idea, or how to disagree might be modeled by the teacher. In addition, the "accountable talk" examples in Figure 10.3 could be posted.

At the end of each meeting, it is a good idea to reinforce the importance of abiding by the norms by asking students in an exit slip whether any norms were violated and, if they were, how they were. These data are then discussed at the next advisory—without naming a person, but just by indicating that, for example, three people felt that not everyone had an opportunity to speak.

Figure 10.3 Accountable Talk Sentence Starters

I say...	When...
Building on the idea of Jim	I want to give someone credit for an idea
I understand what you're saying, but I'm not clear about	I need to understand more clearly what is being discussed
I hear what you're saying, but I don't agree	I disagree respectfully
Can you give me more details	When I want someone to add to their ideas
Thank you	I want to show appreciation to a classmate
What do you think, Paul?	I see that someone hasn't had a chance to enter the conversation

Group Work and Classroom Meeting Activities That Support Social, Emotional, and Academic Development

Learning how to discuss ideas with peers is an ongoing learning process both for social and academic learning. The activities listed below require modeling and practice, followed by feedback and reflection. They support and scaffold improving academic and social-emotional skills. For example, the activity, "Fishbowl" (below) is followed by a listing of both the academic and SEL skills developed in the activity and by the routine itself.

Agree/disagree, vote with your feet, and living Likert scale activator

Academic Skills: Quick formative assessment, active participation, and varying perspectives

SEL Skills: Impulse control, self-discipline, perspective-taking, respect for others, communication, social engagement, teamwork, analyzing situations, evaluating, reflecting, identifying problems, solving problems

The Routine: The facilitator makes a series of statements about a topic—for example, illegal immigration—and students are asked to indicate their level of agreement or disagreement with each statement on a scale along a wall of the class or by going to a specific corner of the class. One way in which this activator can be used to encourage wider class participation is by asking students to imagine a line cutting across the center of the classroom. Designate one side of the room as the "strongly agree" side and the other side of the room as the "strongly disagree" side. Then, read one of the statements on the activator and ask students to stand up and physically move to the spot along the invisible line that represents the strength of their opinion on the particular statement. Once students have assumed their various positions in the classroom, ask students why they feel the way they do (i.e., why did they choose to stand in that particular spot in the classroom?) This activity can be an effective way of generating a lively discussion and of pulling in some shyer students.

Carousel/Carousel Brainstorming/ Scavenger Hunt

Academic Skills: Sharing information and providing feedback

SEL Skills: Impulse control, self-discipline, perspective-taking, respect for others, communication, social engagement, teamwork, analyzing situations, evaluating, reflecting, identifying problems, solving problems

The Routine: Carousel brainstorming provides scaffolding for new information to be learned or existing information to be reviewed through movement, conversation, and reflection. While taking part in carousel brainstorming, small groups of students rotate around the classroom, stopping at various "stations" for a designated period of time (usually one to two minutes). At each station, students activate their prior knowledge of a topic or concept and share their ideas with their small group. Each group posts their ideas at each station for all groups to read. This can work as a "museum" or a science or art fair. Each station of the carousel could have a "docent," a scientist presenting his or her scientific experiment or research, or an artist presenting his or her artwork. Half of the class can become the audience and walk through the stations while the other half presents. Then, the museum, science fair, or art fair has a different set of displays described by different students. Variations: the students can be assigned specific topics to present as steps in the carousel.

Get the Gist

Academic Skills: Improves comprehension, collaboration, and literacy

SEL Skills: Impulse control, self-discipline, perspective-taking, respect for others, communication, social engagement, teamwork, analyzing situations, evaluating, reflecting, identifying problems, solving problems

The Routine: Get the Gist is a comprehension strategy that is used both during reading and after reading. In pairs of two, students are assigned a part of a text to summarize with a specified number of words. When using Gist, students create summaries that are 20 words or less for increasingly large amounts of text.

Fishbowl

Academic Skills: Academic discussion skills, careful listening and giving feedback

SEL Skills: Impulse control, self-discipline, perspective-taking, respect for others, communication, social engagement, teamwork, analyzing situations, evaluating, reflecting

The Routine: Half of the students sit within a circle in a smaller circle, the other half of the students sit around the central group. The students in the inner circle discuss, while those in the outer circle observe and may take notes or evaluate. Then, the two groups switch roles and the inner circle discusses while the outer circle observes. The fishbowl activity allows the teacher to teach routines, SEL skills, and academic conversation skills explicitly. Before the discussion, provide students with the norms for academic discussions, which may include models of how to agree, disagree, or give someone else, a classmate or reference, credit for an idea. Scaffolding and practice can take place before the entire class is divided into an inner and outer circle. Students can practice in smaller groups with the topic that is assigned. Accountability can be supported by asking the outer circle to rate participation on a rubric. Timing: allow half of the time for each half of the class. Provide verbal feedback immediately after the discussion, and provide peer assessments on the following day.

Interactive Annotation/Interactive Reading/Interactive Note-Taking

Academic Skills: Comprehension and deep reading

Specific SEL Skills: Impulse control, self-discipline, perspective-taking, respect for others, communication, social engagement, teamwork, analyzing situations, evaluating, reflecting, identifying problems, solving problems

The Routine: When students work together to annotate the important parts of a text, to read and interpret the text, and to take notes from their reading or from the classroom discussion, they are improving both reading and writing skills. Each partner contributes to the learning. Reading and constructing meaning from a text is a complex and active process; one way to help students slow down and develop their critical analysis skills is to teach them to annotate the text as they read. Suggestions for annotating text can include labeling and interpreting literary devices; labeling and explaining the writer's rhetorical devices and elements of style; or labeling the main ideas, supportive details, and/or evidence that leads the reader to a conclusion about the text. To differentiate, teachers can annotate some of the more difficult parts of a text to aid the students, begin the annotation with the entire class to get them started, or form heterogeneous or homogeneous groups based on skill levels and the teacher's discretion for the best way to proceed.

Jigsaw

Academic Skills: Individual accountability, comprehension, deeper reading, academic discussion skills, and careful listening

Specific SEL Skills: Impulse control, self-discipline, perspective-taking, respect for others, communication, social engagement, teamwork, analyzing situations, evaluating, reflecting, identifying problems, solving problems

The Routine: Students read a section of text assigned to them. When they complete the reading, the students meet for approximately 20 minutes with others assigned to the same topic. They discuss the material, identify the most important learning points, and return to their "home groups" to instruct the others about information in which they have become an "expert." Each student takes turns teaching what he or she has learned to the other home group members.

Numbered Heads Together

Academic Skills: Individual accountability to the group and participation

SEL Skills: Impulse control, self-discipline, perspective-taking, respect for others, communication, social engagement, teamwork, analyzing situations, evaluating, reflecting, identifying problems, solving problems

The Routine: In this activity, students are divided into groups of four, and each one is assigned a letter—A, B, C, or D. The teacher then poses a question or problem for each group to solve. They may work together, but they must make sure that every member of their group can answer the question. After enough time has passed, the teacher says something to the effect of "All right, I will take the answer from anyone who is a *B*." Only the student assigned the letter *B* in each group may answer. The teacher then repeats the process with a new problem, but this time calls on students assigned the letter *D* to answer. This activity creates an opportunity for shyer students to get into the action. If their letter is called, they will likely also receive some positive peer pressure from other members of their group to raise their hands and share the group's response.

Peer-Assisted Learning Systems (PALS)

Academic Skills: Processes are practices for all content area

Specific SEL Skills: Impulse control, self-discipline, perspective-taking, respect for others, communication, social engagement, teamwork, analyzing situations, evaluating, reflecting, identifying problems, solving problems

The Routine: Students work together as a class to describe, step by step, how to solve an algebra problem, for example. The whole class rehearses the protocol of how to solve the problem; the protocol

might be the mathematical order of operations. Then, students alternate as coach and learner in pairs, using the protocol to solve a series of problems until the process is mastered—in this case, until students follow the order of operations effectively. The peer-assisted learning strategy enables teachers to circulate around the classroom and observe students, providing feedback where necessary. The coaches do not "correct," but read the procedure that the student did not follow. Pairs of students are changed regularly, and all students participate as both "coaches" and "players."

A variation of PALS is partner reading. It is a cooperative learning strategy in which two students work together to read an assigned text in any content area. This activity can be a class-wide peer-tutoring program in which teachers carefully partner a student with a classmate or a shared task. The teacher develops the protocol, and the two students follow it carefully. For example, they may each read aloud for five minutes then summarize what they've read. The partner reading strategy allows students to take turns reading and provide each other with feedback to monitor comprehension. Partner reading does not require special reading materials and consequently enables teachers to use the reading material of their choice. The format offers teachers flexibility for incorporating the strategy into various content areas. Partner reading provides direct opportunities for a teacher to circulate in the class, observe students, and offer individual remediation. Each member of the teacher-assigned pair takes turns being "coach" and "player." The coach and the player check their understanding as they read together, alternating every five minutes. The coach reads along and helps the player with any problem words, and then the coach reads while the player reads along. These pairs are changed regularly, and over a period of time as students work. Thus, all students can be coaches and players.

Say-It-in-a-Word and Whip

Academic Skills: Quick formative assessment

SEL Skills: Impulse control, self-discipline, perspective-taking, respect for others, communication, social engagement, teamwork, analyzing situations, evaluating, reflecting, identifying problems, solving problems

The Routine: An activity offered by Walsh and Sattes (2005, p. 71) is called *say-it-in-a-word*. In this activity, the teacher poses a question to the class and asks each student in the class to come up with a single word that best expresses his or her reaction to the question. For example, the music teacher could play a portion of a piece of music, and each student could describe his or her reaction. The teacher could play another and ask for words from each. The students might then be asked if this was probably created by the same composer. This strategy as well can be a powerful tool for drawing in our more reluctant students, and once they have taken a stand on an idea, they are then drawn into a conversation. The Whip or "whip around" is, again, quick answers to a single prompt by everyone in the class.

Scavenger Hunt

Academic Skills: Community building, icebreaker

SEL Skills: Impulse control, self-discipline, perspective-taking, respect for others, communication, social engagement, teamwork, analyzing situations, evaluating, reflecting, identifying problems, solving problems

The Routine: Students are given a list of attributes of other students in the class such as loves puppies, has a blog, has three brothers, etc. Students take the list and need to identify each of the people with the specific characteristics. If the teacher conducts an interest survey, these answers can be used at the beginning of the year to introduce students to one another.

Socratic Seminars, Scaffolded Socratic Seminars, Pinwheels, and Individual/Partner/Small-Group Seminars

Academic Skills: Academic discussion skills, careful listening, giving feedback and deep reading

SEL Skills: Impulse control, self-discipline, perspective-taking, respect for others, communication, social engagement, teamwork, analyzing situations, evaluating, reflecting, identifying problems, solving problems

The Routine for Socratic Seminars: These whole-class discussions explore ideas, values, and issues drawn from readings or works of art chosen for their richness. Teachers and, over time, student facilitators help participants make sense of a text and of their own thinking by asking questions about reasoning, evidence, connections, examples, and other aspects of sound thinking. A good seminar is more devoted to making meaning than to mastering information. Participants are actively engaged in rigorous critical thought. They must involve a relatively short text, piece of art, etc., and after the seminar are often followed by periods of reflection that may be written or spoken. In its simplest form, students are given an unknown work of art and are asked to determine its name based upon the qualities and objects that they see in it. More structured seminars are listed below.

The Routine for Scaffolded Socratic seminars provide more structure to support students' active participation. For example, the class may be divided into four teams that initially study and prepare for the Socratic seminar with an assigned aspect of the topic. One member of each team participates at a time and the team members provide information and feedback, and reflect on their topic after the meeting. The topic could originate in any content area, but, for example, students could research and then take positions on the ethics of genetic research or the data for global warming. In an American history class, students could discuss whether the United States should have dropped atomic bombs on Japan during World War II.

The Routine for Partner/Small-Group seminars are more formal and focused than large-group seminars. A text, graphic, or artwork is selected, and the students analyze the text based on the models and guided practice from class. The students then create a thesis that needs to be supported by evidence and set up the seminar in an outline form. Partners and group members discuss the materials, but each individual is responsible for submitting and presenting his or her own position. For example, students could receive three scientific data collections about the proliferation of the bubonic plague: one that said it was caused by the rise of the city and its lack of cleanliness, another that it was caused by a mutation of the virus, and a third that said it was a "perfect storm" caused by both a mutation and people living so closely together.

Twosomes or Dyads: Turn and Talk, Processing Partners, Paired Verbal Fluency, and Think-Pair-Share

Academic Skills: Time to debrief concepts orally

SEL Skills: Impulse control, self-discipline, perspective-taking, respect for others, communication, social engagement, teamwork, analyzing situations, evaluating, reflecting

The Routine: The following two-person activities can be short (less than a minute) or can be a longer-termed partnership. They can allow the teacher to gradually introduce the students to one another and introduce the idea that all students in this class work with all students.

The Routine for Turn and Talk or Elbow Partners: Two students sitting near one another turn (to the left or right) and discuss. This twosome strategy requires no movement, but gives students time to process the ideas just introduced with little interruption. Teachers can formatively assess students' progress by listening in to some of the conversations.

The Routine for Paired Verbal Fluency: This strategy can be used to activate thinking about a topic or provide an opportunity for review. (1) Establish partners. Have each dyad decide who will be partner No. 1 and partner No. 2. (2) Assign the topic each partner will discuss in turn. Partners listen carefully to each other. During their turn, they try not to repeat anything said by the other person. (3) When the teacher says "go," partner No. 1 begins. After the designated amount of time elapses, the teacher says "switch," and partner No. 2 takes over. The turn-taking can be done more than once if necessary.

The Routine for Processing Partners: This strategy begins with a handout for each student that contains a series of 6 to 10 terms that are content or SEL-skills related terms that will be used during a unit or year. Each term has a line for a signature following it. Students trade their signatures with a different partner for each term. When the teacher asks students to discuss a topic for a limited time, he or she asks students to process the idea with a specific processing partner. This process is a helpful way to get students to work with others for a limited time. This strategy allows for movement.

Possible Terms for Processing Partners

SEL Terms
1. self-awareness _____
2. self-management _____
3. social awareness _____

Academic Terms
1. hyperbole _____
2. cliché _____
3. didactic _____
4. thesis _____

The Routine for Dyads: Think-Pair-Square and Snowballing; Think-Pair-Share: Students may have a partner based upon a protocol such as using a clock as with clock buddies, or they may be asked to turn to a neighbor, as with elbow partners. This process provides an opportunity to process the recently presented information immediately and briefly with a peer. This group can last from a minute or two to five minutes.

The Routine for Think-Pair-Square: In this pairing, two pairs who have already shared become a foursome (a square) and they share. This addition of another twosome allows further sharing and deepening of the ideas. This gives shyer students an opportunity to share their ideas twice before they may be asked to give feedback to the whole class. Once more, it is about adding depth to ideas, stimulating debate, and collaborative thinking.

The Routine for Snowballing: In this case, the groups of four (square) could become a group of eight. Like the square approach mentioned in Think-Pair-Square, the snowballing activity is another simple but very effective way of building on ideas by starting with small groups and expanding the groups in a structured way. As the metaphor of the snowball suggests, you can begin with an individual response to a question, followed by pairing up students, then creating groups of four, and so on.

Conclusion

Chapter 9, Classroom Management Plans, and this chapter provide specific examples of how techniques that support student growth academically, socially, and emotionally can be incorporated into the classroom. These activities not only support SEL growth, but they also support social-emotional and academic growth without any "add-ons" or special programs. The list below reflects the contents of this book, yet each of these areas is already an established, essential component of learning:

- Defining learning and growth mindset in Chapter 1
- Building relationships in Chapter 2
- Classroom organization in Chapter 3
- Cultural awareness of diversity in Chapter 3
- Classroom routines and rules in Chapter 4
- Group work in Chapters 4 and 10
- Cultivating student engagement and maintaining student attention in Chapters 5 and 8
- Setting goals, student self-assessment, reflection, and peer assessment in Chapter 6
- Creating a classroom plan in Chapter 9
- Community building and Classroom Meetings in Chapter 10

The premise of this book is that each teacher can establish a classroom culture that supports academic growth at the same time as it supports social and emotional skills. As an added bonus, these techniques support an engaging and challenging curriculum with meaningful work that students find worthwhile for their time and energy.

Discussion Questions for Reflection

Chapter 10

1. Chapter 10 offers some detailed descriptions of classroom meetings that contribute to creating a SEL culture within the class. **Select a passage that resonates with you and relate it to your practice.**

2. As you review the typical components of a classroom meeting, think of your own current classroom. **What approach do you think would be most conducive to your situation?**

3. **If you have students with special needs in your classroom, or students who are second language learners, how would you provide accommodations to enable these students to participate in a class meeting?**

4. **How would "Peer-Assisted Learning Strategies" benefit students who are second language learners or students with special needs?**

APPENDIX A

Questions That Develop Social-Emotional Skills

Teachers may use the following questions to help students increase their abilities in the following areas: self-awareness, self-management, social awareness, relationship management, responsible decision-making. Initially, posing these questions may feel uncomfortable or "unnatural." However, with some practice, the questions will become a natural part of prompting students' self-reflection about their actions and behaviors.

Note: When you ask these questions, your attitude should be one of sincere curiosity. If the tone of these questions seems negative, the result could be defensiveness—not reflection.

Social-Emotional Competency	Skills Related to Each Competency	Questions That Develop Self-Awareness
Self-Awareness	• Label and recognize their own and others' emotions • Identify what triggers their emotions • Accurately recognize their own strengths and limitations • Identify their needs and values • Possess self-efficacy and self-esteem	• How did it make you feel when he/she called you that name or hit you? • Why do you think he/she called you that name or hit you? • How do you think he/she felt when you called him/her a name or hit him/her? • Did you want to make him/her feel that way? If so, why? **For older students** • How did it make you feel when you were bullied or ignored by a classmate? • Why do you think this happened? • How do you think he/she felt when you bullied or ignored him/her? • Did you want to make him/her feel this way? If so, why? • What do you think you might do differently next time? • You seemed nervous when I announced the upcoming transition. Were you nervous about the transition? If so, why?

Social-Emotional Competency	Skills Related to Each Competency	Questions That Develop Self-Management
Self-Management	• Set plans and work toward goals • Overcome obstacles and create strategies for more long-term goals • Seek help when needed • Manage personal and interpersonal stress	• When do you do your homework? • Where do you do your homework? • What gets in the way of completing your homework? • What can you do to overcome those obstacles that get in the way of completing your homework? **For older students (who reflect on their own)** • How much time do I spend online doing activities that do not relate to homework? • How much time do I need to spend on extracurricular activities? (sports, part-time work, hobbies, etc.) • How much time do I need to spend on family-related responsibilities? (child-care, housework, etc.) • What can we do to help reduce my anxiety before the transition? • Is there a way we structure the transition that will make me feel more confident?
Social-Emotional Competency	**Skills Related to Each Competency**	**Questions That Develop Social Awareness**
Social Awareness	• Identify social cues (verbal, physical) to determine how others feel • Predict others' feelings and reactions • Evaluate others' emotional reactions • Respect others (e.g., listen carefully and accurately) • Understand others' point of view and perspectives • Appreciate diversity (recognize individual and group similarities and differences) • Identify and use resources of family, school, and community	• How do you think people feel when you interrupt them and don't wait your turn to speak? • What impact do you think it has on others when you talk while I'm talking? • Were you able to listen closely and accurately retell the other person's story? • Did the other person understand your point of view? • Did you understand his or her perspective? • How can I tell if my friend or classmate is happy about something? • How can I tell if my friend or classmate is sad about something? • What can I do to help my friend or classmate if they seem sad?

Social-Emotional Competency	Skills Related to Each Competency	Questions That Develop Relationship Management
Relationship Management	• Demonstrate capacity to make friends • Exhibit cooperative learning and working toward group goals • Evaluate one's own skills to communicate with others • Manage and express emotions in relationships with those who can be resources when help is needed • Communicate effectively • Cultivate relationships with those who can be resources when help is needed • Provide help to those who need it • Demonstrate leadership skills when necessary, being assertive and persuasive • Prevent interpersonal conflict, but manage and resolve it when it does occur • Resist inappropriate social pressures	• When you are the leader, how do you determine if someone is doing too much of the talking and not giving others an adequate chance to speak? • If you see this happening, what can you do to correct the situation? • If you see someone bullying a friend or classmate, how can you show that you are an ally? • If you feel lonely or afraid of something or someone at school, who would you feel you could go to? **For older students** • When a group of your friends wants to get involved in an inappropriate activity (e.g., cheating on a test, drinking alcohol, taking drugs, shoplifting), what are some things you can do to resist or remove yourself from the situation?
Social-Emotional Competency	**Skills Related To Each Competency**	**Questions to Develop Responsible Decision-Making**
Responsible Decision-Making	• Identify decisions that are made at school • Discuss strategies used to resist peer pressure • Reflect on how current choices affect future • Identify problems when making decisions, and generate alternatives • Implement problem-solving skills when making decisions, when appropriate • Become self-reflective and self-evaluative • Make decisions based on moral, personal, and ethical standards • Make responsible decisions that affect the individual, school, and community • Negotiate fairly	• In what way will the expectations listed help you learn more effectively in this class? • How can a class meeting help you improve your problem-solving skills? • If you had to design the list of our class rules, what would be your top three items on the list? Why? • If someone in the class breaks one of the class rules, what do you think should happen? • If someone breaks one of the rules, should they get another chance? Why or why not? • The next time you have an assignment that is due in a week, what can you do to avoid doing it all the night before it is due? • Why did you skip my class? • What were the consequences of choosing to skip my class? What can you and I do to make it less likely you will want to skip my class?

Columns 1 and 2 based on Yoder, Nicholas, Ph.D.
Research-To-Practice Brief: "Teaching the Whole Child: Instructional Practices That Support Social-Emotional Learning in Three Teacher Evaluation Frameworks," American Institutes for Research, January 2014. http://www.gtlcenter.org/sites/default/files/TeachingtheWholeChild.pdf, accessed 2/26/2017.

APPENDIX B

Using Effective Praise and Growth Mindset Statements to Support Social-Emotional Learning

Teachers may want to substitute different phrasing in their conversations with students to encourage a more positive environment and apply the characteristics of effective praise as they implement social-emotional learning. Instead of being generic praise, the alternatives provide the students with a very specific description of what merits the comment. Below are some examples of alternate statements that better develop social-emotional learning. Initially, changing your phrasing may feel uncomfortable or unnatural. However, if you stick with this practice, very soon it will become second nature and you will automatically use these types of statements.

Generic Praise Versus Effective Praise

Instead of saying:	Try saying:
"Nice work."	"I noticed that you really took your time working on that story. It has great details and an interesting plot."
"Amazing."	"The colors you chose for this drawing are very eye-catching. What made you think of that color combination?"
"Wrong!"	"Tell me how you worked out that solution. Can you think of another way you might come up with a different answer?"
"Be Quiet! You are too loud!"	"Let's practice our one-inch voices. See how softly you can talk and still have your processing partner hear you."
"I'm really disappointed in you."	"That situation didn't work out too well. What can we do next time to have a better outcome?"
"I'm waiting…"	"As soon as everyone can hear my voice, I will begin."
"Hurry up!"	"Let's see if we can beat our time from yesterday getting our room ready for dismissal."
"You are out of control!"	"Let's regroup everyone!"
"Stop pushing."	"I love to see how everyone is lining up patiently."
"You think you're funny?"	"I love a good sense of humor, but right now, we have work to do."
"Forgot your homework, again?" (*public shaming*)	(*private conversation*) "I noticed that you have missed the last few assignments. Can we discuss this later? Is there something I can help you with?"
"Why did you do THAT?"	"Could you explain to me what caused you to make that decision?"
"I don't know."	"Try to remember one thing we talked about."

Fixed Mindset Versus Growth Mindset Statements

Here are examples of fixed mindset statements that might be said by a student, and teacher statements that support a more positive mindset for the student.

Instead of saying:	Try saying:
"I can't do this." (groan, tears, etc.)	"Wow, look at what you have already done! Let's keep going!"
"I give up."	"Try a couple more and then let's see how you feel."
"It's not fair! Why does he/she get to take the test orally?"	"Right now, Tim needs this accommodation to help him complete his work. We all need different things to succeed in school. I will make sure you receive what you need to be successful."
"This sucks!"	"It sounds like you are frustrated, but we need to avoid disrespectful language in our class. Tell me what is the part of the assignment that is making you feel this way?"
"I need help!"	"I am happy to help you or answer your question after you take a few minutes to check in with your processing partner."
"I'm done!"	"Before you pass in your paper, make sure to do the checklist before you hand it in for grading." (Provide a short checklist that students can readily access.)

BIBLIOGRAPHY

Introduction

Aldeman, G., and Greene, S. "Social Powers and Effective Classroom Management: Enhancing Teacher–Student Relationships." *Intervention in School and Clinic* (originally published online, May 17, 2011).

Aronson, J. *Improving Academic Achievement: Impact of Psychological Factors on Education.* San Diego: Academic Press, 2002.

Brackett, M.A., Palomera, R., Mojsa, J., Reyes, M., and Salovey, P. Emotion regulation ability, job satisfaction, and burnout among British secondary school teachers. *Psychology in the Schools* 47 (2010), 406–417.

Burchinal, M., Peisner-Feinberg, E., Pianta, R., and Howes, C. "Development of academic skills from preschool through second grade: Family and classroom predictors of developmental trajectories." *Journal of School Psychology*, 40 no. 5 (2002): 415–436.

Davis, M., Eshelman, E. and McKay, M. *The Relaxation and Stress Reduction Workbook.* Oakland, CA: New Harbinger Publications, 6th ed. (May 2008).

Duckworth, A. and Seligman, M. "Self-Discipline Outdoes IQ in Predicting Academic Performance of Adolescents." *Psychological Science* 16 (2006): 939–44.

Durlak, J.A., Weissberg, R.P., Dymnicki, A.B., Taylor, R.D. and Schellinger, K.B. "The Impact of Enhancing Students' Social and Emotional Learning: A Meta-Analysis of School-Based Universal Interventions." *Child Development* 82 (2011): 405–432.

Dweck, C., and Elliot, A., eds. *Handbook of Competence and Motivation.* Change to: New York, NY: Guilford Press (2005).

Fraser, S., ed. *The Bell Curve Wars: Race, Intelligence, and the Future of America.* New York: Perseus Books (1995).

Hamre, B., and Pianta, R. "Early teacher–child relationships and the trajectory of children's school outcomes through eighth grade." *Child Development*, 72.2 (2001): 625–638.

Jones, F. *Tools for Teaching.* California: Fredrick H. Jones and Associates (2013).

Jones, V., and Jones, L. *Comprehensive Classroom Management: Creating Communities of Support and Solving Problems* Boston: Allyn and Bacon, 10th ed., (2012).

La Paro, K., Pianta, R. *Experiences in P-3 classrooms: The implications of observational research for redesigning early education.* New York, NY: Foundation for Child Development (2003).

Landrum, T., Lingo, A., and Scott, T. "Classroom Misbehavior is Predictable and Preventable." *Phi Delta Kappan*, 93 2, (2011): 30–34.

Mashburn, A., Pianta, R., Hamre, B., Downer, J., Barbarin, O., Bryant, D. Burchinal, M., Clifford, R., Early, D., and Howes, C. "Measures of classroom quality in pre-kindergarten and children's development of academic, language, and social skills." *Child Development*, 79 no. 3 (2008): 732–749.

Morrison, G., Allen, M. "Promoting Student Resilience in School Contexts." *Theory into Practice.* 45 (2007): 162–169.

National Institute of Child Health and Human Development (NICHD) Early Child Care Research Network. "Social functioning in first grade: Associations with earlier home and child care predictors and with current classroom experiences." *Child Development*, 74 (2003): 1639–1662.

Pianta, R., Cox, M., and Snow, K., eds. *School readiness and the transition to kindergarten in the era of accountability.* Baltimore, MD: Brookes Publishing, 2007), 121–147.

Raver, C.C., Jones, S.M., Li-Grining, C.P., Metzger, M., Champion, K., and Sardin, L. "Improving preschool classroom processes: Preliminary findings from a randomized trial implemented in Head Start settings." *Early Childhood Research Quarterly*, 23 (2008): 10–26.

Raver, C.C., Garner, P., and Smith-Donald, R. "The roles of emotion regulation and emotion knowledge for children's academic readiness: Are the links causal?" *School Readiness and the Transition to Kindergarten in the Era of Accountability*. Baltimore, MD: Paul Brookes Publishing (2007), 121–147.

Tanyu, M. "Implementation of prevention programs: Lessons for future research and practice: A commentary on social and emotional learning: Promoting the development of all students." *Journal of Educational and Psychological Consultation* 17.2-3 (2007): 257–262.

Walker, H.M., Ramsey, E., and Gresham, F.M. *Antisocial behavior in school: Evidence based practices.* Belmont, CA: Wadsworth Publishing/Thomson Learning, 2nd ed. (2003).

Weissberg, R. and Cascarino, J. "Academic Learning and Social-Emotional Learning, A National Priority." *Kappan Magazine*, 95 no. 2 (2013), 1–6.

Zakrzewski, V. "Why Don't Students Take Social-Emotional Learning Home?" University of California, Berkley: The Greater Good Science Center (March 31, 2016). Accessed September, 2016. http://greatergood.berkeley.edu/tag/social-emotional+learning

Chapter 1: Beliefs

Anastasi quoted in Devlin, B., Fienberg, S.E., Resnick, D.P., Roeder, K., eds. "Intelligence, Genes, and Success: Scientists Respond to The Bell Curve." New York: Springer-Verlag, Inc, (1997): 2.

Brigham, C. A *Study of American Intelligence*. Oxford University Press: Princeton (1923).

Davis, M., McKay, M. and Eshelman, E. *The Relaxation and Stress Reduction Workbook*. Oakland, CA: New Harbinger Publications (2008)

Dweck, C. *Self-theories: Their Role in Motivation, Personality, and Development (Essays in Social Psychology) 1st Edition*. East Sussex, United Kingdom, Psychology Press, 1st ed. (2000).

Devlin, B., Stephen E. Fienberg, Daniel P. Resnick, and Kathryn Roeder. "Intelligence and success: is it all in the genes." *Race and intelligence: Separating science from myth* (2002): 355–368.

Diala, C. C., Muntaner, C., and Walrath, C. "Gender, occupational, and socioeconomic correlates of alcohol and drug abuse among U.S. rural, metropolitan, and urban residents." *American Journal of Drug and Alcohol Abuse*, 30 no. 2 (2004), 409–428.

Dweck, Carol. *Mindset: The New Psychology of Success*. New York, NY: Random House (2006).

Fairman, S. "Unconscious Bias: When Good Intentions Aren't Good Enough." *Educational Leadership*, 74, no. 3 (2016): 11–15.

Ferlazzo, L. Larry Ferlazzo blog, "Study: 'Authoritative,' not 'Authoritarian,' Classroom Management Works Best for Boys." (2015) http://larryferlazzo.edublogs.org/2015/06/10/study-authoritative-not-authoritarian-classroom-management-works-best-for-boys/

Fraser, S., ed. *The Bell Curve Wars: Race, Intelligence, and the Future of America*. Basic Books, NY (1995).

Galea, S., Ahern, J., Tracy, M., and Vlahov, D. (2007). Neighborhood income and income distribution and the use of cigarettes, alcohol, and marijuana. *American Journal of Preventive Medicine*, 32(6), 195–202.

Gurian, M. *Boys and Girls Learn Differently*. Chandler, AZ: Gurian Institute (2015). http://gurianinstitute. com/boys-and-girls-learn-differently

Gurian, M., and Stevens, K. "With Boys and Girls in Mind." *Educational Leadership* 61 no. 3 (November 2004), 21–26.

Gurian, M. and Stevens, K. *Boys and Girls Learn Differently! A Guide for Teachers and Parents, revised 10th anniversary ed.* San Francisco, CA: Jossey-Bass (2010).

Hernstein, R. and Murray, C. *Bell Curve: Intelligence and Class Structure in American Life*. New York, NY: Free Press (1994).

Kevles, D. *In the Name of Eugenics: Genetics and the Uses of Human Heredity*. Harvard University Press Cambridge (1998).

Morin, R. "Exploring racial bias among biracial and single-race adults: The IAT." *Washington, DC: Pew Research Center* (2015).

Mueller, C. and Dweck, C. *Implicit theories of intelligence: Malleability beliefs, definitions, and judgments of intelligence*. Unpublished data (1997).

Murray, C. *Real Education: Four Simple Truths for Bringing America's Schools Back to Reality*. Crown Forum (2009).

National Institute of Mental Health. "Any Anxiety Disorder Among Adults." National Institutes of Health (NIH) and US Department of Health and Human Services (HHS).https://www.nimh.nih.gov/health/statistics/prevalence/any-anxiety-disorder-among-adults.shtml (2017).

Perkins, D. *Outsmarting IQ: The Emerging Science of Learnable Intelligence*. New York, NY: Free Press (1995)

Ricks, Dionna, "Educating Boys for Success." National Education Association (1922). http://www.nea.org/home/44609.htm (2017)

Terman, L. "Were We Born That Way?" 44 *World's Work* (1922), 657-659.

U.S. Department of Education; Office of Civil Rights Civil Rights Data Collection: Data Snapshot. http://ocrdata.ed.gov/

Chapter 2: Teacher-Student, Student-Student Relationships

Brackett, M. and Rivers, S. "Transforming Students' Lives with Social and Emotional Learning." New Haven, CT: Yale Center for Emotional Intelligence (2014).

Brophy, J., and Good, T. *Looking in Classrooms* 8th ed. Boston, MA: Allyn and Bacon (2000).

Chang, M. "An appraisal perspective of teacher burnout: Examining the emotional work of teachers." *Educational Psychology Review*, 21 (2009) 193–218.

Collaborative for Academic, Social, and Emotional Learning (CASEL). "Safe and Sound: An Educational Leader's Guide to Evidence-Based Social and Emotional Learning (SEL) Programs." *Mid-Atlantic Regional Educational Laboratory: The Laboratory for Student Success*: Chicago, Illinois: CASEL (2003).

Cotton, K. "Classroom Questioning." Portland, OR: *Education Northwest, School Improvement Research Series. Close-Up*, 5 (2012): 1–16.

Curwin, Richard L. and Allen N. Mendler. *Discipline with dignity*. Alexandria, Va., USA: Association for Supervision and Curriculum Development (1999).

Deci, Edward L and Ryan, Richard M. "The 'What' and 'Why' of Goal Pursuits: Human Needs and the Self-Determination of Behavior," *Psychological Inquiry* 11 no. 4 (2000), 233.

Durlak, J.A., Weissberg, R.P., Dymnicki, A.B., Taylor, R.D., and Schellinger, K.B. "The impact of enhancing students' social and emotional learning: A meta-analysis of school-based universal interventions." *Child Development* 82 (2011), 405–432.

Dymnick, A., Sambolt, M., and Kidron, Y. "Improving college and career readiness by incorporating social and emotional learning." Washington, DC: College and Career Readiness and Success Center (2013). Retrieved from http://www.ccrscenter.org/products-resources/improving-college-and-career-readiness-incorporating-social-and-emotional

Elias, M. "The connection between academic and social-emotional learning" in M.J. Elias and H. Arnold, eds., *The Educator's Guide to Emotional Intelligence and Academic Achievement*. California: Corwin Press (2006), 4–14.

Elmore, M. "Effective Parent Conferences." *Principal Leadership* 8 no. 6 (2008), 7-8.

Kidron, Y., and Fleischman, S. (2006). Promoting adolescents' prosocial behavior. Educational Leadership, 63(7), 90–91Kress, J. Elias, M. "Building Learning Communities Through Social and Emotional Learning: Navigating the Rough Seas of Implementation." *Professional School Counseling*, 10 no. 1 (2006), 102–107.

Marzano, R. *The Art and Science of Teaching a Comprehensive Framework for Effective Instruction*. Alexandria, VA: ASCD (2007).

Mendler, A., Curwin, R. *Discipline with Dignity for Challenging Youth*. Solution Tree. Bloomington, IN (1999).

Mendler, A. *As Tough As Necessary: Countering Violence, Aggression, and Hostility in Our Schools*. Association for Supervision and Curriculum Development. Alexandria (1997).

Minahan, J. and Rappaport, N. *The Behavior Code: A Practical Guide to Understanding and Teaching the Most Challenging Students*. Cambridge, MA: Harvard Education Press (2012).

Reichert, M., Hawley, R. *For Whom the Boy Toils: The Primacy of Relationship in Boys' Learning*. International Boys' Schools Coalition, Pawling, NY (2013).

Ribas, W., et al. *Instructional Practices That Maximize Student Achievement for Teachers by Teachers*. 3rd ed. Norwood, MA: Ribas Associates Publications, Inc. (2017).

Tough, P. *How Children Succeed: Grit, Curiosity, and the Hidden Power of Character*. Mariner Books, NY (2013).

Vitto, J. *Relationship-Driven Classroom Management, Strategies That Promote Student Motivation*. Corwin Press, Thousand Oaks, CA (2003).

Yoder, N. "Teaching the Whole Child, Instructional Practices that Support Social-Emotional Learning in Three Teacher Evaluation Frameworks. Research to Practice Brief." Washington, DC: American Institutes for Research (2014).

Zins, J., Payton, J.W., Weissberg R.P., and Utne-O'Brien, M. "Social and emotional leaning and successful school performance" in Matthews, G., Zeidner, M., and Roberts, R., eds., *Emotional Intelligence: Knowns and Unknowns*. New York: Oxford University (2007), 376–395.

Chapter 3: Creating Physically and Emotionally Safe Spaces

English Learners References

Andrade, H., Valtcheva A."Promoting Learning and Achievement through Self-Assessment." *Evidence-Based Education* (March 2009): 12–13.

Anonymous. "Punishment vs. Logical Consequences: What's the Difference?" *Responsive Classroom Newsletter* 10, no. 3 (1998).

Aronsen, E., Baney, N. Stephin, C. Sikes, J., and Snapp, M. *The Jigsaw Classroom*. Beverly Hills, CA: Sage Publishing Company (1978).

Boyd, L. "Five Myths about Student Discipline." *Educational Leadership* 70, no. 2 (October 2012) 62–67.

Brady, K., Forton, M., Porter, D. *Rules in School*. Greenfield, MA: Northeast Foundation for Children, 2003.

Brophy, J., and Good, T. *Looking in Classrooms* 8th ed. Boston, MA: Allyn and Bacon (2000).

Cloud, N., Genesee, N.F., and Hamayan, E. *Literacy Instruction for English Language Learners: A Teacher's Guide to Research-Based Practices*. Portsmouth, NH: Heinemann (2009).

Crowe, C. "When Students Get Stuck: Using Behavior Agreements." *Educational Leadership* 68 (June 2011).

Danforth, S. and Smith, T. *Engaging Troubling Students*. Thousand Oaks, CA: Corwin Press (2005).

Darling-Hammond, L, and Ifill-Lynch, O. "If They'd Only Do Their Work!" *Educational Leadership* 63, no. 5 (Feb. 2006), 9–10.

Davis, D., Eshelman, E., and McKay, M. *The Relaxation Response and Stress Reduction Workbook*, 6th ed. Oakland, CA: New Harbinger Publications (2008), 2.

Dean, C., Hubbell, E., Pitler, H., and Stone, B. *Classroom Instruction That Works: Research-Based Strategies for Increasing Student Achievement*. Alexandria, VA: Association for Supervision and Curriculum Development (2012).

Denton, P. and Kriete. R. *The First Six Weeks of School*. Greenfield, MA: Northeast Foundation for Children (2000).

Farnsworth, M. and McErlane, J. "Signals for Quiet." *The Responsive Classroom Newsletter* 14, no. 3 (Summer 2002), 1–4.

Ferlazzo, L. "Eight Things Skilled Teachers Think, Say,

and Do." *Educational Leadership* 70, no. 2 (October 2012).

Frey, N. and Fisher, D. (2011). "High-Quality Homework." *Principal Leadership* 12, no. 2 (2011), 56–58.

Gonzalez, N., Moll, L.C., and Amanti, C. *Funds of Knowledge: Theorizing Practices in Households, Communities and Classrooms*. Mahway, NJ: Lawrence Erbaum (2005).

Greene, R.W. "Collaborative Problem Solving Can Transform School Discipline." *Phi Delta Kappan* 93, no. 2 (October 2011), 25–28.

Greene, R. "Collaborative Problem Solving Can Transform School Discipline." *Phi Delta Kappan* 93, no. 2: 25–29 (2011).

Hallowell, E. and Ratey, J. *Driven to Distraction: Recognizing and Coping with Attention Deficit Disorder from Childhood through Adulthood*. New York: First Anchor Books (2011).

Hernstein, R. "Relative and Absolute Strength of Response as a Function of Frequency of Reinforcement." *Journal of the Experimental Analysis of Behavior* 4 (1961), 267–272.

"Formal Properties of the Matching Laws." *Journal of the Experimental Analysis of Behavior* 21: 486–495 (1974).

Jones, F. *Tools for Teaching*, 2nd ed. Santa Cruz, CA: Frederick H. Jones and Associates, Inc. (2007), 187.

Jones, F. *Tools for Teaching*. 3rd ed. Santa Cruz, CA: Frederick H. Jones and Associates, Inc. (2013), Kindle version. 3859-3359 or 8100.

Kidron, Y., and Fleishman, S. "Promoting Adolescents' Prosocial Behavior." *Educational Leadership* 63, no. 7 (April 2006), 90–91.

Landrum, T., Lingo, A., and Scott, T. "Classroom Misbehavior is Predictable and Preventable." *Phi Delta Kappan* 93, no. 2: 30–34 (2011).

Lems, K., Miller, L.D., and Soro, T.M. *Teaching Reading to English Language Learners: Insights from Linguistics*. New York, NY: The Guilford Press (2010).

Lovoie, R. *Understanding Learning Difficulties: How Difficult Can This Be?* Washington DC: F.A.T. City Workshop, PBS Video (1989).

Marzano, R. *The Art and Science of Teaching: A Comprehensive Framework for Effective Instruction*. Alexandria, VA: Association for Supervision and Curriculum Development (2007).

Marzano, R. *Classroom Management that Works*. Alexandria, VA: Association for Supervision and Curriculum Development (ASCD) (2003).

Marzano, R. "Classroom Management: Whose Job Is It?" *Educational Leadership* 69, no. 2 (2011), 85–85.

Marzano, R. and Marzano, J. "The Key to Classroom Management." *Educational Leadership* 61, no. 1 (Sept. 2003), 6–13.

McLeod, J., Fisher, J., and Hoover, G. *The Key Elements of Classroom Management: Managing Time and Space, Student Behavior, and Instructional Strategies*, Alexandria, VA: ASCD (2003).

Mendler, A., Curwin, R. *As Tough as Necessary: Countering Violence, Aggression, and Hostility in Our Schools*. Alexandria, VA: ASCD (1997).

Mendler, A. *Connecting with Students*. Alexandria, VA: ASCD (2001).

Mendler, A. and Curwin, R. *Discipline with Dignity*. Alexandria, VA: ASCD (1999).

Mendler, A. *When Teaching Gets Tough*. Alexandria, VA: ASCD (2012).

NEA Classroom Management E-Book, http://www.nea.org/assets/docs/110527_NEA_E-Book_Classroom_MgmtFINAL.pdf

Quinn, T. "G-R-O-U-P W-O-R-K Doesn't Spell Collaboration." *Phi Delta Kappan* 94, no. 4 (December 2012) 46–48.

Reichert, M. and Hawley, R. "Relationships Play Primary Role in Boys' Learning." *Phi Delta Kappan* 94, no. 8: (May 2013), 49–53. .

Searle, M. *Causes and Cures in the Classroom: Getting to the Root of Academic and Behavioral Problems* (Alexandria, VA: ASCD 2013).

Sams, A. and Bergmann, J. "Flip Your Students' Learning." *Educational Leadership* 70, no. 6: (March 2013) 16–20.

Snyder, J. "Reinforcement and Coercive Mechanisms in the Development of Antisocial Behavior: Peer Relationships. In *Antisocial Behavior in Children and Adolescents: A Developmental Analysis and Model for Intervention*, Reid, J., Patterson, G., and Snyder, L., eds. (Washington, DC: American Psychological Association, 2002) 101–102.

Theobald, M. *Increasing Student Motivation: Strategies for Middle and High School Teachers*. Thousand Oaks, CA: Corwin Press (2006).

U.S. Department of Education Office for Civil Rights and U.S. Department of Justice. "Information for Limited English Proficient (LEP) Parents and Guardians and for Schools and School Districts that Communicate with Them." http://www2.ed.gov/about/offices/list/ocr/docs/dcl-factsheet-le-parents-201501.pdf, 2015.

Vitto, J. *Relationship-Driven Classroom Management*. Thousand Oaks, CA: Corwin Press (2003).

Walker, H., Ramsey, E., and Gresham, F. "Heading Off Disruptive Behavior." *The American Educator*: 1–15 (Winter 2003–2004).

Weissberg, R. and Cascarino, J. "Academic Learning + Social-Emotional Learning = National Priority," *Kappanmagazine.org* v95 no. 2 (October 2012) 8–13.

Additional English Learners Related Readings

Anderson, M. "The Early and Elementary Years/The Leap into 4th Grade." *Educational Leadership* 68, no. 7 (April 2011) 32–36.

Brown, D. "Now That I Know What I Know." *Educational Leadership* 69, no. 8 (February 2010), 24–28.

Crowe, C. "Teaching Children with Challenging Behavior." *Educational Leadership* 67, no. 5 (February 2010), 65–67.

Curwin, R.L. *Affirmative Classroom Management: How Do I Develop Effective Rules and Consequences in My School?* Alexandria, VA: ASCD (2013).

"Eight Classroom Disrupters: Getting Them Back on Track." *NEA Today Professional* (Fall 2011). http://www.nea.org/assets/docs/110527_NEA_E-Book_Classroom_MgmtFINAL.pdf

Frey, N. and Fisher, D. "Making Group Work Productive." *Educational Leadership* 68, no. 1 (September 2010).

Garrett, T. "Classroom Management: It's More Than a Bag of Tricks." *NJEA Review* 86: 17–19 (October 2012).

Goodwin, B. "Research Says/New Teachers Face Three Common Challenges." *Educational Leadership* 69, no. 8: 84–85 (May 2012).

Goodwin, B. and Miller, K. "Research Says/For Positive Behavior, Involve Peers." *Educational Leadership* 70, no. 2: 82–83 (October 2012).

Greene, R.W. "Calling All Frequent Flyers." *Educational Leadership* 68, no. 2: 28–34 (October 2012).

Hansen, J. "Teaching Without Talking." *Phi Delta Kappan* 92, no. 1: 35–40 (September 2010).

Jensen, E. *Engaging Students with Poverty in Mind: Practical Strategies for Raising Achievement*. Alexandria, VA: ASCD (2013).

Jensen, E. "How Poverty Affects Classroom Engagement." *Educational Leadership* 70, no. 8: 24–30 (May 2013).

Kraft, M.A. "From Ringmaster to Conductor: 10 Simple Techniques Can Turn an Unruly Class into a Productive One." *Phi Delta Kappan* 91, no. 7: 44–47 (April 2010).

Landrum, T.J., Scott, T.M., and Lingo, A.S. "Classroom Misbehavior Is Predictable and Preventable." *Phi Delta Kappan* 93, no. 2: 30–34 (October 2011).

Marzano, R.J. "Art and Science of Teaching/The Inner World of Teaching." *Educational Leadership* 68, no. 7: 90–91 (April 2011).

Marzano, R.J. "Art and Science of Teaching/Classroom Management: Whose Job Is It?" *Educational Leadership* 69, no. 2: 85–86 (October 2011).

Marzano, R.J. "Art and Science of Teaching/Ask Yourself: Are Students Engaged?" *Educational Leadership* 70, no. 6: 81–82 (March 2013).

Mirsky, L. "Building Safer, Saner Schools." *Educational Leadership* 69, no. 1: 45–49 (September 2011).

Poplawski, K. "A Principal's Job Is Also to Teach." *Responsive Classroom Newsletter* (Fall 2013).

Poplin, M., et al. "She's Strict for a Good Reason: Highly Effective Teachers in Low-Performing Urban Schools." *Phi Delta Kappan* 92, no. 5: 39–43 (February 2011).

Pudelski, S. "The Option of Seclusion and Restraint." *School Administrator* 70, no. 2: 34–37 (February 2013).

Rappaport, N. "Why ADHD Medication Is Not Reform: Understanding Behavior Is Critical." *Education Week* 32, no. 22: 23, 25 (February 27, 2013).

Rappaport, N. and Minahan, J. "Cracking the Behavior Code." *Educational Leadership* 70, no. 2: 18–25 (October 2012).

Thompson, M.D. "Rethinking Our Approach to School Discipline," article in *New Superintendent's Journal 2014-2015: Together, We Are Champions for Children and Public Education.* The School Superintendents Association, Alexandria, VA.

Vatterott, C. "Five Hallmarks of Good Homework." *Educational Leadership* 68, no. 1: 10–15 (September 2010).

Wong, H., Wong, R. *The First Days of School: How to Be an Effective Teacher*. Mountain View, CA: Harry K. Wong Publications.

Special Education Related Readings

"Addressing Disruptive and Noncompliant Behaviors (Part 1): Understanding the Acting-Out Cycle." IRIS. http://iris.peabody.vanderbilt.edu/module/bi1/.

"Fast Facts: Students with Disabilities." National Center for Educational Statistics. https://nces.ed.gov/fastfacts/display.asp?id=64

Headley, C.J. and Campbell, M.A. "Teachers' Recognition and Referral of Anxiety Disorders in Primary School Children." *Australian Journal of Educational and Developmental Psychology* 11: 78–90 (2011).

Jones, S, Bouffard, S., Weissbourd, R. "Educators' Social and Emotional Skills Vital to Learning," Phi Delta Kappan, 94, 8, 62–65 (May 2013).

May-Benson, T. "Parent Fact Sheet Signs and Symptoms of Sensory Processing Disorder". *The Spiral Foundation*, 2006.

Mashburn, A.J., Pianta, R.C., Hamre, B.K., Downer, J.T., Barbarin, O., Bryant, D., Howes, C. (2008). "Measures of classroom quality in prekindergarten and children's development of academic, language, and social skills." *Child Development*, 79, 732–749.

Rawles, P. "The Link between Poverty, the Proliferation of Violence, and the Development of Traumatic Stress among Urban Youth in the United States to School Violence: A Trauma Informed, Social Justice Approach to School Violence." *Forum on Public Policy Online* 2010, no. 4 (2010).

Schultz, J.J. and Hallowell, E.M. *Nowhere to Hide: Why Kids with ADHD and LD Hate School and What We Can Do about It*. San Francisco: Jossey-Bass (2011).

Vega, V. "Social and Emotional Learning Research Review," Edutopia. November 7, 2012, updated December 1, 2015. Accessed 11.20.2016. https://www.edutopia.org/sel-research-learning-outcomes

Zakrzewski, V. "How to Build an Inclusive School Community During a Divisive Election." April 28, 2016 blog.

Chapter 4: Developing a Classroom Community

Corno, L. *Introduction to the Special Issue Work Habits and Work Styles: Volition in Education. Teachers College Record* 106 (2004), 1669–1694.

Corno, L., and Xu, J. "Homework as the Job of Childhood." *Theory into Practice* 43 (2004) 227–233. http://dx.doi.org/10.1207/s15430421tip4303_9

Dean, C.B., Hubbell, E.R., Pitler, H., and Stone. B. *Classroom instruction that works: Research-based strategies for increasing student achievement.* Denver, CO (2012)

Fisher, D., Lapp, D., and Frey, N. "Homework in secondary classrooms: Making it relevant and respectful." *Journal of Adolescent and Adult Literacy*, 55, 71–74 (2011).

Hampshire, P., Butera, G., and Hourcade, J. "Homework Plans: A Tool for Promoting Independence." *Teaching Exceptional Children*, 46 6: 158–168 (2014).

Jones, F. *Tools for Teaching*. Santa Cruz, California: Frederick H. Jones and Associates, Inc. (2013). Kindle version: 3859 and 3359 of 8100.

Marzano, R. *The Art and Science of Teaching, A Comprehensive Framework for Effective Instruction.* Alexandria, VA: ASCD (2007).

McLeod, J., Fischer, J., and Hoover, G., *The Key Elements of Classroom Management: Managing Time and Space, Student Behavior and Instructional Strategies.* Alexandria, VA: ASCD (2003).

Meier, D. "As Though They Owned the Place': Small schools as membership communities." *Phi Delta Kappan*, 87, no. 9 (May 2006): 657–662.

Neff, L. "Lev Vygotsky and Social Learning Theories" Learning Theories Website. http://jan.ucc.nau.edu/lsn/educator/edtech/learningtheorieswebsite/vygotsky.htm

Quinn, Timothy. "G-R-O-U-P W-O-R-K: Doesn't Spell Collaboration." *Phi Delta Kappan* 94, no. 4 (2012): 46.

Xu, J. "Why do students have difficulties completing homework? The need for homework management," *Journal of Education and Training Studies*, Beaverton, OR: Redframe Publishing, April 11, 2013. http://dx.doi.org/10.11114/jets.v1i1.78

Chapter 5: Engaging Students

Farnsworth, M. and McErlane, J. "Classroom Management and Discipline/Classroom Organization." *Responsive Classroom Newsletter*. 2002. Responsive Classroom Website. https://www.responsiveclassroom.org/signals-for-quiet/

Findley, T. "New Study: Engage Kids with 7x the Effect." *Edutopia*. September 9, 2015. https://www.edutopia.org/blog/engage-with-7x-the-effect-todd-finley/

Hamblin, James. "Exercise is the New ADHD Medication." *The Atlantic*. Washington, DC: Atlantic Media Company.

"What Is Normal Attention Span?" *Day2Day Parenting*. http://day2dayparenting.com/qa-normal-attention-span/ (2017).

Chapter 6: Habits of Successful Students

Bloom, M. "Self-regulated learning: Goal Setting and Self-Monitoring." *The Language Teacher. Taito, Taito-ku, Tokyo, Japan.* Japan Association of Language Teaching: JAlT Publishing (2013), 46–51.

Zimmerman, B.J. "Self-regulated learning and academic achievement: An overview." *Educational Psychologist*, American Psychological Association. London, England: Taylor and Francis Publishers 25, no. 1 (1990): 3–17.

Andrade, H. "Promoting Learning and Achievement Through Self-Assessment." *Better Evidence-Based Education*. New York, NY: Institute for Effective Education, Johns Hopkins School of Education. 3, no. 3 (Spring 2011), 2–13. http://betterevidence.org/us-edition/issue-7/

Chapter 7: Restorative Discipline

Brady, K., Forton, M., Porter, D., Wood, C. *Rules in School*. Greenfield, MA: Northeast Foundation for Children (2003).

Craig, J. and Cairo, L. "Assessing the Relationship between Questioning and Understanding to Improve Learning and Thinking (QUILT) and Student Achievement in Mathematics: A Pilot Study." Charlestown, WV: Evantia, Inc., (2005), 1–20.

Crowe, C. "When Students Get Stuck: Using Behavior Agreements." *Educational Leadership* 68 (June 2011).

Danforth, S. and Smith, T. *Engaging Troubling Students, A Constructivist Approach*. Thousand Oaks, CA: Corwin Press (2004).

Dweck, C. *Essays in Social Psychology: Self Theories*. Philadelphia, PA: Psychology Press of Taylor and Francis Group (2000).

Elias, M. "Why Restorative Practices Benefit All Students." *Edutopia*: Social and Emotional Learning. https://www.edutopia.org/blog/why-restorative-practices-benefit-all-students-maurice-elias

Johnston, Peter H. *Choice Words: How Our Language Affects Children's Learning*. Stenhouse Publishers.

Marzano, R., Marzano, J., and Pickering, D. *Classroom Management that Works: Research-Based Strategies for Every Teacher*. Alexandria, VA: Association for Supervision and Curriculum Development (2003).

Minahan, J. and Rappaport, N. *The Behavior Code: A Practical Guide to Understanding and Teaching the Most Challenging Students*, Cambridge, MA: Harvard Education Press (2012).

Minahan, J. *The Behavior Code Companion: Strategies, Tools, and Interventions for Supporting Students with Anxiety-Related and Oppositional Behaviors*. Cambridge, MA, Harvard Education Press.

Okonofua, J., Paunesku, D., and Walton, G. "Brief Intervention to Encourage Empathic Discipline Cuts Suspension Rates in Half Among Adolescents." *Proceedings of the National Academy of Sciences*, 201523698 (2016).

Searle, M. *Causes and Cures in the Classroom: Getting to the Root of Academic and Behavioral Problems*. Alexandria, VA: ASCD (2013).

Snyder, J. "Reinforcement and Coercive Mechanisms in the Development of Antisocial Behavior: Peer Relationships" in Reid, J. Patterson G, and Snyder, L., eds. *Antisocial Behavior in Children and Adolescents: A developmental Analysis and Model for Intervention*. Washington, DC: American Psychological Association (2002), 101–122.

Walker, H., Ramsey, E., and Gresham, F. "Heading Off Disruptive Behavior." Washington, DC: American Federation of Teachers, *The American Educator* (Winter 2003–2004), 1–15.

Willingham, D. "Ask the Cognitive Scientist: How Praise Can Motivate—or Stifle." Washington, DC: American Federation of Teachers, *The American Educator* (Winter 2003–2004), 1–15.

Chapter 8: Engaging Teaching

Bandura, A. and Schunk, D. H. "Cultivating competence, self-efficacy, and intrinsic interest through proximal self-motivation." *Journal of Personality and Social Psychology, 41* 3: 586–598 (1981).

Deci, E.L. and Ryan, R.M. "The 'what' and 'why' of goal pursuits: Human needs and the self-determination of behavior." *Psychological Inquiry* 11, no. 4 (2000), 227-268.

Delale-O'Connor, L., Farley, C. Lippman. L.; Walker, K. E. "Essential self-management skills: Summary of research." Washington, DC: *Child Trends* (2012).

James, N., "Student Engagement: Golden Rules for Engaging Students in Learning Activities" *Edutopia*, originally published December 8, 2014, updated December 11, 2015. https://www.edutopia.org/blog/golden-rules-for-engaging-students-nicolas-pino-james?utm_source=twitterandutm_medium=socialflow

Massachusetts Curriculum Framework for English Language Arts and Literacy, Massachusetts Department of Education. Boston: March 2011.

Schlechty, P. *Shaking Up the Schoolhouse: How to Support and Sustain Educational Innovation*. San Francisco, CA: Jossey-Bass (2004).

Searle, M. *Causes and Cures in the Classroom: Getting to the Root of Academic and Behavioral Problems*. Alexandria, VA: ASCD (2013).

Snipes, J., Fancsali, C., and Stoker, G. "Student academic mindset interventions – a review of the current landscape." (2012). Retrieved from http://www.impaq-int.com/files/4-content/1-6-publications/1-6-2-project-reports/impaq%20student%20academic%20mindset%20interventions%20report%20august%202012.pdf

Theobald, M. *Increasing Student Motivation: Strategies for Middle and High School Teachers*. Thousand Oaks, CA: Corwin Press (2006).

Ribas, W., et al. *Instructional Practices That Maximize Student Achievement for Teachers by Teachers*. Norwood, MA: Ribas Associates Publications, Inc. (2017).

Wiggins, G. "How Good Is Good Enough?" Alexandria, VA: ASCD: *Educational Leadership* 71, no. 4 (December 2013–January 2014): 10–17.

Chapter 9: The Classroom Management Plan

Durlak, J.A., Weissberg, R.P., Dymnicki, A.B., Taylor, R.D., and Schellinger, K.B. "The impact of enhancing students' social and emotional learning: A meta-analysis of school-based universal interventions." *Child Development* 82 (2011), 405–432.

Dymnicki, A., Sambolt, M., and Kidron, Y. "Improving college and career readiness by incorporating social and emotional learning." Washington, DC: College and Career Readiness and Success Center (2013).

Elias, M.J. "The connection between academic and social-emotional learning." In Elias, M.J., and Arnold, H. (eds.), *The educator's guide to emotional intelligence and academic achievement*. Thousand Oaks, CA: Corwin Press (2006), 4–14.

Loeb, P., Tipton, S., and Wagner, E., "Social and Emotional Learning: Feedback and Communications Insights from the Field," Edge Research, Inc. The Wallace Foundation (2016). http://www.wallacefoundation.org/knowledge-center/Pages/SEL-Feedback-and-Communications-Insights-from-the-Field.aspx

Zins, J., Payton, J.W., Weissberg, R.P., and Utne-O'Brien, M. "Social and emotional learning and successful school performance." In Matthews, G., Zeidner, M., and Roberts, R.D., eds., *The Science of Emotional Intelligence: Knowns and Unknowns*. New York: Oxford University Press (2007) 376–395).

Chapter 10: SEL Classroom Meetings

Allen-Hughes, L. "The Social Benefits of the Morning Meeting: Creating a Space for Social and Character Education in the Classroom." School of Education and Counseling Psychology, Dominican University of California, San Rafael (April 2013).

Bafile, C. "Morning Meetings in Middle School: An Elementary Ritual Grows Up." Education World (2009). http://www.educationworld.com/a_admin/admin/admin523.shtml

Brock, L.L., Nishida, K.K., Chiong, C., Grimm, K.J., and Rimm-Kaufman, S. E. "Children's perceptions of the social environment and social and academic performance: A longitudinal analysis of the Responsive Classroom approach." *Journal of School Psychology* 46 (2008): 129–149.

Dabbs, L. "The Power of the Morning Meeting: 5 Steps Toward Changing Your Classroom and School Culture." Edutopia.

Education Northwest "What the Research Says (Or Doesn't Say): Advisory Programs (January 10, 2011).

Gardner, C. Morning meeting and science—a winning combination. *Science and Children*, 50(1), 60–64 (2012). Retrieved from http://search.ebscohost.com

Gibbs, J. *Reaching all by creating tribes learning communities*. Windsor, CA: CenterSource Systems, LLC (2006).

Grant, K., and Davis, B. H. "Gathering Around." *Kappa Delta Pi Record* 48 no. 3 (2012), 129–133..

Halaby, M. *Belonging: Creating community in the classroom*. Cambridge, MA: Brookline Books (2000).

Kagan, M., Robertson, L., and Kagan, S. *Cooperative learning structures for classbuilding*. San Juan Capistrano, CA: Kagan Cooperative Learning (1995).

Kriete, R. Start the day with community. *Educational Leadership* 61 no. 1 (2003), 68–70.

McClure, L., Yonezawa, S., and Jones, M. "Can school structures improve teacher student relationships? The relationship between advisory programs, personalization and students' academic achievement." *Education Policy Analysis Archives* 18, no. 17 (2010), 1–21.

Rimm-Kaufman, S. E., and Chiu, Y. I. "Promoting social and academic competence in the classroom: An intervention study examining the contribution of the Responsive Classroom approach." *Psychology in the Schools* 42 (2007), 397–413.

Rimm-Kaufman, S.E., Fan, X., Chiu, Y.I., and You, W. "The contribution of the Responsive Classroom approach on children's academic achievement: Results of a three-year longitudinal study." *Journal of School Psychology* 45 (2007), 401–421.

Rashid. T. "Development of social skills among children at elementary level." *Bulletin of Education and Research* 32, no. 1 (2010), 69–78.

Responsive Classroom Center for Responsive Schools, Turners Falls, MA (2017). https://www.responsiveclassroom.org/about/printables/

Stack, B. "Morning Meetings: Creating a Safe Space for Learning." Edutopia: Schools That Work (2015). https://www.edutopia.org/practice/morning-meetings-creating-safe-space-learning

Webster-Stratton, C. and Reid, M.J. "Strengthening social and emotional competence in young children—the foundation for early school readiness and success." *Infants and Young Children: An Interdisciplinary Journal of Special Care Practices*, 17, no. 2 (2004), 96–113.

INDEX OF KEY TERMS AND AUTHORS CITED IN THIS BOOK